SUDAN

1950–1985

DEATH OF A DREAM

SUDAN
1950–1985
DEATH OF A DREAM

BY

GRAHAM THOMAS

FOREWORD BY

ROY JENKINS
(Rt. Hon. The Lord Jenkins of Hillhead P.C.)

DARF PUBLISHERS LTD
LONDON

FIRST EDITION 1990

© Graham Thomas, 1990

Published by
Darf Publishers Ltd, 50 Hans Crescent, London SW1X 0NA

ISBN 1 85077 216 9

Cover by Sue Sharples

Printed in Great Britain by
BPCC Wheatons Ltd, Exeter

*This book is
dedicated
to the Sudanese People
in gratitude
for their friendship*

ACKNOWLEDGEMENTS

I should like to record my thanks to Bushra Fadallah (Press attaché Sudan Embassy), Mahdi el Helu, Yassin Kallas, Nasr Eldin Imam el Hadi, Sherif Touhami, Dr Yusif Bedri and many other friends for their help and encouragement, and to Mrs Jane Moore for typing the script. There are two people who I must especially thank, namely Abdel Rahman Abdel Gader without whose generous support in research this publication would never have come to fruition, and secondly my wife for her constant support.

The author acknowledges with gratitude permission to use the photograph of the Mahdi, held in the Mansell Collection, the picture of the Mahd's Tomb which is in the National Army Museum collection, and the picture of Sayed Abdel Rahman's arrival in London which is in the Press Association picture library.

Thanks are also expressed to the Mahdi family, the Ministry of Information and the Archives of the Sudan Government. The remaining photographs are from the author's own collection.

CONTENTS

PREFACE   xi

FOREWORD   xiii

CHAPTER I   SUDANESE HERITAGE   1

CHAPTER II   THE LAST DAYS OF THE BRITISH   17

CHAPTER III   INDEPENDENCE AND SOVEREIGNTY   53

CHAPTER IV   EXPERIMENTS IN DICTATORSHIP
                 AND DEMOCRACY   87

CHAPTER V   NUMIERI—THE STRUGGLE FOR
                 SUPREMACY   104

CHAPTER VI   ATTEMPTS AT RECONCILIATION   135

CHAPTER VII   ABSOLUTISM AND DISINTEGRATION   181

CHAPTER VIII   TOWARDS DEMOCRACY   224

CHAPTER IX   POSTSCRIPT   234

                 BIBLIOGRAPHY   245

                 INDEX   249

ILLUSTRATIONS

Page

xii The Author Graham F. Thomas

 6 (a) The Mahdi
    (b) One of the flags of the Mahdiya
 8 (a) Osman Digna
    (b) The Mahdi's Tomb

12 (a) Sayed Abdel Rahman el Mahdi as a young man
    (b) Sayed Ali el Mirghani—an early portrait

14   Sir James Robertson
         —last Civil Secretary of the Sudan

44   Sayed Abdel Rahman el Mahdi arriving in London

48 (a) Muhammed Saleh Shingetti
    (b) Abdel Rahman Ali Taha
    (c) Ibrahim Ahmed
    (d) Abdel Rahman Abdoun

50   Sayed Abdel Rahman greeting President Neguib of
         Egypt

60 (a) British Troops being replaced by Sudanese
    (b) Hoisting the Independence Flag

62   Ismael el Azhari 1st Prime Minister of the Sudan

64 (a) Dardiri Muhammed Osman
    (b) Yahia el Fadli

77 (a) The Supreme Council
    (b) Abdullah Khalil

ix

78   The Sudanese welcome self-government

79   Muhammed Ahmed Mahjoub

84   General Ibrahim Abboud, Head of State

92   The Ansar celebrating

96   Sadig el Mahdi, Muhammed Ahmed Mahjoub, and
      Ismael el Azhari

114   The author with Dr Abdel Kader Hatem in Cairo

119   Graham Thomas presenting a letter from Rt Hon
      Harold Wilson to President Numieri

124   The Author with General Muhammed el Baghir,
      Vice-President

136   President Numieri in the London Embassy on his
      official visit to England to 1973

141   Sherif Hussein el Hindi

156   General Joseph Lagu, Vice-President of Southern
      Sudan under Numieri

163   Hassan el Turabi, Leader of the National Islamic
      Front

218   Mahmoud Muhammed Taha

236   Muhammed Ibrahim Nugud, Communist Leader

238   Sayed Sadig el Mahdi

242   Sayed Ahmed el Mirghani, Head of State

PREFACE

"There is a history in all men's lives"

W. SHAKESPEARE

This book is a personal history of certain aspects of the Sudan. It is not intended as a definitive history of the period, it could not be so for two reasons. Firstly, it is written by a non-Sudanese. Secondly, as an onlooker I was caught up in some events, and absent on others so that the narrative must offer an intermittent commentary both on events and personalities.

There is, however a certain sense of continuity, of intimate relationships extending over a period of some forty years. As one British Ambassador to the Sudan put it—"You have a time span of knowledge while we have only a fragmented view of developments." Or as Sayed Sadig el Mahdi expressed it—"There have been five generations of the family including the Mahdi and you have known four of them".

My wife and I are grateful for the rich and varied experience we have enjoyed by being caught up in a little of Sudanese history, and we are deeply appreciative of all the friendship so generously given to us by literally hundreds of Sudanese from all areas of the country, and from a wide range of background and political viewpoint. We hope that in some small way we have been able to repay this affection.

I am fully conscious of the shortcomings of such a work and realise that what is offered cannot possibly give the whole truth, but merely a glimpse of some aspects of the truth.

GRAHAM THOMAS

xi

The Author

FOREWORD

Graham Thomas is a remarkable amalgam of political Welshman and dedicated servant of the Sudan. By the time he was thirty-two he had already gained two degrees from the University of Wales, fought a parliamentary seat against a future Conservative Chancellor of the Exchequer, married his wife, Ismay, who was a councillor and alderman at the high tide of responsible Labour power in South Wales, and become a member of the Sudan Government service.

In the nearly forty years since then he has been a sort of supplementary ambassador for the Sudan in Britain, except that he has not represented a particular government so much as the underlying needs and problems of the country, which from the days of Gordon and the Mahdi through the exceptional Sudan Political Service of the 20's and 30's has always aroused a British interest far beyond the scale of its population size.

Now, drawing on this experience and his almost unique knowledge of all the major figures, he has produced this book, succinct, highly informative, sympathetic and penetrating.

Roy Jenkins

CHAPTER I

SUDANESE HERITAGE

"The spirit of the Mahdi roused the fires of patriotism and religion . . . and freed his native land of foreigners"
                                                    SIR WINSTON CHURCHILL

The most dominant feature of the Sudan is the magnificent, life-giving river Nile, or rather the two Niles; the Blue Nile rising in the mountains of Ethiopia and the White Nile flowing North from Lake Victoria, converging at Khartoum. It is Africa's largest country covering almost a million square miles in the North East of the Continent. The area is not a homogeneous one, stretching as it does from latitude 22° North to latitude 4° North at its Southern boundary.

In the South the river has created the vast swampy area known as the Sudd, where, in an area as large as France, the water is ever changing its course, making navigation extremely slow and difficult. Here are Equatorial forests and mountains alive with exotic flowers and fruit and inhabited still by the great beasts of Africa. Herds of elephant, rhinoceroses, hippopotami, lions, leopards, monkeys, and gazelle of many varieties abound as do snakes and game of all descriptions. The region, because of its climate and terrain has always been difficult to control and develop. Its people, mainly Nilotic have traditions and affinities more akin to the African tribes of Uganda, Kenya, and the Congo rather than with the Arabic speaking peoples of the North.

1

The Anglo-Egyptian Condominium Government in the Sudan deliberately pursued a closed area policy in the South, fearing that the Arab merchants would exploit these simple African peoples. Three provinces were created (Equatoria, Bahr el Gazal and the Upper Nile) which were administered by a special cadre of British personnel (known as the 'Bog-barons'). As their expectation of life was short, because of tropical diseases, they were employed on short contracts with gratuities in contrast to their colleagues in the North who were permanent, pensionable, and retired at the age of forty five.

Following the Nile northwards, the terrain changes to savannah lands, where there is some rainfall, enabling cultivation to take place and cattle to be raised. Here too, wild life is plentiful, and during migration seasons the sky is thick with multi-hued birds. Away to the West are the great, mainly arid provinces of Kordofan and Dafur peopled by nomadic beduin tribes, and by the Fur people who for hundreds of years had an independent Sultanate with El Fasher as its splendid, if barbaric capital. Along the river at Malakal live the magnificent Dinka tribe, often over seven feet tall with splendid physiques, and by the time the White Nile reaches Kosti and Wad Medini, cotton crops extend over many feddans producing most of the revenue for the country. To the North of Khartoum and the confluence of the two Niles lies the vast deserts, part of the Sahara, but called in the Sudan the Nubian desert. To the East the Red Sea Hills are inhabited by the fiercely independent Beja tribe, one of whose leaders Osman Digna had the distinction of leading the only native troops to break a British (military) Square.

The North, arid, and almost without rain, covers almost two thirds of the country, and probably the same proportion of the population. This area is mainly Arab and Muslim by tradition contrasting sharply with the South.

This division has, from time immemorial bedevilled the history of the Sudan and despite nearly two hundred years of varying attempts to unify the whole area little progress has been made; it was not an entity, neither ethnically nor geographically. Its people were as complex as its boundaries were vague. Some six hundred separate tribes, with no common language, no common identity, and no common culture inhabited this vast territory which for centuries had been left virtually un- disturbed.

The early history of the Sudan can be traced only in the chance remarks of travellers. The Northern area (Nubia) was occupied by the Pharaohs of the Middle Kingdom (2000–1700 BC), and after capturing Egypt in 1700 BC, the Hyksos introduced the horse into the country. Tutmosis I records that in conquering the Northern Sudan he had "Penetrated the Valleys which the Royal Ancestors had not". Perhaps the most valuable evidence exists on the murals which decorate the walls of Queen Hatshepsut's Temple on the West Bank at Luxor which indicate clearly, in the representation of expeditions returning laden with treasures from the land of Punt, that the Ancient Egyptians had explored deeply into the Sudan, The remains of Egyptian Temples, now imaginatively rescued from the flooding by the High Dam Project, and re-erected in the National Museum at Khartoum show that their occupation continued throughout the years 1500–1100 BC, and it also documented that Nero, in the years between 54–58 AD dispatched two centurions into the area. They reached the Sudd (South of Khartoum) before reporting that the Sudan was not worth conquering. By 1500 AD the Black Sultanate of the Fung was known, and it was at this time that conversion to Islam within the Northern Sudanese tribes began and prospered. However, many Christian communities survived, and evidence of Christianity continued until the seventeenth century in the Kingdoms of Meroë and Napata. By the beginning of the nineteenth century only the coastal strip around Suakin remained subject to the rule of the Turkish Empire, which up to that time had vaguely asserted some sovereignty; while the European penetration of Africa had scarcely affected the vast expanses to the West and South of the Sudan of which little was known other than in myths. The influences exerted by Christianity and Islam were to affect the whole future history of this country. Thus geographical as well as political and religious factors have tended to divide the country into the Northern Islamic area with its racial and linguistic affinities with Egypt and the Arab World, and the Southern Provinces populated by a variety of proud warlike conservative Nilo-Hamitic and Negro tribes. It was not, however, until the nineteenth century that the challenge came from an alien invader with superior forces and a more advanced political organisation. The acquisition of the Sudan by Muhammed Ali Pasha of Egypt in 1821 united for administrative purposes this virtually unknown area.

Muhammed Ali had motives which were many and varied. Primarily he wished to procure slaves as soldiers, and increase the financial stability of Egypt by appropriating the gold which he believed existed in great quantities. He also wished to overthrow the remnants of the Mamelukes (the Military Elite) who had controlled Egypt before him and who had fled to the Northern Sudan; and were now ruling in the Dongola area. It was this expansion of Turkish-Egyptian influence, which at first, indirectly, brought the Sudan within the sphere of British interest, and this was precipitated by the sweep of French interventions in Africa in general and specifically in Central Africa. Initially, after a brief experiment with direct Egyptian rule, the various local populations were left under traditional tribal or district sheiks, but the Government was centralised to some extent by the appointment of Governors-General based in Khartoum, which became the administrative Capital.

More frequent contact with the centres of Islamic learning encouraged a more positive approach to religion and a few of the religious orders became powerful. One of these, the Khatmiyya, was particularly favoured by Egypt who encouraged their leaders, the Mirghani family; and indeed, to the present day the Mirghanis have kept close links with Cairo. The Sudan, however, remained an area over which the Egyptians had intermittent control, either because of inertia or corruption; the extension of control was seen as a priority by the successors of Muhammed Ali, and it was not without significance that Sir Samuel Baker and General Gordon were appointed by the Khedive Ismael to weaken the slave trade and to improve communications. However, after Ismael had been deposed in 1879 and General Gordon's resignation in 1880, the situation in the Sudan deteriorated and the slave trade increased again. Taxation had become extortionate, corruption prevailed; the time was ripe for revolution.

The catalyst who was to spark off the attempt to expel the Turks was an unlikely one, for Muhammed Ahmed was the son of a Dongolawi boat builder, but a man who combined personal magnetism with the zeal of religious fervour. He was to be the first truly national leader that the Sudan had experienced. It has been asserted that the Mahdiya was a result of the oppression and misgovernment of the Turco-Egyptian conquerors, but a single theory can only inadequately reflect the complexity out of which it arose. It was a response to a set of social, political, and economic circumstances and was religious in essence and radical in intent. Only a 'Jehad'* could provide the necessary impetus. At first the authorities greatly underrated the

---

*Religious War or Struggle.

The Mahdi

One of the flags of the Mahdiya

strength of the Mahdist movement but to many Sudanese Muhammed Ahmed is 'Abu el Istiglal' (the Father of Independence), the man who united the tribes by the passion of his Islamic appeal, drove out the alien rulers, and laid the foundations of a nation state.

During this period the Sudan was considered not to be directly within the sphere of British interest.

> "Thus an illogical assembly of political, financial and moral considerations led the British Government, not only to evade involvement in the Sudanese problem but also to check the attempts of the Khedival Government to promote resolute action in the threatened provinces"[1]

In an effort to save the prestige of Egypt and to check Muhammed Ahmed, who had taken control in the western Provinces of Kordofan and Dafur, an expeditionary force was dispatched by a reluctant British Government to organise a withdrawal. General Gordon was sent to the Sudan to complete this mission, but his personal commitment to confrontation with the Mahdi, resulted in his death. This humiliating failure made future British involvement inevitable. The overwhelming of the garrison at Khartoum, and the killing of General Gordon meant that the Mahdi's control over the greater part of the former Egyptian-dominated Sudan was complete.

The Mahdi did not live long to enjoy the fruits of his victory and after his untimely death, probably of typhus, in June 1885 the leadership passed to his chosen successor, the Khalifa Abdullahi, who built up an administrative system reflecting the religious ideology of the Mahdist movement. The particular significance of the reign of the Khalifa was that the greater part of the Sudan was united under Mahdist rule. Power was exercised by the Khalifa through a constitution with a bureaucracy of civil servants and military

---

[1]Holt, Modern History of the Sudan, p. 82.

Osman Digna

The Mahdi's Tomb after being shelled by Kitchener's Troops 1898

commanders, but the necessity of sustaining the military character of the government prevented general stabilisation. By many Europeans, particularly Colonel (later General) Wingate and Slatin Pasha, the Khalifa Abdullahi was portrayed as the personification of evil.

Remoteness and geographical obstacles prevented the Equatorial Provinces in the South from effective integration, thus the foundations were laid for the dichotomy which has bedevilled the Sudan until now. The European scramble for Africa also exerted its influence. The Nile Valley was in the "diplomatic market", and the Southern Sudan was recognised, ultimately, as being within the sphere of British influence. Thus, the freeing of the Sudan from the Islamic despot began to be seen by the British as a mission of civilisation as well as retribution for the death of Gordon.

Sir Evelyn Baring, the British Agent-General controlling Egypt, at first resisted Egyptian pressure to reconquer the Sudan, but the construction of the Aswan Dam in 1895 was seen as necessitating the control of the upper reaches of the Nile, so by 1898 a full scale military expedition was mounted under General Kitchener, to reconquer the Sudan which culminated in the Battle of Omdurman in 1898. Since the early part of the nineteenth century Egypt had, in effect, become a protectorate of Britain so it was out of the question that Egypt itself should be allowed to control the Sudan. Equally unacceptable was the creation of an undisguised British colonial administration. Thus a compromise solution was proposed which was to have far reaching effects on the future political development of the Sudan. This was the Anglo-Egyptian Convention which was signed in 1899 thus forming the Condominium Government which was to continue until 1955. This meant that Britain extended its power in Africa, with a show of legality which its European competitors did not possess. Henceforth the British and Egyptian flags flew side by side in the Sudan and the Condominium instrument gave formal recognition to the situation although the Egyptians were never satisfied with their meagre share of power and this led to pressures and strains for many years; in brief, Egypt paid but Britain administered. The first priority of the Condominium Sudan rule, was the restoration of law and order; so, initially, the Government was a military one. The Governor-General was also Sirdar (Commander-in-Chief) and ruled as an autocrat with military Governors in the Provinces. Both Kitchener, and Wingate who succeeded him as Governor-General in 1899 had many problems; the three most crucial were the Mahdist elements which remained, particularly in the West, various local uprisings, and the pagan primitive tribal areas of the Southern Sudan. The reconquest was a slow process as the borders were redefined, so the work of reconstruction had to wait until pacification, but a civil administration was gradually developed. Islamic Law was enacted for family and matrimonial affairs while the penal and criminal code was based on the British Imperial System. With the onset of World War I the military personnel were required elsewhere and they were gradually replaced by a cadre of carefully selected young British civilians of good health, high moral character, and fair abilities with athletic prowess. These governed the Sudan under a triumvirate of principal officials—the Civil, Legal, and Financial Secretaries. A political service was created to handle the heterogeneous affairs of about a million people with the aid of

"good intentions and a classical education"[*2]

or as H A L Fisher was to express it

"The Sudan is the land of the Blacks ruled by the Blues".[3]

The service built a high reputation for efficiency, organisation, and integrity but exhibited a tendency to paternalism

---

[2]Henderson. The Making of the Modern Sudan Intro xxx.
[3]Ibid 476.

and parochialism which inevitably led to the growth of national feeling among the Sudanese.

The decision by Kitchener that the Southern Sudan was to be converted to Christianity while the North remained Muslim was to have a divisive effect. It led to the segregation of the Southern Provinces and the development of a different value system. One of the major problems confronting the administration has always been the integration of the South into full participation in Government.

Increasingly after the First World War there was growing tension in Anglo-Egyptian relations, Egyptian nationalism emerged with explosive force; and the development of irrigation and agriculture in the Sudan was seen in Cairo as a threat. It was also becoming clear to the Sudanese and the Egyptians that the so-called Anglo-Egyptian control in the Sudan was in fact dominated by the British who held all the senior posts, and who had introduced both legal and educational systems based on British models. These senior British Officials behaved with dedicated benevolence towards the rural areas but they profoundly distrusted the educated urban Sudanese, thus stimulating the very opposition they feared, as the educated class developed a very nationalistic outlook. Political consciousness was beginning in the early 1920's with the formation of the White Flag League, and the reaction of the Sudan administration to the assassination of Sir Lee Stack, the Governor-General in Cairo in 1924 sharply increased the activities of the nationalist intelligentsia. There were immediate traumatic effects, as virtually all Egyptians were demoted from senior posts, and the Egyptian troops were expelled from the Sudan. The administration attempted to revive authoritarian indirect rule through tribal chiefs, and deliberately slowed down the extension of secondary education. As a result of their alienation the educated Sudanese became more politically active, forming the Graduates Congress which they

Sayed Abdel Rahman el Mahdi as a young man

Sayed Ali el Mirghani — an early portrait

saw as a vehicle for defining their political aims and the promotion of education. By 1942 they were in a position to present a political manifesto, which included demands with clear political and constitutional implications. The brusque response and rejection of their demands by the then Civil Secretary led to a crisis of confidence; and differences of opinion within the Congress led to the formation of political parties. Ismael El Azhari, President of Congress—(later to become both Prime Minister, and President) created the Ashigga Party in 1943 to promote the Unity of the Nile Valley and to counter the Independence Party (The Umma) which was under the patronage of Sayed Abdel Rahman el Mahdi, the posthumous son of the Mahdi, who had over the years rebuilt the Mahdist cause. It was felt in some quarters that the Umma Party were prepared to cooperate with the existing administration and were the 'tools' of British Imperialism. It was inevitable that at that stage of development an alliance between the religious sects and political parties should exist, and in some ways would even be advantageous, although it marked a polarisation of the Northern Sudan into two deeply divided groups which was ultimately incompatible with sound political growth.

World War II had given a great jolt to the Sudan and the Administration. It was immediately caught up in the great struggle—the Italians in Ethiopia were poised to enter the Sudan, while Rommel and the Africa Corps swept across Libya towards Cairo and the Nile Valley. The cordial relationships which the British Officials had built up with most of the Sudanese ensured the cooperation of the country with the allied powers. There was none of the hostility that existed in Egypt where the Palace and the Government truculently refused to declare war on the Axis or support the Allies wholeheartedly.

Inevitably the war not only had a physical impact on the Sudan but as with the rest of Africa and Asia there was a

Sir James Robertson

quickening of national aspirations. This was immediately recognised by the Civil Secretary, Sir Douglas Newbold, and, as early as 1942, proposals were being considered for the institution of a consultative body. Newbold worked with some speed. The Advisory Council for the Northern Sudan Ordinance 1943 was promulgated and the first step in what was seen as a slow progress towards representative institutions was taken as it was certainly not expected at that time that, within a decade, Sudanese self-government would have become a reality. It was a forum for discussion and its recommendations were not binding. It was criticised as being over weighted by tribal chiefs and because of the exclusion of the Southern Provinces. The fears, that it was the intention of the Administration to cede the Southern Sudan, were not allayed by the publication of the Siddky-Bevin protocol in 1946, in which it was implied that, according to the Egyptians, self-determination and self-government was envisaged for the South.

The Sudanese adopted the new form of procedures with great dignity, so the progression to formality was a natural one as Sudanese Society was essentially democratic with tribal communities habitually deliberating on topics of concern. Sir Douglas Newbold did not live to guide this development to its fruition for in March 1945 he succumbed to an infection and died. He had not the stamina to fight it, having been exhausted by overwork during the war years.

Fortunately for the Sudan and the Sudanese, James Robertson had been appointed as Deputy Civil Secretary two years earlier. He was physically a big man, with tremendous energy and a strong personality; above all he had vision. He appreciated that a radical and forward policy was essential in the changing circumstances. The formation of the United Nations, the declaration of the Four Freedoms and, above all, the surge of nationalism throughout the colonial parts of the world dictated that the Sudan had to go forward to a new future. By 1946 constitutional changes were proposed and the formation of a Legislative Assembly and Executive Council was undertaken unilaterally by Britain, as Egypt totally opposed this and the pro-Egyptian Sudanese boycotted the Assembly.

The election of a Labour Government in the United Kingdom meant that the old imperialism was dead. With the departure of Sir Winston Churchill from office there could no longer be any question of delaying tactics nor the use of repressive measures to hold on to power. Political opinion, both in the United Kingdom and throughout the world would not countenance such methods, and the Labour Party, with the Rt Hon Clement Attlee as the new Prime Minister, was totally committed to the colonial freedom movement.

CHAPTER II

THE LAST DAYS OF THE BRITISH

"Not lust of conquest but love of order is at the basis of Empire"
Sir A. Duff Cooper

The sweep of nationalism across the world had its effect, not only in the Sudan, but in Egypt as well. Inevitably the nationalists in Egypt urged on by the Nahas Pasha, the Prime Minister and Wafd (the largest party), saw their opportunity to escape from the tutelage of British control. The action of the British in surrounding King Farouk in the Abdin Palace with British tanks during the War, when they effectively ordered him to change not only his government but also his attitude to the war, had rankled deeply in Egyptian hearts. They were quick to encourage the Sudanese in their political aspirations and, in March 1946, an all-party delegation went from the Sudan to Cairo. Sayed Abdel Rahman and the Umma Party, however, quickly grew suspicious that the Egyptians had ulterior motives and withdrew from the delegation.

At the same time the negotiations, on the renewal of the Anglo-Egyptian Treaty, were in grave difficulties. By 7th October, 1946 the Governor-General and Civil Secretary of the Sudan received news of the Siddky-Bevin protocol which was open to the interpretation that the future of the Sudan was linked with Egypt. The Egyptians saw it in this light and the Sudanese were deeply concerned. Sayed Abdel

Rahman flew immediately to London to see the Prime Minister, while simultaneously the Sudan Government vigorously lobbied His Majesty's Government and the Foreign Office to stand by the Sudanese. Sayed Abdel Rahman returned reassured and by 9 December, 1946 Siddky had resigned and had been replaced by Nokrashi Pasha who was more acceptable to the British. However, members of the Advisory Council of the Sudan were still very apprehensive and the Governor-General had to explain the British position, to reassure them. Huddleston's period of office as Governor-General was coming to an end and on the 6 May, 1947 he retired, and his successor Sir Robert Howe arrived with Lady Howe to take up his duties as Governor-General. Sir Robert was always regarded as a protegé of the Rt Hon Ernest Bevin, whose confidence he certainly enjoyed. It is politically significant that he arrived in May—the hottest month of the year when the temperature soared often to 125°F. Air conditioning had not reached the Sudan and ceiling fans only whirred the hot air from one side of the room to the other. The arrival of His Excellency at such a time indicated the seriousness with which His Majesty's Government viewed the Sudanese and Egyptian situation. Rightly so, for the Egyptian Government took Britain to the United Nations Security Council but to no avail.

Sir James Robertson and the new Governor-General moved swiftly to forestall any further Egyptian moves, and created a Legislative Assembly which was formally opened by the Governor-General on the 23 December, 1948. It was composed of ten members directly elected by ballot in the main towns, forty-two rural representatives elected by electoral colleges; twelve from the newly elected Southern Provincial Councils, ten nominated by the Governor-General and eleven members of the Executive Council of which six were British. Muhammed Saleh Shingetti was elected as Speaker, and Abdullah Khalil (Secretary- General of the Umma Party), the Leader and Minister of Agriculture.

Sayed Ali el Mirghani and the pro-Egyptians boycotted the elections and refused to participate, which gave the Umma Party and Sayed Abdel Rahman a considerable advantage in that they held the key posts and dominated the Assembly. The Umma Party Ministers were Dr Ali Bedri (Minister of Health), Abdel Rahman Ali Taha (Education), Abdel Rahman Abdoun (under-secretary Irrigation), Muhammed Ali Shawki (under-secretary Justice) and Ibrahim Ahmed (Minister without Portfolio).

The Assembly proved a useful training ground in Parliamentary procedure and Ministerial responsibilities. It was to stand them in good stead in the years which followed. As Sir James wrote in his memoirs:-

> "Towards the end of 1950 political excitement began to build up again and once more the Egyptians were involved".[1]

And so they were. The speech from the Throne in the Egyptian Parliament once again enunciated the doctrine of the 'Unity of the Nile Valley'. Reactions in the Sudan were swift, the pro-Egyptians (Unionists) were delighted while the Mahdists led by Sayed Abdel Rahman were infuriated. Rumours were rife and tempers ran high. It was widely reported that the Mahdists would fight and that Egyptian troops in the Sudan would support the unionist cause.

It was into this cauldron of political ferment and feverish nationalism that Ismay and I entered on the 16 November, 1950. We quickly found ourselves involved in Sudanese politics. On our way to Khartoum we sat next to a charming, if formidable 'grand dame', Mrs Waller, the wife of the Resident Chief Inspector of the Nile Waters, who although British, was the representative of the Egyptian

---

[1] Sir James Robertson. Transition in Africa, p. 140.

Government. After her husband's long and distinguished service and by seniority and force of personality Mrs Waller had become the doyenne of expatriate wives. She, rather condescendingly, enquired into which branch of the Service we were attached and when Ismay replied "Education" she commented in anguished tones "Oh, you won't be invited to the Palace for years". It was our first taste of the old Imperial snobbery from which, luckily, the Sudan was largely free. It was with great delight that we were able to greet her at a Palace Garden Party within a few weeks of our arrival.

Society was small and in those days it was essential to make your own entertainment which, apart from the physical sports of polo, riding and shooting, meant cocktail, luncheon, and dinner parties. The Sudan political service only numbered some four hundred in the whole period from 1899 to 1956 and the other Government Departments had relatively few British Officials despite the fact that the Sudan was nearly the size of India.

At one of our first social ventures when we were invited to a drinks party I spoke to a large man, obviously with years of Sudan experience behind him, and with all my Welsh and Socialist fervour I told him how the country should be run. After all, I had just fought a Parliamentary Election for the Labour Party. He told me bluntly that I should tell all this to the Civil Secretary and I retorted that I would be happy to do so. Within the week we had an invitation to drinks at the home of the Civil Secretary and Lady Robertson. As we went in my 'large man' said "Well, now you can tell the Civil Secretary how to run the country". There was no point in retracting but I apologised for my rudeness and continued to express my views. It was the beginning of a rich and valued friendship which only ended with his death thirty-four years later. Let me pay tribute to a truly great man whose vision was a great inspiration to me, and whose tolerance was outstanding. He had his failings and did not suffer fools gladly, but he generated much empathy and was an effective leader of men. Sir James was blessed by his marriage to Nancy who is a considerable woman in her own right. She is a decisive and caring individual of much energy and courage, totally devoid of condescension or snobbery. She quickly captivated both Ismay and I, and we have enjoyed her friendship to this day.

I suppose, at first, Sir James was amused to have an ex-Labour candidate in the Sudan service, but both Ismay and I are political animals and I think he enjoyed listening to our different approach to the Sudan's problems. The Sudan Government Service was almost totally composed of Oxbridge 'Blues' from upper middle class family backgrounds and when we arrived most of the Senior Heads of Departments had been in the Sudan since the 1926 General Strike and, as students, had driven buses or in some way participated in attempts to break it. In the main they were intelligent, creative, industrious, and courageous men, but were conditioned (as we all were) by birth, background, education, and experience. The English among them had no conception of nationalism, although they were intensely patriotic. I often thought that it was our Welsh background that gave us an understanding of nationalist aspirations. Certainly at first, Sir James was suspicious of me, thinking (as he told me years later) that I was "subversive and very left wing". He later said that this was his reason for transferring me from education into the Labour Department in his office, where "I could better keep an eye on you". There can be no doubt that a number of senior officials in the Political Service viewed with grave disquiet and some hostility the arrival of two members of the Labour Party. (A few years later I was told that there had been *one* other socialist in the 1930's). I was grateful for the friendship and

support of Sir James and Lady Robertson and during the
next few months we saw them frequently.

The house we had been allocated in Omdurman was not
completed when we arrived, so we had to take up residence
in the Grand Hotel. It was "Grand" in those days, especially
to us. We had Room 32 with a balcony overlooking the
terrace and the Nile. The weather was glorious and it was a
sheer sensual joy to sit watching the majestic river with
fellucas idling by. The great avenue of trees, planted, it is
said by Kitchener, ran alongside the river giving welcome
shade from the heat of the sun. Along this avenue lived the
hierarchy of the Sudan. At the far end from the hotel was
the rebuilt Palace of the Governor-General, rather resem-
bling a white iced wedding cake and, in between, were the
large lofty and cool houses of the great, the Kaid, the Legal
Secretary, the Civil Secretary, and Sayed Ali el Mirghani to
name a few. Their gardens were a riot of colour and oriental
fragrances, frangipani, hibiscus, and bougainvillaea, with tall
palm trees tossing their heads high into the brilliant blue
sky.

We were immensely fortunate to live in the Grand Hotel
at this time. As the only hotel, it was the focal place for
Sudan Government Officials, distinguished visitors, Sudanese politicians, and international journalists. It was a
multi-racial meeting place. It was here that we met Abdel
Rahman Abdoun who was our first Sudanese friend. He was
the Under-Secretary for Irrigation and a staunch supporter
of Sayed Abdel Rahman el Mahdi. We soon became close
friends; his was a fascinating story. He was born when
Khalifa Abdullahi ruled and lived until 1984. He was one of
the first Sudanese to be educated at the Gordon Memorial
College and the first Sudanese engineer, being responsible
for the construction of the great canal through the Gezira
for the cotton scheme which was to become the main
source of revenue for the Sudan. He introduced us to Sayed

Sir Abdel Rahman el Mahdi Pasha, KBE, CVO, the posthumous son of the Mahdi. This was the beginning of a close relationship with the Sayed and his family—his sons, especially his successors Imam Siddig and Imam el Hadi and his grandson, Sadig el Mahdi, later Prime Minister of the Sudan. In fact, to many of the younger members of the family I became known as 'Uncle'. On one occasion Muhammed Ahmed, the five year old son of Sayed Sadig, on being asked who we were replied, "Oh they are the British part of the family".

The re-assertion of Egyptian claims to the Sudan led to an immediate and vigorous reaction. Tensions rose quickly and the Umma Party (Mahdists) held a vast rally in Omdurman at which Abdullah Khalil and other ministers spoke. Indeed Abdel Rahman Ali Taha was so passionate and persuasive that Nahas Pasha was provoked into telegraphing a protest to the Governor-General. Abdullah Khalil retaliated by protesting against Egyptian interference in the Sudan. Sayed Abdel Rahman seized this opportunity and the Umma members of the Legislative Assembly tabled a motion calling for immediate self government. This placed Sir James Robertson and the British officials in a difficult situation and long hours of discussion took place with Sudanese leaders of all persuasions to see if a compromise solution could be reached. I suspected at the time that Sir James was not averse to the motion (this impression was to be confirmed in later years) but he was in an unenviable position for, if he opposed the motion, he risked a rupture with the Umma Party. Abdullah Khalil and Sayed Abdel Rahman quite easily might have taken a decision to withdraw from the Assembly and boycott constitutional developments. On the other hand, if he had supported the attitudes and wishes of non-Ansar tribal leaders in the North the Southerners would have felt betrayed. A further complication at this time was that the Egyptian Foreign

Minister was in London for talks with the British Foreign Secretary.

On the day of the debate, 14 December, 1950, we hurried as soon as we could to the Legislative Assembly Building. The debate had continued from 9.30 am until 1 o'clock and resumed again at 4.30 pm. When we arrived at about half past five we were dismayed to find long queues of Sudanese waiting for admission to the Visitors Gallery. Fortunately, a friend (The Under-Secretary of Transport) drove up and a place was found for us. The atmosphere in the Assembly was tense and highly reminiscent of the House of Commons. The Umma Party was vociferously demanding the right of self-government; the Southerners were hesitant and the Tribal leaders reluctant to be swept along too quickly. Sir James Robertson had put up an amendment to the effect that the aim was self-government but that it should be delayed. The debate lasted until one o'clock in the morning, when the amendment was defeated by one vote (41 votes to 40) and then the motion was carried by 39 votes to 38.[2]

The Government in Cairo was predictably angry and incensed and the Prime Minister of Egypt telegraphed the Governor-General demanding an explanation; while the British Foreign Secretary also expressed his annoyance, particularly at the timing of the debate. I am sure Sir James was right in advising His Excellency the Governor-General not to stop the debate as that would have been the worst of all worlds. Internally, the results satisfied most people. The Umma had seen their motion carried. The non-Mahdists had strongly recommended delay and it had clearly indicated to Cairo that the Independence Movement was a real force in the Sudan. The Governor-General was able to avoid taking action because of the narrowness of the

---

[2]Ismay Thomas. Mss letter, 15.12.51.

vote. The indecisiveness was a clear indication of the fact that no one in the Sudan then nor in the three decades which followed had been in a position of having an outright majority, and this has been tragic for the Sudan.

A few days before this fateful debate the 'Joint Commission for the Amendment of the Constitution', which had been convened by the Government, had been formulating its proposals. Muhammed Ahmed Mahjoub a retired lawyer and the Leader of the Opposition in the old Legislative Assembly had become a member and his contribution to its deliberations was monumental. He was a brilliant advocate and it was largely by his efforts that a 'Transitional Constitution' was formulated which became the basis of Sudanese democratic Government and, even after two military dictatorial regimes, is still in use in 1985/86. Sir James had taken the pulse of the country and realised that it was vital to continue to press on towards complete self-government.

Another major problem faced the Sudan Government at this time. After the war, Trades Unions appeared on the scene and the Government was under pressure from the Labour Government in Britain to introduce legislation to recognise and register these. Not only was this legislation introduced, but Sir James went further and appointed David Newman (a British Trades Union Official) as an adviser to management and the unions. The most powerful of the Sudanese Trades Unions was the Sudan Government Railway Union. They were in a vital position as the railway system was essential to the economic life of the country. The Sudan Railways had been started by Kitchener for the purpose of The Reconquest (from Halfa to Khartoum). Later the lines had been extended east to Port Sudan, south for the cotton at Wad Medani, and west to El Obeid for the gum arabic trade.

By the time we arrived in the Sudan the Unions were

flexing their muscles and the British administrators viewed with horror this 'new subversive movement'. I could understand, although not sympathise with, their views. It must have been hard for officials who had, for twenty or thirty years, ruled with their authority unquestioned to be suddenly confronted by organised labour. Some of them resented deeply the appointment of an official to help and organise the masses, for what they anticipated would be a revolution. The constitutional crisis was heightened by a series of threatened or actual strikes. By the second of December Ismay was writing home that the strike was effective.

"nothing was coming from Port Sudan, no mail, no food"

and the next day she also reported a

"complete stoppage of the railways".[3]

However, when we lunched with the Robertsons, Sir James was unperturbed by either the political temperature or the industrial attacks on his Administration. Egypt, naturally encouraged and financially supported the railway workers; Nahas Pasha was only too delighted to give comfort to anyone who would embarrass the British Officials. Many senior officials urged that repressive measures be taken for, to them, the excellent ordinances passed between 1948 and 1951 were an incitement to the unions and a reward for their previous militant activities.[*]

The Sudan Government managed to convince most of the trades unionists that the Legislation was in their own interests, but the militants, some of whom were communist inspired, continued to press their claims and were branded as subversive for activities which would have been con-

---

[3]Ismay Thomas. Mss letter, 2.12.51.
[*](The Trade Union Ordinance; A Regulation of Trade Disputes Ordinance; An Arbitration Ordinance; A Workman's Compensation Act; A Work Shop and Factories Act; An Industrial Relations Act).

sidered, in the United Kingdom, legitimate and justified in attempting to raise the living standards of their workers. Many Government officials; the expatriate business and commercial interests, the Levantine families who had contributed so much to the Sudan, and even the emerging Sudanese entrepreneurs believed that the structure of Sudanese society was threatened by the Trade Union leadership.

There were serious internal difficulties within the Sudan Government service over policy. Sir James had no doubt that self-government and independence were inevitable and consequently he worked towards that end as quickly as possible. Most of the Governors and District Commissioners believed in the objective but were convinced that at least two or more years were essential for a smooth transition. The Civil Secretary believed that any appearance of delaying tactics would inevitably bring strife, riot, and possibly bloodshed which might force the use of British troops. This he was determined to avoid, but in doing so he faced considerable opposition from within. R J Hillard, General Manager of Sudan Railways which was the largest single industrial undertaking in the country, was a senior and formidable member of the political service with considerable experience in the Sudanese hierarchy. John Hillard was a powerful, vigorous personality probably only matched by Sir James and was an advocate of a 'hawkish' policy towards the Trades Unions, the Unionists, the urban intellectuals and the graduates. Sir James was supported by his own political advisers, especially by the Hawksworth brothers, and he received much help from Sir Arthur Gaitskell, Managing Director of the Sudan Gezira Cotton syndicate, but he was a gentle, almost academic character and no match for Hillard. Both served on the Governor-General's Council and the Executive Council, but Sir Arthur unlike his brother Hugh Gaitskell had little taste for politics and soon resigned to devote himself to the Gezira. It was natural for Hillard to wish for an aggressive policy from the Sudan Government, for, as General Manager of the Railways he faced the largest and best organised Trade Union, militantly led by alleged communists, who directed a series of crippling strikes which almost brought the Sudan to economic crisis. Hillard wanted the strikes crushed for obvious reasons but Sir James, who was more aware of the possible political repercussions both internally and outside (notably the reaction of Egypt) resisted all pressures for arbitrary or ruthless action. There is no doubt that there were critical divisions and the Civil Secretary faced tremendous yet delicate problems but even Sir James was surprised at the speed of developments and his critics were silenced.

Despite rail strikes and shortages we thoroughly enjoyed our first Christmas away from home. The British were determined to keep the traditional festivities alive and an endless round of parties began. It was, of course, de rigeur to attend service at the Cathedral on Christmas morning but perhaps one of the most attractive features of life in Khartoum then was the genuine sense of tolerance on the part of the Sudanese themselves. They readily joined in the party spirit, reciprocating with breakfast, lunch, tea or dinner parties. Although devout Muslims, they completely accepted the 'People of the Book'. The Virgin Birth is indeed recorded in the Koran and in the 'Hadith' the Prophet Mohammed states, "If you want friends, find them among the Christians". They appreciated our celebrations, as they did their own Eids (Festivals). One of the pleasures of serving the Sudan was that we enjoyed the public holidays of Britain and of Egypt because of the Co-Domini. The King-Emperor's day was celebrated as was that of King Farouk. In addition to the Muslim Festival holidays, we had the two distinct Christian holidays as the Coptic and Orthodox Churches differed from the Western Christians in their dates for the celebration of Christmas and Easter. We looked forward to 1951 with interest and excitement.

New Year 1951 opened on a Hollywood note, for in January Prince Aly Khan and Rita Hayworth arrived in Khartoum where they had taken the whole first floor of the Grand Hotel. Naturally Khartoum was agog; British and Sudanese alike were curious to see these internationally famous personalities. Our first glimpse came at lunch time when we had gone, as usual, to the dining room. As the normal daily procedure of shutting all the windows because of the heat, had made the room quite dark, it was rather a surprise to see them wearing dark sun glasses which were most incongruous. Their identity was well known, so there could be no question of them being 'incognito'. As the majestic Ahmed Adam, the head waiter, ushered them to their table they gave an impression of being unwashed and grubby, but Rita Hayworth's hair was truly her crowning glory. The visit gave some light relief during a period of troubles and tribulations. A series of strikes had led to the prosecution of some workers and Trades Union Leaders, which in turn led to a further five-day general strike. I had been trying to persuade Sir James Robertson to send some of the leaders to the Trades Union College, Ruskin, at Oxford but this was resolutely opposed by the Commissioner of Labour, who viewed that institution as a hot-bed of subversives. I was also trying to introduce the Training-within-Industry scheme for Supervisors, especially for the Sudanese, as a step forward in management training.

In March there was the announcement of the convening of the Governor-General's Commission on the Constitution, composed of thirteen Sudanese. The Civil Secretary was anxious that work should begin speedily so the first meeting was held on April the twenty second. The Egyptians were very annoyed at this development, but their attention was distracted from it by the sudden decision of King Farouk to divorce his beautiful and popular wife Farida, who had given him three daughters, but had not produced an heir to the throne of Egypt. The people of the Nile Valley both Egyptian and Sudanese were astonished, when on the sixth of May the King married a young Egyptian girl called Narriman (whom it was reported he had seen in a jeweller's shop). She was already betrothed, but the King insisted on the marriage, which incensed many devout Muslims in whose tradition a betrothal was as binding as marriage. Much ribald amusement was expressed by the Sudanese, when, eight months later Queen Narriman produced a son.

We were increasingly involved with Sudanese politicians of every shade of opinion, and had been received by both the main religious leaders Sayed Abdel Rahman and Sayed Ali el Mirghani. In fact both our letters home and Ismay's diary reveal a constant round of breakfast, lunch, tea, and dinner parties. We soon formed many deep friendships which have only been severed by death. In a situation which was unique we not only had very close relationships with friends of Sayed Abdel Rahman el Mahdi—including his son Sayed Siddig, Muhammed Saleh Shingetti (Speaker of the Legislative Assembly) Abdel Rahman Abdoun, Ibrahim Ahmed and Abdullah Khalil (Secretary-General to the Umma Party and Leader of the Assembly), but also the trust and confidence of Sayed Ali el Mirghani's supporters, especially Mirghani Hamza, Dardiri Muhammed Osman, Mubarek Zarroug, and later Ismael el Azhari. There were also the independent grouping which included Abdel Fatah Mograbi, Zubeir Hamad el Melik, Muhammed Ahmed Mahjoub and even the virulently anti-British Khidr Omar (founder member of the Ashigga Party) who were all frequent visitors to our home. Indeed, our small house on the river front in Omdurman was the meeting place for all, including many young people of our own age, people such as Muhammed Tewfig Ahmed, Kamil Shawki, Ishaq Khalifa

Sherif, Kamal el Jack, Jamal Muhammed Ahmed, Shefig Shawki, and Mansour Khaled. I am sure that many of the old guard of the Sudan Political Service viewed our association with some of these people with horror, but Sir James and Lady Robertson gave us generously of their time and patronage. Looking back through our diaries and letters, I am amazed how much time Sir James gave to us in spite of working between fifteen and eighteen hours a day at that time. In one letter written in 1951 he said "I am a little submerged by work, though that is nothing new".[4]

Certainly I had difficulties with some senior colleagues who considered me to be a militant socialist. Perhaps it had not helped when I refused to join the Sudan Club, of which British Officials were expected to become members. Sir James questioned me on the subject and I replied that I considered it repugnant to have a club based on race, and that "if Sudanese were allowed to join I would happily take up membership". He was taken aback and replied vigorously that the Egyptians, Greeks, Armenians, and Copts had their own clubs and asked why not the British. I told him that I thought it absurd, with the Sudanese advancing to self-government and possibly independence that they should be prevented by an alien ruling group from joining a club on Sudanese soil. To me, it was insulting as well as unnecessarily bad policy. He accepted my position although he did not agree.

In April, Sir James transferred me to the Labour Department of the Civil Secretary's Office, and I was, to my great joy, sent on an industrial tour of Egypt, but in effect, to assess the mood and economic strength of that country. Fortunately, Ismay who was teaching at the Girl's Teacher Training College in Omdurman was able to come with me. It was a wonderful adventure for we travelled the whole

---

[4]Sir James Robertson. Mss Letter. 9.12.51.

length of Egypt, by train and boat, seeing for the first time
Abu Simbel (then on its original site) Aswan, Luxor, Cairo,
and Alexandria. For part of the time I was the guest of the
Shell Oil Company, visiting their huge refinery at Suez and
crossing into Sinai, even managing to visit Moya Musa
(Moses' Well) from which the prophet had reputedly drunk.

I was appalled by the contrasts in Egypt, the vulgar
ostentation of the Pashas, compared with the squalid
poverty of the peasants (fellahin). Luxurious palaces and
private gardens were surrounded by mud shacks in which
lived the peasants. We were, technically, officials of the
Anglo-Egyptian Co-Domini which meant (it was a nice
fiction) that we took our rank as Egyptian Officials. It also
meant that we had considerable status in Egypt. The
country was Muslim but not Arab—it was still essentially
pharaonic. The bureaucracy was incredible; inertia was a
blight all over the land and until 'Pharaoh' nodded—
nothing was done.

The Egyptians never gave up their claim to Sovereignty
over the Sudan, and bitterly resented the Sudan Government's insistence on safeguarding the rights of the Sudanese.
Consequently there was always perpetual strain on relations
between Cairo and Khartoum. Egyptian propaganda was
powerful and emotive. "We are brothers, bound by Islam"
was the constant and repetitive theme. The Egyptians too
were investing much money in providing places for
Sudanese students in Egyptian schools in the Sudan, and
having many politicians and journalists from the Sudan on
their 'pay-roll'. Lavish entertainment was provided for these
when they visited Egypt. By 1951, Egyptian penetration in
Sudanese society was deep. First they launched a campaign
for the 'Unity of the Nile'; the Egyptian newspaper, 'Al
Ahram' then reported that nearly half a million Egyptian
pounds were being spent on social welfare in the Sudan, in
addition to the support given to one hundred and thirteen

mosques and wakfs (Religious Endowments). The Egyptian Ministry of Education proposed opening more schools, and the Ahlia School in Omdurman to which I was first posted was wholly financed by them and was quite blatantly a centre of pro-Egyptian propaganda—the students were manipulated for that purpose. To be fair to the Egyptian Government they saw this activity as merely redressing the balance, as they felt that the whole British presence in the Sudan was solely in the interest of Britain and they felt at a disadvantage.

While we were in Egypt, the Sudan Agent reported that the Egyptians were going to abrogate the Co-domini agreement, but this was received with scepticism by both Khartoum and London. They felt that with King Farouk on his honeymoon, and Nashas Pasha on holiday this was unlikely. The Governor-General had visited Cairo shortly before this and Sir James had spent two hours talking with Ibrahim Faraj Pasha, (the Foreign Minister) in Alexandria, recording in his diary that 'the talks were of little use'[5]. But the rumours persisted, and while we were enjoying our Egyptian Tour the Egyptians were fermenting trouble in the Sudan. The police had been complaining for some time about their poor pay and conditions and had, in my opinion, genuine grievances. They wanted their own union and to affiliate to the Trades Union Federation, but they were curtly told that the newly introduced Trade Union legis-lation did not apply to the police. Early in June the Police went on strike, and political agitators and the criminal elements saw their opportunity to take advantage of the situation. Looting took place, mainly against the Greeks and the Copts (ironically these were Egyptian Copts). The Com-mandant of Police who was British and his Coptic assistant mismanaged the situation, and very unfortunately two

[5]Robertson. Transition in Africa, p. 146.

Sudanese were killed in the disturbance. The Federation at that time was led by Al Shafiee el Sheikh, reputedly a Communist, and, it must be said, acting quite irresponsibly. The leadership was militant and left wing, but not Communist as no Marxist would have acted so stupidly in 'trying' to exacerbate the situation.

Sir James Robertson acted swiftly and with great coolness by recognising their genuine grievances, as he was under great pressure from his senior officials, both in the political service and the heads of the other great departments of the Sudan Government. The Civil Secretary ordered the Sudan Defence Force to be ready to take over if necessary but the two battalions of British troops were confined to barracks. He had no intention of allowing what was essentially an industrial dispute to develop into a political crisis. The position was critical as the SDF* were hesitant, but remained a disciplined force. The Police were ordered to return to duties and over seventy percent of them did so. Sir James deserved the highest praise for his wisdom in handling an explosive situation.

The heat in the Northern Sudan was intense, and we were enduring our first experience of Ramadan, the month long Muslim fast. We marvelled at the tenacity of the Sudanese, adhering to this discipline in such conditions, as we could not contemplate abstaining from drinking anything from sunrise to sunset. Food in that heat was no problem, but the desire to drink was almost impossible to suppress. Everyone was glad to celebrate the Bairam at the end of the month and tensions were eased. We were urged, by Sayed Siddig el Mahdi with whom we were sharing the end of Ramadan breakfast to visit the Island of Aba, the birthplace of Mahdism, as guests of his father. It was at this time that Sayed Abdel Rahman el Mahdi was taken

*Sudan Defence Force.

seriously ill, but as the situation was so fraught his admission to a clinic in Switzerland for treatment was kept secret, and publicly he was said to be on holiday. He was by this time the unquestioned leader of the Independence Movement, and there was no one else of his stature to replace him.

An official tour of the Gezira Cotton Syndicate allowed us to pay a visit to Gezira Aba where we met, for the first time, Sayed el Hadi, Abdel Rahman's second son, later to be the Imam of the Ansar. Until then he had been rather remote from affairs, and it was at my suggestion, that his father brought him to Khartoum where he could be more involved.

Before leaving Khartoum in August for a six week tour of various training schemes in England I had a series of meetings with both Umma and Khatmiyya leaders so that I could inform my old friends the Rt Hon Jim Griffiths, the Rt Hon Hilary Marquand and the Rt Hon Herbert Morrison of the Sudanese view. I spent much time conveying my impressions about the Sudan and Egypt, but the Labour Government, with a bare majority, was fighting for its existence and not really interested in overseas affairs, although, Herbert Morrison, then Foreign Secretary, was struggling with the problems of Mossadeck and the Iranian oil crisis; and with threatening noises from Cairo. Sir James Robertson had written to me on Morrison who had succeeded Ernest Bevin that he considered him to be "a most capable administrator with an unbiased mind, but the Egyptian problems will test his ability".[6]

Sayed Abdel Rahman, who had returned from his treatment in Switzerland summoned us on October the eighth to take tea with him at his Abbas'iya Palace in Omdurman, which surprised us somewhat as he had been

---

[6]Sir James Robertson. Mss letter, 9.8.52.

living very quietly because of his heart condition. When we arrived at the family residence we were very shocked at the Sayed's appearance: he was grey and drawn, and walked slowly leaning heavily on his stick. He was immaculate, his white gallabia was covered by a dark brown cloak delicately embroidered with a light gold thread, but an incongruous note was struck by his vividly coloured and patterned socks.

Sayed Abdel Rahman immediately asked me for my views on the present situation as there was an obvious deterioration in the relationship between Britain and Egypt. As we were talking Zein el Abdin carried the telephone into the garden. The short conversation (I never knew to whom he was speaking) brought a flush to the Sayed's face In some way the atmosphere became electric as he put down the receiver. Before saying anything he swallowed a pill which he took from a small case and then said (in Arabic) "Egypt has abrogated the Condominium Treaty". There was a stunned silence, for such unilateral action had not been anticipated, or even considered by the Sudanese as being a remote possibility. Its evident political consequence would be that Egypt had no legal status in the Sudan. Muhammed Ali Shawki, who was present with Sayed el Hadi, struggled to his feet as he was very lame, and threw himself at Sayed Abdel Rahman's feet saying "Now we must declare the Independence of the Sudan. This is the moment". He went on to elaborate, saying that both His Excellency the Governor-General and the Civil Secretary were out of the country, so that Speaker Shingetti could convene the Assembly and a motion could be passed. Tears were streaming down Shawki's face as he volunteered to pull down the flag of Egypt from the Palace. El Hadi joined the pleas of Shawki, vehemently begging his father to seize the moment. Sayed Abdel Rahman turned to me asking "What would you do, if you were me?" I was embarrassed as I was a Sudan Government Official, if only a junior, and a British subject. I was truly in a dilemma. Had I been in Sayed Abdel Rahman's place I would have done as Shawki urged as it would have forced the British Government to choose between accepting a fait accompli or imprisoning the Sayed and his Umma followers. This would have united the country behind them and ultimately given them the Independence they longed for, freeing them from the taint of being 'British stooges'. As I was reviewing the possibilities Abdullah Khalil came hurrying in with Abdel Rahman Abdoun followed by Sayed Siddig. Everyone seemed to be talking at the same time, but the Sayed silenced them and asked Khalil to state his view, which he did clearly and emphatically, saying, "I have given my word to Sir James Robertson that the Umma Party will proceed to Independence by constitutional means and that I will not deviate from that path". His view was endorsed by Abdoun, and by Sayed Siddig, the son of Sayed Abdel Rahman. Tempers flared, Abdullah Khalil threatened to resign; and Shawki retorted "Let him go". The Sayed sat quietly for a few minutes and then indicated that would accept Khalil's point of view.[7]

I am convinced that had Sayed Abdel Rahman not had his heart attack he would have made the decision to declare Independence as he did not entirely trust the British and had deep reservations about the policies of the Governor-General and Sir James. So Shawki was not to tear down the Egyptian flag, but he was to live to see it lowered, together with the Union Jack, and the Sudanese flag of Independence raised above Gordon's Palace.

When the full information reached the Sudan it revealed that Nahas Pasha, the charismatic head of the Wafd Party and in effect the popular leader of Egypt, had not only abrogated the Treaty but had declared King Farouk to be

---

[7] G F Thomas. Mss notes.

King, not only of Egypt but of the Sudan. On the sixteenth and seventeenth of October, King Farouk signed two Acts in the Egyptian Parliament. In addition to the declaration on Farouk's Sovereignty over the two countries, it detailed the methods by which the Sudan would be governed. The Sudanese Cabinet was to be appointed by and dismissed by the King; the House of Representatives would, with Farouk's consent, make laws and approve the budget, but he would have the right to dissolve the House at will. Matters of Foreign Affairs, Defence, the Armed Forces, and Currency were to be exclusively the prerogative of the Egyptian ruler.

The Umma and Ansar reaction to these announcements was immediate and decisive; but the pro-Egyptian factions in the Sudan, even including Sayed Ali el Mirghani were acutely embarrassed. They had not been prepared or consulted. Azhari, and even Egypt's staunchest supporter in the Sudan, Muhammed Nur-el-Din, were astonished. The Civil Secretary once said to me when I had expressed dismay at the progress of Egyptian influence "You need never worry for you can always rely on Egypt doing the wrong thing at the right time".[8] He was to be proved right on many occasions.

The British Government's reaction had a true Churchillian ring, as the Conservatives had gained power at the previous Election, for in the King's Speech at the opening of the new Parliament it made it clear that the British Government regarded the unilateral abrogation as illegal and totally without validity. The determination of Britain not to accept the abrogation negated it completely, Nahas was all "hot air and talk". A side effect on the Sudan was that, rather pettishly, Egypt held up surface mail for a period. At this time I was able to air my views on these matters by

---

[8]Conversation with Sir James Robertson.

contributing articles on the Sudan and Egypt to the London "Observer" under the pen name of Richard Russell. These articles, which were written with the tacit approval of Sir James Robertson were syndicated in British Newspapers, and throughout the world.

Political agitation continued, the students were increasingly militant resulting in the closure of schools for a period. My work took me all over the Sudan and it was at this time that I had the pleasure of meeting William Luce, Governor of Blue Nile Province and later the Constitutional Advisor to the Governor General. Our first year in the Sudan was coming to an end and we celebrated Christmas at Port Sudan as guests of Bill Clark, the very hospitable Commissioner of the port.

Shortly before the New Year of 1952 Tom Driberg MP, the then Chairman of the Labour Party paid a visit to the Sudan, where his brother (a distinguished anthropologist) had served as a District Commissioner, in the South where he died and was buried. I had arranged for the visit and his expenses were being met by Sayed Abdel Rahman. At the time he was an effective journalist with a weekly column in the now defunct Reynolds News. Sir James detailed me to look after him; whether he knew of my role in the arrangements or of the involvement of Sayed Abdel Rahman I never knew. A series of meetings was arranged with leading politicians and journalists, and the usual round of official receptions and dinner parties took place. He embarrassed us quite considerably by producing two gay RAF boys whom he had met at their base in Suez and brought with him—he insisted on their going with him everywhere, and meant to take them to the Governor-General's dinner. He was only dissuaded when I threatened to telephone The Rt Hon Clement Attlee, then Leader of the Labour Party. I arranged for the two service personnel to be recalled to duty in the Suez Canal Zone.

He wrote some very sympathetic articles about the Sudan in Reynold's News so Sayed Abdel Rahman was fully satisfied with the visit. Sir James was highly amused by his activities and his reports, but he was becoming disturbed at the attitude of the British Foreign Office. At lunch he said to me "Rumours have it that Churchill is thinking of selling out to Farouk. If that happens many of the Sudanese will revolt"[9]—I took this to mean that he wanted this to be conveyed to my Labour Party friends in London which I did.

Internally matters were quite difficult, a further three day General Strike had had a deleterious effect on the economy, and there was much political unease as even the pro-Egyptian Unionists were disturbed by recent events in Cairo and the lack of consultation. The unionists were once more thrown into confusion and the Observer reported a statement from Anthony Eden in which he said "The pro-Egytian parties in the Sudan have never been more disunited, divided and confused".

Nahas Pasha had been completely frustrated and his authority utterly weakened by His Majesty's Government's refusal to respond to the Egyptian action on the Abrogation. It was a non-event. So in a desperate attempt to shore up his collapsing authority he resorted to violence, inciting the mob led by indoctrinated students to rampage on the streets of Cairo. The symbols of British Imperialism, the Gezira Club and Shepheard's Hotel, were burned and scores of British lives, together with hundreds of Egyptians were lost in the carnage which followed. Nahas deliberately delayed calling out the police, and he and King Farouk watched Cairo burn. Eventually the King and his Army Officers took action, Nahas Pasha was dismissed and law and order imposed. Ali Maher Pasha, a liberal and decent

---

[9]Conversations with Sir James Robertson.

man, formed a new administration and leaders from the various Sudanese pro-Egyptian groups hastened to Cairo for talks. In the Sudan there was an easing of relations between the two major groupings, who had reached an understanding that the Sudan should have the right of self-determination. This was made very clear to me in talks with Mirghani Hamza and Dardiri Muhammed Osman, although Sayed Ali el Mirghani had made no reference to the developments in Egypt or the Sudan in our regular usual meetings, but in a devious way he had shown that he was interested in the attitude of Britain. The respect with which Ali Maher Pasha was held seemed to indicate that the situation was improving.[10]

These events in Egypt had their repercussions in the Sudan. The Civil Secretary was pressing for an Independent Sudan Government although he had received a coldly worded dispatch from the Foreign Office which read 'It is not Her Majesty's Government policy that the Sudan should be prepared for self-government by 1953'[*][11] Sir James' reaction was revealed in a comment to the Governor-General which was merely to say "We must play for time". There had been much discussion since the abrogation relating to the constitutional basis for the Sudan Government. The main question at issue was where did sovereignty of the Sudan reside (after the Abrogation) until the country could achieve self-determination. The British insisted that the question was theoretical as the Egyptian action had been both 'illegal and invalid', but to Dardiri Muhammed Osman and Muhammed Ahmed Mahjoub (the leaders of the two largest pressure groups) both of whom had had legal training it was vital and urgent. The Constitutional Commis-

---

[10]G F Thomas. Mss letter.

[*]NB. This is in direct conflict with Eden's statement to the House of Commons (15 November 1951) in which he had said "HMG is glad that the Sudan is now rapidly moving in the direction of self-government".

[11]Muddadhir Abdel Rahim-Imperialism and Nationalism, p. 181.

sion sent a cable to the United Nations asking that a Commission to supervise the country during the interim period should be appointed. No reply was received.

With an acute political grasp of the immediate situation, Sir James Robertson requested the Chairman of the Commission, Judge Stanley Baker to draw up a report, including the agreed recommendations to date. One result of this was that the Report when presented to the Legislative Assembly in April was only slightly amended before being passed in May 1952. It was a considerable achievement. Unfortunately, then the Assembly adjourned, and in effect, this was to be its last sitting although it had already had its life extended beyond the original deadline. It was hoped that elections could be held before the 1952 rains, but events made that impossible. The consequence was that the Sudan lacked an effective representative body to articulate Sudanese aspirations at this most critical point in their history. Sir James recognised this in his book and described it as 'One of the greatest mistakes I made as Civil Secretary'[12]. No one really protested at the time of the adjournment of the Legislative Assembly although Shingetti had felt some reservations.

In Cairo, the United States Embassy was using its powerful influence to revive the old Siddky-Bevin idea of the 'Symbolic Sovereignty' of the Egyptian Monarch over the Sudan and Hillali Pasha, by then Prime Minister of Egypt, tried to conciliate Sayed Abdel Rahman, and succeeded in so far that a 'Personal Mission' was sent by him to Cairo on the twenty seventh of May, but when the details were revealed it was impossible for Sayed Abdel Rahman to accept any form of Egyptian sovereignty. The mission returned to Khartoum on the twelfth of June no agreement having been possible.

---

[12]Robertson. Transition in Africa, p. 146.

I went on tour to the Southern Sudan which was fascinating and stimulating. The problems there were in sharp contrast to those of the North. We returned to Khartoum but only for a short time before Leave, but it was an eventful period. In early June we were telephoned by Shingetti to ask us to go immediately to the Gubba where Sayed Abdel Rahman wanted to speak with me urgently. We were there within minutes only to be asked to wait as the Sayed was engaged. We were intrigued as the Governor-General's Rolls Royce was in the drive. As we were being served with fresh lemon juice the door of the salon opened and the Sayed emerged. As he greeted us courteously I noticed that he was not his usual self for he was obviously much agitated, which was always indicated by the impatient tapping of his stick, and his complexion had a peculiar greyish white hue. He said "I am so angry you must forgive me. I must lie down for a while. Abdullah will tell you what has happened this morning". As he left, Abdullah Khalil came out with two individuals—obviously American, and bade them farewell ushering them into the Rolls Royce, before joining us. He explained that the two men, one of whom was Robert Murphy (later an Under-Secretary at the Pentagon) had asked Sayed Abdel Rahman to recognise Farouk as King of the Sudan. In return the Sayed could have whatever title he wished and a guaranteed income of £3 million a year. We were speechless. It was unbelievable as Sayed Abdel Rahman had spent his life and wealth opposing union with Egypt. When I enquired about the title, Abdullah said "Viceroy or Khedive, and what the Sayed wanted to know was if you had heard anything and if the British were behind the approach".[13] I had heard nothing, but I was certain that Sir James who detested the regime in Cairo, would not only have

---

[13]G F Thomas. Mss notes.

Sayed Abdel Rahman el Mahdi arriving at London to see Winston Churchill

disapproved but would never have contemplated such a proposition. He was working only in the interest of the Sudanese which had always been his approach. I assured Abdullah of this, but when asked to explain the tacit support indicated by the use of the official car I could only surmise that the Americans were pressuring the British Government to find a way to support Farouk. Sayed Abdel Rahman who was furiously angry had coldly but courteously told them that their proposition was "wholly unacceptable". Within six weeks the Egyptian Revolution had taken place; Farouk had been exiled and was no longer King of Egypt. When I later asked Sir James about the incident he had no recollections, and certainly made no reference to it in his memoirs.

Our leave in England was not a holiday, as we continued our campaign on behalf of Sudanese Independence. With the consent of Sir James Robertson, I addressed a gathering of members of Parliament in one of the House of Commons' Committee Rooms and spoke to a number of MP's and ex-Ministers including Griffiths, Marquand, Michael Stewart, and Morrison.

While we were still in England, the Armed Forces in Egypt deposed King Farouk and established General Muhammed Neguib as President; and Farouk sailed away to obscurity and an early death. He had always said that soon there would be only five kings left in the World—those of hearts, clubs, diamonds, spades, and the King of England. He had cynically added that he would only remain king of Egypt as long as he had control of the Army. He had now lost this, and as he said farewell to Neguib his final words were—"You will find Egypt harder to rule than you think".

These events in Egypt had reactions in the Sudan. Neguib had Sudanese connections for he had lived in Khartoum when his father was serving in the Egyptian Army, and his brother Ali had been the Egyptian ADC to the Governor-

General and was extremely popular. The Unionists were concerned as the new leaders were an unknown quantity, and while the Umma party were delighted to see the end of the monarchy, they were still apprehensive, although it was believed that Neguib favoured self-determination for the Sudan. Sir James Robertson, as Civil Secretary was also carefully monitoring events, commenting that "The Sudanese took the Egyptian Revolution very quietly and are watching the melodrama from their seats. I do not think we will have much bother, unless things in Egypt alter"[14] and a few weeks later he was saying that he was hopeful that "our political and constitutional position will clear up so that we can go ahead with all the elections. Sayed Abdel Rahman and Sayed Ali el Mirghani are both menaces to the Sudan with their personal and sectarian rivalry".[15] But things were altering in Egypt. Neguib and Nasser believed that having deposed Farouk, the Egyptians could beat the British at their own game simply by calling their bluff.[16] The new Government in Egypt opened discussions with the Umma Party and the Independence Front, and as they were prepared to concede to the Sudanese self-determination, agreement was quickly reached.

On September the twenty third Sayed Abdel Rahman, anxious to know the views of the British Government, flew to London for talks with Churchill and Eden, who quite frankly admitted that they had been outmanoeuvred by the Egyptians and could not object. Churchill received Sayed Abdel Rahman at No 10 Downing Street, reminiscing about the Mahdi and the Battle of Omdurman, and eulogising the value of monarchy to a country. Shingetti, who was acting as interpreter had some difficulty in explaining to the Sayed that Churchill was referring to the United Kingdom and was

---

[14]Sir James Robertson. Mss letter, 22.3.51.
[15]G F Thomas. Mss notes.
[16]Neguib. Egypt's Destiny, pp. 241–2.

not urging Sayed Abdel Rahman to take the Crown of the Sudan. Sayed Abdel Rahman, having satisfied himself that the British accepted the situation, returned to Cairo where an agreement was signed with Neguib on the twelfth of October. Five days later sixty-five leading members of the Umma Party flew to Cairo to greet the Sayed, and I noted that "It seems certain that we shall have a general election here before Christmas. I think Neguib wants to arrive at a real settlement"[17] and I wrote home at the end of the month to say that "All Sudanese politicians are coming home today, Great crowds are assembling and the Mahdists are chanting and marching".[18] At this time, Hilary Marquand wrote to me, saying that he had had a long talk with Sayed Abdel Rahman and his friends who expressed their satisfaction with the talks they had had with Eden, and had no wish for the Labour Party to intervene, but the British opposition leaders had assured them that they would be glad to help if necessary. Certainly the Umma Party was jubilant as Sayed El Hadi reported when he came to tea.[19]

The agreement was essentially based on the self-government statute which Sir James had been anxious to achieve, but there were certain important amendments. Neguib had opened discussions with the British Government, and Sir James flew to Cairo for talks with Sir Ralph Stevenson (the British Ambassador), Neguib, and Mr Caffery (the American Ambassador). The Americans had been pressing Britain to settle with the Egyptians "Even at the price of selling the Sudanese".[20] One of the Americans sent to the Sudan to negotiate even referred to the Sudanese as "ten million bloody niggers"[21] which incensed

---

[17]Conversation with Shingetti.
[18]G F Thomas. Mss letter, 3.10.52.
[19]G F Thomas. Mss letter, 31.10.52.
[20]Robertson. Transition in Africa, p. 150.
[21]Ibid.

Muhammed Saleh Shingetti

Abdel Rahman Ali Taha

Ibrahim Ahmed

Abdel Rahman Abdoun

Sir James, who was strenuously trying to persuade Neguib that the Sudan needed more time, that they could not run the country without a "considerable amount of outside help" and above all that he feared great troubles if the Southern Sudanese were handed over without any safeguards. His appeal for time did not succeed, for Neguib knew that he had already achieved agreement with the major Sudanese parties. Alas, Sir James was to be proved right. The Civil Secretary was deeply concerned at the emphasis on speed in the Sudanisation of the Service, particularly in the fields of administration, the police, and the armed forces. The tide was flowing too strongly towards Independence and London was urging a quick settlement in the hope that it would ease matters concerning British bases in Suez while Cairo was well aware of the political appeal of Sudanisation. Sir James considered that the Sudan had been thrown into the melting pot "Of course it has, and it has been thrown in by the Foreign Office, and by the Cairo Embassy because in spite of all we have said they thought they could buy a settlement on the Canal at the price of the Sudan. That is why in October 1952 Anthony Eden had told Sayed Abdel Rahman to go to Cairo and make an agreement with Neguib".[22]

It was at this time that we gave a party to which were invited Sayed Siddig, Abdullah Khalil, Shingetti, and other Umma Leaders, and we also invited the leaders of the Khatmiyya and Unionists including Dardiri Muhammed Osman, and Mirghani Hamza. It was the first time that the 'great divide' between the two groups had been bridged in over twenty years. I confess that at first we were nervous, but after an initial period of coolness, the atmosphere became more relaxed and informal, as Ismay put everyone at ease. After an hour Sayed Siddig asked whether there was

---

[22]Conversation with Sir James Robertson.

a private place where he and Dardiri could talk. The only available room was our bedroom, but they were quite happy to retire there for their discussions. One and a half hours later they emerged and announced that, subject to Sayed Abdel Rahman and Sayed Ali el Mirghani being agreeable, they would contest the next elections. This was a huge step forward as for nearly a decade the Khatmiyya and Unionists had refused to participate in any elections.

By January 1953 all the Sudanese parties signed a further agreement with Egypt. Even the Socialist Republican Party signed. An Egyptian Embassy was sent to the Sudan (led by the notorious Major Salah Salim, the Dancing Major). Abdullah Khalil had some misgivings but Sayed Abdel Rahman was convinced that Neguib had conceded on the most important point, that of self-determination and this should not be put in jeopardy by insisting on other safeguards which could be determined on Independence. Sir James gloomily reports in his diary "What then are we to

Sayed Abdel Rahman greeting President Neguib of Egypt

do? There seems little point in struggling when all the political parties are in agreement with Egypt. But, would we desert the South or the Nazirs if we gave in? Have we the power to stand out any longer?"[23] This was the crucial point. There was no power left to sustain the Sudan Government, and their objections on the two vital matters of the South and the speed of Sudanisation were both ignored by the British Government and on the fourteenth of February the Anglo-Egyptian agreement was signed in Cairo.

Assessing the situation accurately now that the agreement was signed, Sir James decreed that the Celebrations marking the occasion should be attended by all expatriate officials, and His Excellency the Governor-General initiated a ceremonial gathering under the statue of Field Marshal Lord Kitchener where he delivered a speech of welcome to the Agreement in front of thousands upon thousands of rejoicing Sudanese.

In March the Rt Hon Selwyn Lloyd flew out to review the situation, especially as there was a danger that many British Officials would leave too quickly. He attempted to persuade Sir James himself to stay a little longer "to steady the situation". Sir James replied that "there were many reasons why I should not . . . . I also told him that I was responsible to the Governor-General, not the British Government and that if the Governor-General wanted to re-open the matter that was up to him".[24] This was an interesting point indicating the autonomy of the Sudan Political Service. Within a few weeks, Sir James and Lady Robertson left. It was a highly emotional occasion and many tears were shed as they entrained for Port Sudan, and their final leave. It was the end of an epoch which had begun with the death of General Gordon. Sir James was the last of the Proconsuls.

---

[23]Robertson. Transition in Africa, p. 151.
[24]JRobertson. Transition in Africa, p. 158.

An interesting postscript was Sayed Ali el Mirghani's vituperative comments on Sir James' departure, when we visited him shortly after leaving the station. He exploded with rage, denouncing Sir James in the most violent of terms blaming him for all the trials and tribulations of the Sudan. Sir James' greatest sin had been to create Sayed Abdel Rahman el Mahdi into a man of influence and that had been the cause of all the problems. Sayed Ali questioned why had Sir James wanted to change everything. He and his family had been content until the Civil Secretary had interfered. "That man" had made the Mirghani family look towards Egypt for support, "for they had no trust in either Sir James or Sayed Abdel Rahman". It was most vehement and no attempt was made at dissimulation. It was most revealing.[25]

Major Salah Salim managed to persuade the various factions in the pro-Unionist group to form a National Unionist Party under the leadership of Ismael el Azhari and this was followed by the reconciliation, at least publicly between Sayed Abdel Rahman and Sayed Ali.

Britain, even had she wanted to do so, had no alternative but to accept the situation, agreeing that the Sudan Government Statute would come into effect on the thirty first of December 1955, which, with later amendments, became the Transitional Constitution of the Independent Sudan. This has remained virtually the only constitutional instrument since that date despite dictatorships.

Neguib announced in Cairo that he hoped the Sudanese would join Egypt, but they were free to choose Independence; he denied their right to join the British Commonwealth. Britain weakly said that this was not so but no one in the Sudan was enthusiastic about joining the Commonwealth except Muhammed Ali Shawki. It was not a realistic proposition.

---

[25] G F Thomas. Mss notes.

CHAPTER III

INDEPENDENCE AND SOVEREIGNTY

"The first of all earthly blessings, independence"

GIBBON

During the stipulated three years to self-determination the task of Government fell on A C Beaton, Gawain Bell, (his deputy) and Sir William Luce who was designated Adviser to the Governor-General on Constitutional and External affairs. Three bodies were established to prepare the way for self-determination. These were the Electoral Commission, the Governor-General's Advisory Commission, and the Sudanisation Committee. Of these, the Electoral Commission was the first to become active under the chairmanship of a distinguished Indian, Sukamar Sen. He led a commission of one British member, one American, one Egyptian, and three Sudanese, and was much respected by all. We became good friends and saw him and his wife frequently during this period. Having made a few changes in the electoral law and procedures he then supervised the elections, which, largely thanks to his efforts and the natural good temper of the Sudanese went off smoothly and peacefully.

The Egyptians had naturally made vast donations to the pro-unity parties and to individuals. As I drove to work one morning I followed an Egyptian army lorry which I noticed stopped at various gateways, and on each occasion a fair

53

sized box was carried in. After this had occurred twice I decided to tail the lorry, and watched the same thing happen at some ten or twelve doors before it returned to barracks. When I reached the office I telephoned security, reported what I had seen and then forgot about it until about half an hour later when a young Sudanese arrived at my office claiming to be a telephone engineer. I was nonplussed as the telephone appeared to be functioning, but when he insisted that I follow him so that I could be shown the problem I complied. I was astonished when he produced his identification from security and asked whether I could point out the precise houses. I went with him and pointed out approximately six or seven including one which belonged to a well known Egyptian doctor. I was told later that the houses had been raided, and thousands of pounds of Egyptian money had been found. All the houses belonged to Egyptian sympathisers.[1] After the elections I described this episode to Colonel Abdel Fatah Hassan, the Commander-in-Chief of the Egyptian troops in the Sudan and questioned the morality of bribing the electorate. He laughed and replied "Graham, I really don't understand you British, you will spend millions of pounds conquering a country by force—that is valour and patriotism—our distribution did not create any widows or orphans and three million is a relatively cheap way of conquering a country".

The constitutional boundaries had been drawn up by the political section of the Civil Secretary's office and I am convinced that they were drawn up as honestly and fairly as a group of individuals could achieve, but in my opinion there was a bias towards the towns and against the rural areas. This gave the National Unionist Party an advantage as they were strongest in the Capital and the Northern Province. I had a good idea of the situation as my job in the

---

[1] Ismay Thomas. Mss Journal, p. 159.

Labour Department not only required me to travel widely, but meant that I was constantly in touch with the Labour offices in all the areas and with many Sudanese of all persuasions. I could 'take the temperature' so to speak, and my background enabled me to interpret and assess. My views were widely sought after by many senior politicians, and by Sayed Abdel Rahman.

The election was foremost in everyone's mind. Sayed Abdel Rahman was being accused of wishing to become the King of the Sudan, and in spite of statements repudiating this the rumours persisted especially as Sayed Abdullahi el Fadl and Sayed Muhammed Khalifa Sherif were constantly advocating a royal dynasty but the Sayed appreciated that kingship had no place in his country.

Shortly before the election Ismay and I were invited to an informal dinner by Sayed Abdel Rahman at the Mahdi's house adjacent to the Gubba. At first the conversation was general without anything of importance being said until Muhammed Ali Shawki suddenly said "Graham has great reservations about Sayed Siddig standing at the election". Rather sharply I was asked by the Sayed whether this were true and what were my reasons. My reply was to the effect that the public feared the monarchical aspirations; were not convinced by the denials, and that if Siddig stood for parliament this would confirm their fears. I then added that Siddig would be put in a very humiliating position as the Umma Party would not win the election. No bomb could have caused a greater effect. Everyone spoke at once, and I was convinced there was a strong feeling that I was a British stooge, spreading alarm and despondency. I very quickly intervened to assure them that I had always tried, without fear or favour to speak the truth as I saw it, and the good friend sometimes had to give unpalatable as well as pleasant news. The Sayed nodded and asked for my evidence. In detail I told them of our contacts both through our professional connections, and through the open house policy we had always followed, entertaining Sudanese of all shades of opinion. Siddig was furiously angry and challenged me to forecast the number of seats which would be taken by the Umma Party. Fortunately I had done my calculations, and suggested that the Umma would only gain between twenty-four and twenty-six seats. All were incredulous, and tempers ran high. The evening ended by Sayed Abdel Rahman assuring me that he knew that I was a passionate believer in the Independence of the Sudan, that he was sure I spoke from my heart as well as my head. He was equally certain that I was wrong as all reports reaching him indicated otherwise, and that the Umma Party would have a massive victory. We left saddened for it was the first major disagreement with our friends, and Siddig was bitterly resentful. Ismay felt I had been too brutal and frank, and maybe that was true for I was young.[2]

There was no doubt in my mind that the result was a foregone conclusion because of the electoral boundaries. The representation was heavily biased in favour of the areas where the unionists were strongest. This had not been a deliberate ploy, but although the electoral commission had been utterly scrupulous that was what had happened. I am glad to say that there was no break in my relations with Sayed Abdel Rahman although Siddig was decidedly cool until after the elections.

Another incident of some interest happened a few days later when I was discussing the most violently pro-Egyptian candidate Muhammed Nur-el-Din with Sayed Abdel Rahman. I pointed out to him that if Nur-el-Din was unopposed in his constituency of Halfa it would give him the freedom to use his considerable energies elsewhere, and give the impression to the world press that the Wadi Halfa

---

[2] G F Thomas. Mss note.

area was unanimously in favour of Union with Egypt. I suggested that an Independent candidate should be found to contest the area where the Umma Party had no support. So it came to pass that Muhammed Tewfig Ahmed, a young colleague of mine in the Labour Dept was sponsored to contest the seat and ensure that Muhammed Nur-el-Din was kept busy.

Prior to the elections, Sir James Robertson had made, in my view, an error of judgement (in allowing a new party to be formed), which was rare for him as he was a truly outstanding man with a deep insight into the Sudan and Sudanese based on thirty years experience. As self-government came nearer, it seemed that it would be a battle between the NUP (Sayed Ali el Mirghani) and the Umma (Sayed Abdel Rahman el Mahdi). Many of the British officials feared that years of devoted service might end in chaos and even a blood-bath because, for a lifetime, relations between Sayed Ali and Sayed Abdel Rahman had been strained to the point of utter detestation. So the idea of a middle party was floated. Current gossip in Khartoum indicated that the 'putative father' of the idea was Desmond Hawksworth, then working in the Civil Secretary's office. He certainly denied it and Sir James in his book denied that it emanated from his office[3] but such was the power and influence of the Civil Secretary that at least tacit approval must have been given for its formation. Essentially the Socialist Republican Party as it was called, appealed to Sudanese Government officials and the intelligentsia of liberal persuasion. Later Sir James, in a letter, admitted to me that it had been 'inspired'. 'I agree with you that as things worked out the SRP may have been a mistake. The idea was to try to build up a non-marxist party supporting independence because *I felt sure* (my italics) there were many

---

[3]Robertson. Transition in Africa, p. 151 footnote.

Sudanese who did not want to be associated with Sayed
Abdel Rahman el Mahdi, but who were equally against
Union with Egypt. Without some centre party there was no
way in which they could express their views. However it
doesn't seem to have worked".[4]

Curiously, in his book Sir James calls it the Sudan
Republican Party but the title had been carefully chosen to
indicate to Sayed Ali el Mirghani that it was non-sectarian
and to Sayed Abdel Rahman that it was anti-monarchical.
Ibrahim Bedri became the Secretary-General. The Bedri
family was traditionally Mahdist, but had tended to support
the British who had encouraged the family's interest in
education, both for girls and boys.

When the news of the formation of the SRP broke, Sayed
Abdel Rahman el Mahdi was furious because he regarded it
as an attempt to weaken the Umma Party and divide the
Independence Front. It was equally disliked by Sayed Ali el
Mirghani, who saw it as another sinister attempt on the part
of the Civil Secretary's office to confuse the whole issue.
Sayed Abdel Rahman vigorously expressed his views to Sir
James while Sayed Ali became even more uncooperative
with the Sudan Government. So much so, that the Civil
Secretary sent a very senior member of the political service
to warn the Sayed against being so hostile. He lectured
Sayed Ali for over half an hour during which he was
listened to in silence. Then, after a pause Sayed Ali el
Mirghani replied in his usual allegorical way, "For many
years I have complained to Sir James about the noise made
by the lions in the zoo (situated near his Khartoum home)
These have for years disturbed my tranquility, but he has
chosen to ignore my protests and take no action against the
lions (meaning Sayed Abdel Rahman and the Umma Party).
Now he has let the monkeys (SRP) out all over the place".[5]

[4]Sir James Robertson. Mss letter, 10.9.53.
[5]Conversation with Sir James Robertson.

I personally felt that the time was not right for such a new political development and that its influence would be minimal. It was so—it withered and died but it embittered relations between the British and Sudanese at a critical time. When the election results were known Sayed Abdel Rahman and the Umma were appalled. Fifty one seats went to the NUP, only twenty two to the Umma. The Southern Party had nine while there were eleven non-party. Only three seats were won by the SRP while there was one anti-imperialist front (Communist). Muhammed Ahmed Mahjoub was elected in the graduates' section.

Sayed Abdel Rahman felt deeply humiliated and betrayed by the British. It appeared that his life's work had been in vain. He was gracious to me saying that my forecast had been accurate, and he was later to say to his grandson Sadig that if he wanted honest advice he could get it from Graham Thomas.

The National Unionist Party's gain of the majority of seats at the election was analysed by Sir James, by then in retirement, as being the result of a number of factors. In his view there was dislike by true Moslems of the heresy of the Mahdists; also dislike of Sayed Abdel Rahman and his friends because of their bad 'nouveau riche' manners. It was also felt that they had been too reliant on the British. Egyptian propaganda and money he saw as having a crucial impact, as did the reputation of Neguib and the fear that Britain was no longer an important power in the Middle East.[6]

What was very evident was that the Unionists had never defined what they meant by 'Union with Egypt' and I did not think that either Sayed Ali or the Khatmiyya wanted to be under the domination of Egypt. Sir James expressed the view that 'some of those elected' would not back Egyptian

---

[6]Sir James Robertson. Mss Letter, 13.12.53.

British Troops replaced by Sudanese

The flag of Independence

rule. He said that people like Fadlallah Ali el Tom, Muhammed Said Telba, Muhammed Ahmed Abu Sin and others were anti-Sayed Rahman but not pro-Neguib.[7]

The situation did not appear to augur well for the Independence Front, but there was never a suggestion that the Ansar (Mahdists) would resort to violence to achieve their aim of Independence. The year ended quietly but with an air of apprehension, yet of expectation and excitement. The Sudanese all looked forward to the first meeting of their Parliament on the first of January 1954. British rule of the Sudan was now effectively at an end, and the few British Officials who remained no longer had any executive role but were purely advisory in the transitional period and the process leading to Sudanese Government.

The Parliament duly met on the first of January 1954, and on that very day, two of the principal supporters of Azhari, the Prime Minister, were in dispute. Mubarek Zarroug admitted to me he had quarrelled with Mirghani Hamza.[8] One source of disagreement was over the nomination of Ibrahim Mufti as Speaker which the Governor-General, with the approval of his Council, had rejected although the votes had been 54 to 43. It was evident that the Unionists were "badly divided between the Khatmiyya and Ashigga factions.[9] However, by 19 January, Mubarek Zarroug and Mirghani Hamza had been reconciled for they came to dinner to bid farewell to Ismay on her departure to England.

Azhari formed his government, taking the post of Minister of the Interior as well as that of Prime Minister. Mirghani Hamza had the Ministries of Education, Agriculture and Irrigation, which was a ridiculously large portfolio, while Mubarek Zarroug became Minister of Communications and Transport Overland. Others included

---

[7]Ibid, 28.10.53.
[8]G F Thomas. Mss letter, 26.2.54.
[9]Ibid, 13.2.54.

Ismael el Azhari, 1st Prime Minister of Sudan

Ibrahim Mufti at Commerce, Hamad Tewfig at Finance, Nur el Din at the Public Works Department, while Amin el Said was Minister of Health.

Within a few weeks quarrels broke out among the Unionists, principally over the nominations for the Sudanis-ation Committee. This was hardly surprising (as I noted in a letter)[10] "as they had nominated five ridiculous people" one a junior clerk, another a journalist, and the others had no idea of administration. Even Mahmoud el Feki, a staunch unionist was incensed, while Yahia el Fadli, (one of the leaders of the NUP) was furious at not being given a post and declared he would get 'Dardiri Muhammed Osman off the Governor-General's Commission'.[11] Mirghani Hamza threatened to resign and was supported by Muhammed Nur-el-Din. Yahia had the backing of about twelve NUP members, and even tried to obtain support from the Umma Party. Major Salah Salim, the Egyptian dancing major, was being severely criticised and told to 'keep his nose out' of Sudanese affairs. The Government was being openly abused in the market place. Certainly in those first few weeks the outlook appeared bleak. Azhari, no doubt to rally the NUP, made an anti-British pro-unity of the Nile Valley speech, and the Government announced that "No further recruit-ment of expatriates would take place, and that there would be no extensions of terms whatsoever".[12]

While all this was happening, and probably to Azhari's relief, trouble broke out in Egypt (I remembered Sir James' prediction that Egypt could always be relied on to do the wrong thing), by the twenty-fifth of February the secret struggle between Neguib and Nasser erupted into the open. Neguib offered his resignation as President to the Revolu-tionary Council and it was accepted. I saw Sayed Abdel

[10]Ibid, 28.2.54.
[11]Ibid, 26.2.54.
[12]G F Thomas. Mss note.

Dardiri Muhammed Osman

Yahia el Fadli

Rahman the same day and found him depressed by the news from Cairo, as he thought Neguib was a good and fair friend to the Sudan.[13] The Sudan was horrified by events in Cairo and when Mubarek Zarroug came to tea the following day, he was aghast.[14] Abdullah Khalil took me aside at the Khartoum Races, telling me that Sayed Abdel Rahman wanted to send another letter to Attlee, as he was very unhappy. General Neguib was exceptionally popular throughout Egypt and in the Sudan, and the mob went on the rampage in Cairo. Mohieddin, and his tanks supported Neguib and Nasser was forced to give way. The effect of Nasser's attempt to depose Neguib sent a profound shock wave through the whole of the Sudan. Over two hundred thousand telegrams of protest were sent from the Sudan.[15] The Unionists were in a state of confusion although Azhari was still advocating the Unity of the Nile Valley. I saw Sayed Abdel Rahman that day, and he was perplexed by developments; by a strange coincidence the Rt Hon Clement Attlee had written to Sayed Abdel Rahman urging him to exercise caution, and to be a restraining influence.[16]

That evening, Mubarek Zarroug came to see me, and I was astonished to see the change in him. He looked completely exhausted and was very depressed and disturbed at events in Egypt. I was to write the next day "You have no idea of the scorn with which Egypt is held by all Sudanese. Their contempt has to be seen to be believed. Nasser and Salah Salim are the laughing stock".

The Sudanese Parliament was to be opened on the first of March 1954, and many countries throughout the world were invited to attend the inauguration. British and Sudanese officials were deputed to look after these VIP's

---

[13]Ibid.
[14]G F Thomas. Mss Diary, 26.2.54.
[15]Ibid, 3.2.54.
[16]G F Thomas. Mss note.

and I was responsibe for Rao Raja Rajwadi, representing Pandit Nehru for India. He was a charming person, married to one of the most beautiful women I have ever met. He was the Indian Ambassador to Egypt, and very sociable. General Muhamed Neguib announced his intention to come to the opening of Parliament which caused some consternation among the Independence groupings, who were uncertain of how they should react. A series of meetings were held, in some of which I was involved. The Umma Party were still very bitter and shocked at the election results. They were at this time, still convinced that Azhari would lead the Sudan into a union with Egypt. So it was decided that they would organise a huge demonstration to prove to the world and the world's press that, despite the election results, all the Sudanese did not want union with Egypt. They were determined that such a gesture was essential, but Sayed Abdel Rahman was totally committed to a non-violent approach. At the informal meeting of the Sayed, Sayed Siddig, Abdulah Khalil, Shawki, and others including myself, at his farm by the Nile in Omdurman, the final strategy was planned. It was agreed that the Ansar would congregate near the airport and then line the route along which the procession would go. The 'Baraka' (blessing) by Sayed Abdel Rahman would be given from the balcony of Sayed Siddig's house which, at that time, was almost the last house on the road leading to the airport. The slogan was to be "Welcome to Neguib but no union with Egypt". There was no personal animosity against Neguib as an individual, and it was unanimously agreed that he was to be welcomed.[17] It was estimated that some half-a-million of the Ansar would answer the call, coming from the Blue Nile and Dueim areas.

On the first of March, I was driving down Gordon

---

[17]G F Thomas. Mss note.

Avenue (since renamed) when I was enveloped by thousands upon thousands of Ansar running away from the centre of Khartoum. Some were carrying heavy sticks (not unusual in the Sudan), and as I leaned out of the window to congratulate them I was shocked as they hit out at my car with their sticks. Needing petrol, I drew into the filling station only to find it deserted. I called and waited for service and ultimately a small boy crept out from behind an oil drum saying "Go home, Sartek Mudir, go home, they are shooting, people are dead". Thus I heard first of the tragedy of March the first. The boy refused to serve me with petrol, so I crawled on towards the Grand Hotel. I could not go past the Government Secretariat on to the Corniche, but I drove down a parallel road until I reached a police barrier which I was allowed to pass to get to the Hotel. There were gathered a number of phlegmatic British officials, who had like me, been marooned. Sukamer Sen, the Chairman of the Electoral Commission, had managed to reach there too, and it was he who told me that McGuigan (the Commissioner of Police) due to go on final leave six weeks later, and twenty six others had been killed, and that a state of emergency had been declared. We remained on the verandah, sipping our beers, and surrounded by barbed wire, little realising that a few yards away the dead lay where they had fallen. Radio Omdurman made continuous appeals to people to go home and stay home.

It was only later that I learned of the sequence of events that had so marred what should have been a day of rejoicing. The Ansar had gathered as agreed and having received the "baraka" they waited the arrival of the Egyptian President. Then they discovered that Neguib was not using the route planned, as someone from the Administration had decided that it was too dangerous for him to do so and had smuggled him out of the airport through a back gate. The Ansar spontaneously decided to march on the

Palace to which Neguib had been taken. So, tens of thousands marched towards the Palace, chanting as they had agreed. As they reached the main square near the Palace, the Police threw a cordon across the road which was disastrous. It was a case of those in front crying back, while those behind were still pushing forward. The pressure built up, and as the police line was in imminent danger of breaking the Assistant Commissioner of Police Mahdi Mustafa drove his car into the crowd in an attempt to stop the Ansar. This enraged them, so Mahdi Mustafa, himself a Mahdist, was seized and killed. In order to attempt a rescue McGuigan rode into the crowds on his horse, only to be plucked from the saddle and stabbed to death by the now frenzied mob. A detachment of the Sudan Defence Force opened fire and chaos ensued leaving some twenty six dead. It took a long time for the true casualty figures to be discovered but, in addition to some eleven policeman, there was a total of thirty three killed. The mob fled, and I have since marvelled that I, in my car, had not suffered the same fate as that of Mahdi Mustafa.

Later in the day I decided to make my way back to our house in Omdurman, mainly to ensure the safety of all our possessions as everything was packed and ready for my departure for final leave on the seventh of March; Ismay had left two months earlier. Friends and colleagues tried to dissuade me, but I carefully motored to the White Nile Bridge and persuaded the Army to allow me to cross. The Omdurman streets were littered with the debris, burned out buses and cars, chunks of rock, broken glass and overturned stalls. I eventually reached home to find my neighbours barricaded in, my servant terrified, and a message from the District Commissioner's Office to say I must evacuate, as all British in Omdurman were at grave risk. This I refused to do. For several days there was a state of seige, no electricity, no telephone, and not much food as I had few supplies left in store because of my near departure. Luckily my Sudanese friends came to my rescue. Not only was I not in any danger but I was under Ansar protection. News was difficult to come by, and the Government feared an onslaught of Ansar from the West but in a few days normality returned. Shingetti telephoned me on the third of March to tell me that Sayed Abdel Rahman had been placed under house arrest, his personal servant Baballa (very old, very fat, and utterly non-political) had been imprisoned with other Ansar for leading the rebellion. The idea of Baballa as a revolutionary was ludicrous.

As soon as the White Nile bridge reopened I drove to Khartoum to bid farewell to Sayed Abdel Rahman before I left for the United Kingdom. I was shocked to be, at first, refused admission by armed guards placed at the Sayed's gate by the Government, but as a British official I persuaded them that I did not need a 'Waraga' (permission). Sayed Abdel Rahman was seated on the patio with a few faithful old Ansar seated around his feet. He looked drawn, tired, and grey. As I drew near, the Sayed did something which he had never done before, he rose to his feet embracing me warmly in the Sudanese fashion, kissing me on both cheeks. As we stood there I realised that tears were running down his face which shattered me as I had never expected to see him cry. After a few quiet moments he said "Habibi (my dearest friend) you are the one and only British person to come see me in my desolation. No one has been near me, they just put me under house arrest. They know that I had no part in this tragedy They know the truth. Why am I so humiliated?" After a further pause he continued "I never believed that the British would allow this to happen. I have worked with them all my life. I have given them a lifetime of cooperation. Why has not Luce been to see me?" I was overcome because this man was a truly great leader of his people with a tremendous personality. I loved the man. We sat without speaking, our hands clasped together. No other words were spoken. It was a deeply emotional farewell.[18]

During the State of Emergency armed troops mounted guard over the public buildings, trains were searched, and one hundred and seventy-six Ansar were arrested, while the death toll mounted as more of the injured died in hospital. Cairo Radio repeatedly and deliberately broadcast that Sayed Siddig had been arrested, which was quite untrue but was meant to provoke the Mahdists in the Gezira and Kordofan into rebellion. My farewell party was rather sombre as events had overshadowed us. Discussion with my old friends including Muhammed Ahmed Mahjoub, Kamil Shawki, Muhammed Tewfig Ahmed was clearly affected by the recent disastrous events. Muhammed Hamad el Nil (Ambassador to London) voiced all their fears when he confessed that he did not know what the outcome would be. Mubarek Zarroug who entertained me on my last evening was also very subdued, and as I left early the next morning, travelling up the Nile to Cairo for what I thought might be the last time; I was very apprehensive about the future of the Sudan.

My departure from the Sudan service was not the only one. By the end of 1954 most of the senior British had left. The few that remained acted in an advisory capacity to the Sudanese. I felt that I had perhaps become too identified with the Umma Party and the Independence group to be allowed to carry on. It appeared at that time that the strength of the tide was going with the extreme group of pro-Egyptian Sudanese politicians and that union with Egypt now seemed a real possibility. I was wrong and on reflection, I should have stayed on, but I joined Her Majesty's Overseas Civil Service and moved to Kenya to experience another form of Colonial Rule, and Mau Mau.

---

[18]G F Thomas. Mss letter, 3.3.54.

But I continued to be involved with the Sudan and Sudanese, and followed very closely subsequent events.

Egypt continued to throw long shadows over the Sudan. The Umma Party was dismayed, but the Unionists were seriously embarrassed. As I was travelling up the Nile Valley on the first stage of my homeward journey, Nasser had made yet another abortive attempt to dislodge Neguib. I was greatly surprised on reaching Aswan to be told that I could go no further as there were "problems in Cairo". The situation was explained to me by the Governor of Aswan (at that time always a Sudanese) and when I asked which side he was on he replied "I'll tell you tomorrow". I persuaded him to let me go on to Luxor, which I did by road with an army escort. Luxor had been cleared of foreign visitors so I had a wonderful three days visiting all the monuments without being surrounded by tourists. Special pleading enabled me to continue to Cairo where I had telephoned Raja Rajwadi to meet me. After a slow, overnight journey I arrived at Cairo Station to be greeted by the Station Master, resplendent in top hat and tails, and Raja. From the comparative quiet of the station master's office we could hear the roar of the Cairo crowds. It was later reported that a million people had taken to the streets. Raja was concerned for my safety as the crowd was volatile and an "Englishman" would be at grave risk, but shortly after I had arrived Cairo Radio announced that General Neguib was still President. Roars of approval greeted the news, the atmosphere in the streets was totally changed. We left in the Embassy car with the Indian flag flying, and when I enquired what was to be our destination I was told "The safest place in Cairo The Abdin Palace". The crowds were huge but they let us through, and we were relieved that they were in a happy mood. We drove into the heavily guarded courtyard and as we reached the Palace we were met by Colonel Abdel Fatah Hassan, the Minister for

Sudanese Affairs and my first Egyptian friend. As we sipped another coffee we were joined by General Banna, a Sudanese who was ADC to Neguib. I asked if it was possible to see the Egyptian President and to my surprise General Banna said "Why not?" I was taken to the President's room.[19] It was just 10.30 am. I spent an hour and a half with Neguib and as we talked we shared a light meal. We touched on Sudanese affairs which I think he found confusing, but genuinely wished the Sudanese to do well. On N.A.T.O., he particularly spoke out against the inclusion of Turkey into the Western Alliance, and then he showed considerable interest in British domestic politics and the organisation of the Party System.

He was surprisingly short, dressed simply in his uniform, wearing no decorations. His face was lined and his eyes friendly. He was amazingly frank and most courteous and as I left he asked whether there was anything I would like to see while I was in Egypt. When I replied "The Royal Palaces', he teasingly asked why socialists should be so interested in royalty. The next day the Head of the Antiquities Dept came to my hotel and I spent several days looking at the Palaces in Cairo and Alexandria (which were not open to the public at that time). It was especially interesting to see the Montazah Palace at Alexandria from where Farouk left for exile in 1952. Everything was exactly as he had left it. There was only one telephone in the Royal bedroom, but a large collection in the next room where his valet monitored the calls. Heads of the Army, Air-Force, Navy and even the Prime Minister, all had to approach the King by courtesy of Hassan his valet, a powerful influence indeed (I had in fact met him, when shortly after the coup, he had arrived destitute in Khartoum and had been befriended by Muhammed Tewfig Ahmed.) The Royal bath

---

[19]Egyptian Gazette.

still contained the charred remains of the State papers which Farouk had ordered Hassan to set alight with kerosene. Even the jerry-can still stood beside the bath. It was a strange relic of a vanished dynasty.

Immediately after the riots of March the first, tension heightened throughout the Sudan. British women and children were evacuated from the Blue Nile Province and from the Western Sudan where the Mahdists were powerful and there was talk of arresting Sayed Siddig and the other Mahdist leaders, but this did not happen and slowly the tensions eased.

Much of the credit for this must go to Sir Robert Howe, (The Governor-General) and Prime Minister Ismael el Azhari. The Governor-General had acted not only correctly but with great sympathy and understanding. He built a rapport with Ismael el Azhari, and gained his respect and confidence. He was equally successful in his dealings with the advisory Commission which was designed to neutralize the influence of the Governor-General particularly in the South. The Chairman Mian Ziauddin of Pakistan was a lightweight, while Hussein Zulfikar Sabri was so impossible that even the pro-Unionist Dardiri Muhammed Osman was disgusted and declared himself to be an Independent. The Southerner, Siricio Iro, constantly intrigued with all and sundry, but the quiet patience and persistence of Howe, together with the skills of Sir William Luce, outmanoeuvred the irresponsible members.

Early in May, I went to London, staying with the Rt Hon James Griffiths and his wife, Winnie. For some months past Her Majesty's Government had been discussing future policy in Egypt,[20] and it was clear that it was hoped to reach an understanding on British bases in the Canal Zone. Eventually, the proposed Agreement meant the withdrawal

---

[20]Selwyn Lloyd. Suez, p. 21.

of British troops within twenty months, maintaining the 1888 Canal Convention. A section of the base was to be kept in working order, capable of immediate use if any attack was made on Egypt or any other member of the Arab League. The Egyptians raised objections about Turkey and the wearing of uniforms by the British technicians.

On the third of May, I saw the Rt Hon Clement Attlee and gave him my views of the Sudan and Egypt, including my interview with President Neguib. Attlee was already deeply shocked at Eden's "Sell Out" of the Sudan, saying "we had always refused to discuss Suez and the Sudan', adding "I would never bargain the Sudan for Suez—quite immoral". Attlee told me that he would "go into action with the Foreign Office" and asked for suggestions.[21]

A few days later, when I was lunching with Sir James and Lady Robertson, he told me that he was very worried about the Sudan. He added that Eden had severely reprimanded him for pressing on with the Legislative Assembly Constitution when the British Government was in the middle of delicate negotiations with the Egyptians. He had retorted that Eden's advisers, including Sir James Bowker (later Ambassador to Turkey) were sitting there and said nothing against the proposals.

Sir James had contemplated going to see Selwyn Lloyd and had even had doubts about the wisdom of his leaving the Sudan. He had felt that the Governor-General was too retiring and had not emerged. There was not any doubt that he was frightened that British troops "would eventually be involved after all that we have done".[22]

After my arrival in the United Kingdom I had received many messages, particularly from my friends in the Umma Party, over developments in the Sudan where the Government and some of its leading members appeared determined

---

[21]G F Thomas. Mss Diary, 3.5.54.
[22]G F Thomas. Mss Diary, 8.5.54.

on the policy of union with Egypt. Tensions were certainly increasing amongst the Mahdists. I received an urgent request from Sayed Abdel Rahman to arrange a meeting with as many British leaders as possible as Sayed Siddig was bringing a delegation to England, which included Ibrahim Ahmed and Muhammed Ahmed Omar. I arranged for them to meet the Rt Hon Clement Attlee at his room in the House of Commons. I opened the meeting by outlining recent political developments in the Sudan and the stance of the Umma Party. Attlee appeared uninterested, continuing to doodle on his blotter. Ibrahim Ahmed, who was most statesmanlike, and his colleagues put their viewpoint while Clement Attlee continue to doodle. As I intervened, I was questioned by the ex-Prime Minister, who said "Thomas, twenty-five minutes ago you said . . ." and then proceeded to quote me verbatim—concluding by saying "this appears contradictory to your last remark. How do you reconcile these two comments?" I was devastated but he was quite right. He had listened keenly to what we had to say, and with his incisive mind had absorbed it all. The delegation had conveyed very clearly their resentment over Egyptian influence in the Sudan. His remarks, as he concluded the meeting which had taken over an hour, was to say "The Labour Party has always believed in self-determination and I have made a note of all that has been said".[23] The Rt Hon James Griffiths joined us during the discussions.

I saw everyone I could possibly see, including Captain Charles Waterhouse (a former Minister) and Patrick Maitland, both right wing members of the Conservative Party, who were highly critical of the Government's policy towards Egypt and the Sudan.[24]

However, on 27 July, her Majesty's Government and the Egyptians initialled an agreement that the British troops

---

[23]Ibid, 17.6.54.
[24]G F Thomas. Mss Diary, 26.7.54.

should leave the Canal Zone. The same day, Jim and Winnie Griffiths' daughter Sheila, was married. Among the guests were Attlee, Marquand, Frank Beswick MP, Bernard Taylor (both later created life peers) and Lady Isabel Cripps (widow of Sir Stafford). This gave me another opportunity to press both Attlee and James Griffiths.

Attlee made a forceful speech in the House of Commons on 29 July, accusing the Government of "having sold the Sudanese down the river" and prophesied that there was very great danger of the Sudanese falling again into the hands of the Egyptians.[25]

Before the debate, I had sent telegrams to Attlee, Griffiths Driberg and Maitland. My telegram to Attlee said "Respectfully suggest Egypt will violate new Treaty as Sudan Agreement. Believe we should abstain from voting and advocate international control. New Agreement will compel Sudanese to join Egypt".[26]

The debate was followed by a vote of two hundred and fifty nine for the Government, with twenty eight against. A few Liberals and Labour members voted with the Government but the rest abstained. All those against were Tories.[27]

The Commission on Sudanisation was under intense pressure, and completed its task in nine months instead of the original plan of three years. It was the end of a great service. Dedicated officials, who although they had many limitations, had devoted their energies to the Sudan, now mostly opted for retirement and left for the United Kingdom. Most had left by the end of the year. Sir Robert and Lady Howe also made ready to leave. He had gained the respect of the Sudanese who at first had been very suspicious, but had recognised the integrity with which the Governor-General had fulfilled his task. During the early

---

[25]Selwyn Lloyd. Suez, p. 20.
[26]G F Thomas. Mss Diary, 29.7.54.
[27]Selwyn Lloyd. Suez, p. 26.

The Supreme Council
from left to right, Siricio Iro, Abdel Fattah Mograbi, Dardiri Mohd Osman,
Ahmed Mohd Yassin and Ahmed Mohd Saleh

Abdullah Khalil

Sudanese welcome self-government

days of 1955 the new Administration was facing formidable tasks, and there were soon signs of deterioration in internal affairs. The Governmental machine carried on under its own momentum, but on the eighteenth of August a mutiny occured in the Equatorial Battalions of the Army. What Sir James Robertson had foreseen and dreaded had come to pass, in spite of his warning to all the parties. All the Equatorial Province was in rebellion, Bahr el Ghazal Province was in jeopardy, but the Government managed to keep the Upper Nile under control.

Azhari came quickly to the view that union with Egypt would only add to the problems; so early in December he met privately with Muhammed Ahmed Mahjoub (the Leader of the Opposition) and agreed on an immediate declaration of Sudanese Independence. They were due at a State Dinner at the Palace given by Sir Knox Helm who had replaced Sir Robert Howe earlier in 1955. He was completely unaware of these developments even though they had to make excuses for their late arrival. Mahjoub and Mubarek Zarroug spent long hours drafting the Independence Resolution* declaring the Sudan to be a free and sovereign state which the Sudanese Parliament ultimately passed unanimously.† Instead of the Governor-General there was to be a Council of State, comprising of five Sudanese. These were Ahmed Muhammed Saleh; Ahmed Muhammed Yassin, Dardiri Muhammed Osman, Abdel Fatah Mograbi and Sirocio Iro. Most British and Egyptian troops had left and His Excellency the Governor-General left after serving only a few months. Within a month Azhari had formed a National Government which included the Umma Party. A very interesting development followed. The Prime Minister favoured a secular system, which was not

---

*Dec. 15th, 1955.
*To be effective, 1.1.56.

Muhammed Ahmed Mahjoub

approved of by Sayed Ali el Mirghani. After two decades of rivalry the two religious leaders (Sayed Abdel Rahman el Mahdi and Sayed Ali el Mirghani) drew closer together and exerted presure on Azhari, who had been growing more restive especially after the formation of the Peoples' Democratic Party[28] in June 1956. Within a few weeks Sayed Ali withdrew his support from Azhari, several of his ministers resigned and Azhari fell from office. This meant a sweet moment of success for Sayed Abdel Rahman as Abdullah Khalil became Prime Minister of a Coalition Government of the Umma and Peoples' Democratic Party.

It was at this time that Egypt once again startled the Sudan, and indeed the world by declaring the nationalisation of the Suez Canal. With the invasion of the Suez in October 1956 by Israel, Britain and France, the Sudan with other Arab States, rallied to the support of Egypt, and Mahjoub (Foreign Secretary in the Coalition Government) played a leading and constructive role. The sad story of Suez has been told elsewhere, but the tragedy cast a shadow once more down the Nile Valley. This was only lightened by one event, that of Sudan being accepted into the United Nations. Sudan as an Independent State had "come of age" and taken her place in the Comity of Nations on the twenty first of November 1956.

What at the time seemed a relatively unimportant event took place in December 1956. Mahjoub (intellectually the most outstanding and forceful Independent), joined the Umma Party; but its consequences in the years to come were to be fateful for that Party, the Ansar, and for democracy in the Sudan. At the time Mahjoub allied himself with the Umma, prospects were reasonably favourable, and it looked as if the future of the Sudan was assured. Prime Minister Abdullah Khalil had long and varied experience in

---

[28]U.S.A. Govt. Sudan. Area Study 1973, p. 173.

office, and led a team of competent, efficient Ministers, with high levels of intelligence, personality and energy. What was more, they had had considerable administrative experience.

Economically, in the first half of the year there had been a bumper cotton crop, but this had not sold well, so that a heavy burden was placed on the revenue. It was essential to develop economic growth. These factors put a strain on the alliance for not only were there political and religious disagreements but there were great controversies about economic policy. The coalition was a realignment of conservative factions, but ones which were traditionally hostile to each other. The Umma members of the Cabinet saw the PDP as a temporary compromise in the face of what they regarded as increasing secularisation, but internal differences escalated, with the Southern representatives agreeing with no one. They did hold together for the remaining tenure of that Parliament, and after adjourning in July 1957 they cooperated in the preparation for elections to be held in February 1958.

Two weeks before the Sudanese elections, Nasser, who had finally ousted Neguib, led Egypt into a abortive union with Syria which was to be known as the United Arab Republic and opened a boundary dispute with the Sudan by insisting that the area around Halfa was Egyptian territory. The Sudan reacted vigorously, pointing out that the areas concerned had participated in at least 3 Sudanese elections. At the time of the dispute Sayed Abdel Rahman was sailing towards Aba in his boat "Tahra" accompanied by guests including some Egyptians. As they were travelling toward Gezira Aba a rowing boat came alongside the paddle steamer, bringing a cable from Abdullah Khalil. Once he had read this Abdel Rahman told his guests who had been resting, what had happened, saying "How can you sleep when Egypt is invading our country?" There was a discussion as to whether they should return to Khartoum but it was decided to proceed to Gezira Aba where a cable from Nasser awaited the Sayed in which the Egyptian leader accused him of being in league with Britain and of seizing Egyptian territory. There were tears in Sayed Abdel Rahman's eyes and fury in his voice, as he asked how Nasser could accuse him of such a thing when he himself had been wounded by the British and twelve of his brothers and cousins had been killed. Eventually, when his temper had abated the Sayed drafted a reply in which he calmly and courteously told Nasser that the area annexed by Egypt had returned two MPs to the Sudanese Parliament and had always been Sudanese territory. He continued by saying that he was sure that the "two Governments could find a satisfactory solution".[29] This indeed was done by holding a referendum in which the Sudanese sovereignty was upheld and the Egyptian troops withdrew.

The Egyptian attempt to sieze Sudanese territory immediately unified the country politically and ended any real hopes of the movement for union with Egypt. By the time Parliament recessed in July the economic situation had deteriorated and there was an increasing feeling of discontent. The Government had been much criticised both inside and outside Parliament, there were further disagreements in the cabinet, and no effective leadership was evident. There were rumours and counter-rumours and the atmosphere became tense. During the whole of 1958 Abdullah Khalil was subjected to unprecedented, sustained and vicious attacks. Cairo Radio, day in and day out, poured a stream of propaganda against him accusing him (correctly) that he was pro-British and pro-western and (incorrectly) that he was a traitor to the Sudan, the Arab cause, and Islam. Khalil was quite contemptuous about Nasser. As he

---

[29]G F Thomas. Mss notes.

General Ibrahim Abboud, Head of State

once said to me about the Aswan Dam "Every Pharaoh has to have his pyramid".

It became clear that there were serious differences within the Umma Party on outstanding issues, namely the Southern Question and the fact that for the second successive year the Sudan had failed to market its valuable cotton crop. There was a move to make Abdel Rahman Ali Taha Prime Minister in place of Abdullah Khalil. Certainly Sayed Siddig favoured this for he disliked Abdullah Khalil. However Sayed Abdel Rahman was vehement in his loyalty to Abdullah for he had "been with me in the bad weather".[30] It is a fact that shortly after this Abdel Rahman Ali Taha returned to his home village and totally withdrew from politics. The day Parliament was due to reconvene (the seventeenth of November) a military coup d'etat organised by General Abboud took place. There is little doubt that it was planned in conjunction with the Prime Minister, himself an old military man.

There were persistent reports that Egypt was inspiring a coup, and it transpired that after long consultations in early November both Khalil and Azhari had agreed to pre-empt any Egyptian attempt by inaugurating one of their own. It was a strange twist of history that the great advocate of unity of the Nile Valley was engaged in an act to prevent such a development. Khalil, with his long British tradition was suspicious of and despised the 'riff-raff' among the Unionists. He was convinced that they would ultimately ruin the country, if they went unchecked, believing that the new state would be safer in the hands of the military, most of whom had been trained by the British and had absorbed their general outlook and traditions. He believed that Sayed Abdel Rahman was too indulgent to the unionist urban rabble. No doubt by this time Azhari, too, was dis-

---

[30] G F Thomas. Mss notes.

illusioned by some of his wildest supporters.[31] Muhammed Ahmed Mahjoub was arrested as it was well known that he would not agree to replacing a democracy with an army dictatorship run by Ibrahim Abboud (a staunch Khatmiyya) with Ahmed Abdel Wahab as his deputy (who was an equally staunch Ansari). The interesting point is whether Sayed Abdel Rahman was informed of, or indeed approved of the coup. There was a suggestion at the time he had been surprised. There is something too convenient about the arrangements for the two men heading the new régime as General Ibrahim Abboud was a staunch member of the Khatmiyya and loyal supporter of the pro-Egyptian Sayed Ali el Mirghani. Was his support conditional upon Khalil agreeing to a non-Mahdist being President? It may have been that he and the Khatmiyya, in return, pledged that they would not support Egyptian intervention in the Sudan, I personally cannot believe that after a lifetime of service and devoted loyalty to the Sayed, Khalil would take such a momentous step without consulting him. Sayeda Fatma, daughter of Abdel Rahman confirmed to me that her father knew and approved of the coup "Feeling there was no alternative".[32] Sayed Sadig el Mahdi was equally emphatic on the matter.

The first experiment in democracy had failed; the first experiment in dictatorship had begun.

---

[31]Conversations with Sadig el Mahdi.
[32]Conversations with Fatma Abdel Rahman.

CHAPTER IV

EXPERIMENTS IN DICTATORSHIP AND DEMOCRACY

"The weight of too much liberty"

W WORDSWORTH

With the army take-over, the Transitional Constitution was abrogated, Parliament was dissolved and all democratic institutions were abolished. As Muhammed Ahmed Mahjoub wrote "The army did not bother to have any form of constitution".[1] The Supreme Council of the Armed Forces held all constitutional powers, while General Abboud took over legislative, executive, and judicial authority in addition to commanding the armed forces. The Supreme Council, as one of its first acts, made a declaration stating that it intended to honour all pacts, that all the laws remained in effect, and ordered all officials to remain at their posts. As justification for their actions they declared that they had been compelled to take over the Government because of corruption, instability, and economic chaos. Military dictatorships always put forward these three points when they murder democracy, yet, strangely history has recorded that all dictatorships without exception lead directly to cor-

---

[1]Muhammed Ahmed Mahjoub. Democracy on Trial, p. 176.

ruption, instability, and finally economic chaos. It was indeed to be so with Abboud.

Within months, two army commanders, Brigadier Abdel Rahim Shannan (Northern Command) and Brigadier Mohieddin Ahmed Abdullah, (Eastern Command) who had been ousted from the Supreme Council, initiated a coup in which they moved their troops in the early hours of the morning of the second of March 1959, and besieged Abboud in his house. They also arrested three other members of the Council, Abboud was forced to accept their terms and a new Supreme Council was formed in which were included both Brigadiers Shannan and Mohieddin as was Mahboul el Amin (ousted also from the Government on an earlier occasion).[2] Lt General Wahaab of the Supreme Council refused to take the oath of allegiance to the new Council arguing that the initiators of the coup deserved a court martial, and that any other action would completely destroy the discipline of the army. Wahaab was promptly pensioned off, given a good gratuity and three thousand acres of Government land.

As the struggle for power continued within the higher echelons of the armed forces Mohieddin, who had not been content merely to have a seat in the Council, moved yet again bringing some of his troops into Khartoum on the twenty second of May. This time, however Abboud was ready and prepared. The plot was checked and both Abdel Rahim Shannan and Mohieddin were arrested, tried, and sentenced to death (later commuted to twenty years imprisonment). Another member of the council Lt General Ahmed Abdullah Hamid was charged but only found guilty of 'knowing' of the plot and not informing his seniors. He was cashiered. Yet another insurrection was to occur before the end of the year, and five young officers at the Military

---

[2]Ibid, p. 182.

School in Omdurman were caught, sentenced to death and hanged.

In spite of the unsettled state of affairs within, the regime did reach an agreement with Egypt (now called the United Arab Republic), over the Nile Waters and received fifteen million pounds compensation for damages caused by the High Dam. The previous administration had claimed thirty-five million pounds, and the actual cost was sixty million pounds which was expended on moving fifty thousand people from Wadi Halfa who had been displaced by the waters.

Additionally the Government were able to sell the backlog of cotton for the two previous years which did mean a financial improvement. Despite this, the revenues were dissipated. By this time a constitutional committee had been established, but its deliberations were never published and it withered away.

On the twenty fourth of March 1959 Sayed Abdel Rahman, who had spearheaded the movement to independence died, having had another heart attack. Dr Abdel Halim was with him, as was the doctor sent by Sir Chapman-Andrews, (the British Ambassador), but, as Dr Yusif Bedri arrived at the door to pay his respects, he was told by His Excellency the Ambassador, who was leaving, that there was little hope. As Dr Yusif entered, the wailing of the women informed him that the son of the Mahdi was dead.[3] He had lost a good friend and the Sudanese had lost a leader of great stature. No other Sudanese compared with him. His death was universally mourned, not only by his Ansar followers, and among the chief mourners was his old rival Sayed Ali el Mirghani. It is estimated that three million Sudanese attended his funeral. His son Siddig el Abdel Rahman succeeded him, both as Imam of the Ansar, and the

---

[3]Conversation with Dr Yusif Bedri.

Head of a United Opposition Front composed of the Umma, National Unionists, Communist, and other parties.

The United Front continued their opposition to the military regime sending constant letters of protest, and memoranda to the Military Council but all to no avail. Their demands for a return to civilian rule and for the army to return to the barracks provoked no response. Muhammed Ahmed Mahjoub favoured forcible resistance if further arrests were made but Sayed Siddig declared "I do not wish to meet God with the blood of Muslims on my hands".[4] On the tenth of July 1961, in the early hours, Mahjoub was arrested by troops (three armoured cars and eight soldiers carrying machine guns), and having been taken to the Officer's mess, was banished to Juba in the Southern Sudan for seven months detention. Eleven other politicians were sent with him, including Ahmed Sulieman (later Minister, and Ambassador to London), Abdel Mahjoub of the Communist Party, and Muhammed Abdel Rahman Nugdallah (Secretary-General of the Umma Party).

A further blow to the United Front came with the untimely death of Sayed Siddig on October the second, 1962 at the age of fifty two. For months he had been worried by the rising tensions, and in particular by the serious fighting which had broken out in Omdurman between the Ansar and the Police. For two further years smouldering resentment continued amongst the students, workers, and the professional groups. The deterioration in the North had been intensified by the open revolt in the Southern Sudan, where by 1963 the Anya Nya rebellion was gaining control in Equatoria. A year later the Government decided to expel all foreign clergy (mainly Anglicans and Roman Catholics) from the South because they believed that it was these missionaries who had initiated the

---

[4]Mahjoub. Democracy on Trial, p. 184.

rebellion. These actions, not unnaturally had an adverse effect outside the Sudan.

The regime was both paternalistic and technocratic. It had no real grass roots support, and by the end of 1964 was suffering from many problems. The suppression of Parliament had meant that the Sudanese had no legitimate way to express their grievances, and this had caused the disturbances in the North and the open rebellion in the South. The final crisis in the North was precipitated by student demonstrations in which one student was killed. Inexplicably the regime arrested two judges, one of them Babiker Awadallah, whom I had known when he was Registrar of Trades Unions at the time I was serving in the Labour Dept. More killings were to follow, and the Sudan Military Council collapsed. The people's revolution had triumphed, and Sir-el-Khatim el Khalifa, a distinguished educationalist, became the Prime Minister of the newly instituted civilian administration. The Transitional Constitution was restored, and two old friends were back in office—Mahjoub as Minister of Foreign Affairs and Zarroug in Finance. Abboud, who was worried about his house and his pension hung on until these matters were settled, but having been granted them he retired on the fifteenth of November. The six year military régime of General Abboud had no lasting effects on the Sudan except to inspire later military personnel into believing that power could be obtained by the gun and the bullet. However the first military dictatorship was over, and the second attempt at democratic Government began.

Sir-el-Khatim el Khalifa, who became the civilian Prime Minister, had a sound administrative background. He had been one of the first group of Sudanese trained in supervisory techniques when I introduced the scheme into the Sudan in 1951. He had considerable charm and an ability to get on well with people, but I felt he lacked the strength and aggression required for the demanding post of Prime

Ansar celebrating

Minister. However, he was acceptable to most people at a critical time and provided an excellent bridge to democracy.

The new government consisted of five members from the old established parties, and eight from the united professional front which had led the October Revolution. This was composed of lecturers, teachers, students, civil servants, trades unionists and the tenants of the vast Gezira cotton scheme. It was radical, vaguely to the left and, of course, included the communists. Two posts were given to Southerners. The Southern Provinces were divided into two main political groups, the Sudan African National Union, led by William Deng, later assassinated, and the Southern Front. After the abortive peace conference in 1965 SANU and SF merged to participate in the elections, but the moderate approach of Deng did not satisfy thousands of those who fled after the massacres in 1965.

The guerrillas in the field eschewed any involvement with the political groupings and Anya Nya was split by tribal and religious differences. There was also a clash between the old leaders who had been fighting for years and the younger, better educated and trained; among them Joseph Lagu, a former Captain in the Sudanese Army ,who had only returned to the South in 1964.

The Government had wanted elections in March 1965 but it was obvious that this would be prevented by the strife which existed in many constituencies in the three Southern Provinces. There was a great debate in the North as to whether the elections should take place or be postponed. The Peoples' Democratic Party, the Sudan Communist Party and the Southern elements loyal to the Government argued for postponement as they feared losing ground. The refusal of the Southerners to participate in the elections forced the Government to resign. An appeal was made to the President of the reconstituted Supreme Council, who directed that elections should be held wherever possible. The P.D.P. naturally rejected the Presidential decision and called for a boycott. The Umma, on a lower poll scored a decisive victory, gaining seventy five out of one hundred and fifty eight seats, while the N.U.P. secured only fifty two. However, because of the low turn-out and the vast number of candidates in many constituencies a large number were elected on a minority vote. The election was important in that it was the first time that women had the vote. This was a remarkable sign of progress as it had only been 15 years earlier that the first six girls had entered Khartoum University.

Muhammed Ahmed Mahjoub became the Prime Minister of a coalition Government with the N.U.P., and Azhari achieved his ambition of becoming Head of State by being made the permanent President of the Supreme Council. The previous ludicrous arrangement, whereby five heads of state acting in rotation had ruled, was now dead.

Mahjoub had two objectives, but he was becoming increasingly conservative, forgetting his early ideas of radicalism and socialism. He was determined to crush the Southern rebels, and to remove the communists from Parliament and positions of influence. As a result of the new military campaign the bitterness in the South increased. Undoubtedly atrocities were perpetuated by both sides but the Government were accused of destroying churches, schools, cattle and crops and with decimating the civilian population. Popular support for the Anya Nya guerrillas increased inevitably as repression was the policy of the Government.*

The Administration was rather more successful in removing the S.C.P.; Parliament passed an expulsion order for the eleven Communist members of Parliament, and abolished

---

*NB. 5th June—6 Day War—Nasser resigned, Sudan declared a state of National Emergency.

the party. The Marxists simply went underground and created cells. It must be said, however, that although the S.C.P. was definitely Marxist it was essentially first and foremost nationalistic.

Unfortunately the coalition broke up over the control of foreign policy. Azhari, as President, asserted that he should conduct foreign relations. The Prime Minister refused to give way and held on to office until a vote of no confidence was passed in July 1966, compelling him to resign. These events produced a split, for the first time, in the Umma Party, between the traditionalists, politically led by Mahjoub and spiritually supported by the Imam el Hadi who had succeeded to the Imamship on the death of his brother the Imam Siddig in 1962; and the Radical Wing. The Umma Party's majority in Parliament was loyal to the Imam's nephew Sadig el Mahdi, who was the official leader of the Umma Party. I knew both very well. El Hadi was the second son of Imam Abdel Rahman. When I met him first he was a young man, recently married.[5] He had the charm with which many of the Mahdi family were endowed but had been limited in his education and experience. His life was centred on Gezira Aba, and he had little knowledge of the outside world. I raised this with his father, pointing out that if anything should happen to Sayed Siddig then El Hadi was the next in seniority. Sayed Abdel Rahman appreciated the point and El Hadi came to Khartoum for a period. We gave a number of breakfast and dinner parties for him and became very fond of him. He was a devout man and had great piety. I think he was the most religious of the Sayed's sons, but was very conservative and traditional in his approach. He lacked flexibility and political acumen, and was much influenced by his father-in-law, Sayed Abdullahi el Fadl who certainly had royalist aspirations.

---

[5]Ismay Thomas. Mss Journal.

Sadig el Mahdi, Mahjoub and Azhari

When Imam Siddig died the Mahdi family naturally considered who was to be his successor. In his will Imam Siddig had nominated his son Sadig, but at the time of his death Sadig was not yet twenty seven years old. In Islam, primogeniture does not always apply as other considerations such as age, experience, suitability and capability are taken into account. Abdullahi el Fadl favoured the appointment of El Hadi (his son-in-law) and as he was the most senior member of the family his view carried much weight so that it was agreed that El Hadi should become the Imam.[6] Tragic consequences were to follow.

Sadig was quite different from his uncle. He came to see me first when he was just 15 years old and he had been deputed, as he solemnly told me, "to represent my grandfather and my father who have heard that you were ill and both are away from Khartoum". Even then he was a great strapping boy of considerable physique. That visit began a long and continuous friendship. We spoke for two hours. He was vehemently anti-Imperialist and anti-British. his personality and intellect were quite outstanding and I was so impressed I wrote a note to Sir James Robertson saying, "You need look no further than Sadig el Siddig—he will be the future leader of his country."

Many years later Sadig told me that our first meeting had caused him to change his plans. At that time he was determined to go to the United States to read history. I apparently retorted that to read history Oxford was the only place and that the United States had no history. He took my advice—graduating from St. John's as one of the youngest graduates ever.[7]

Imam el Hadi was conservative while Sadig was radical, although a convinced Mahdist and Muslim. He believed in a secular state and had personally championed the South-

---

[6]Conversations with Sayed Ishaq el Khalifa Sherif.

[7]Conservations with Sayed Sadig el Mahdi.

erners' cause when he demanded an investigation into the atrocities. Sadig had not long been in Parliament and only just qualified to stand for premiership as the minimum age for candidature was thirty years. He was a young man in a hurry when he took office as Prime Minister on July the twenty sixth, 1966. He had virtually requested Mahjoub to stand down and let him take his place, but Mahjoub, an old, wise and very experienced politician and campaigner with a national and international reputation, had no intention of so doing. Sadig was advised to wait, as Mahjoub was ageing and within a few years Sadig's elevation would have been inevitable. Nugdallah the Secretary-General of the Umma Party was a prime mover in urging Sadig on to become leader of the party and Prime Minister replacing Muhammed Ahmed Mahjoub. There was a group of 'Young Turks' at this time, ardent for a radical policy and impatient with the conservative and traditional elders of both the political and religious sections of the movement. A clash was unavoidable. Sadig was convinced that both Mahjoub and the Imam el Hadi were out of touch with the younger, better educated members, not only of the Umma Party but also of Sudan society as a whole. Mahjoub had become an ultra conservative and Sadig could see that changes were needed. He took office with high hopes and great expectations for he had an excellent Parliamentary majority. His ideas for economic reform were good, and he wanted to use economic development to balance the disparity in the Regions and would have moved towards regional government. The Southern Sudanese liked and trusted him so there was hope for a settlement. He proposed that there should be a President, a Southern Vice-President (instead of the Supreme Council) and wanted to introduce a considerable devolution of Government by granting some autonomy for the South.

Sadig was, however, opposed, strangely by an unholy

alliance of right-wing traditionalists and the left-wing of the students, communists, and so called intellectual elitists. To the one he was seen as too progressive, while to the left he was 'a Fabian". The right wing had its strength in the rural areas, the 'leftists' were vociferous and highly organised in the towns. Sadig had increased the resentment of the left for refusing to honour a High Court ruling overturning Mahjoub's legislation which had banned the Communist Party. A more experienced politician would have realised it was unwise to fight on two fronts and would have neutralised one side or the other. Some communists with a few army supporters attempted a coup but it was abortive.

Despite his opposition, Sadig's Umma group won fifteen seats in the pacified areas of the South. The federalist SANU took ten seats and the N.U.P. five. The conservative traditionalists were becoming restive; for in order to tranquilise the Southern Sudan Sadig supported a policy of religious freedom and he had no desire to declare an Islamic State. Imam el Hadi became alarmed and Mahjoub seized this opportunity for revenge and when the N.U.P. joined Mahjoub's group Sadig's administration was at an end. In May 1967 Mahjoub once more became Prime Minister in yet another coalition Government. His cabinet included N.U.P. and P.D.P. members as well as those belonging to his wing of the Umma Party. Azhari, seeing the disarray within the Umma, rallied the P.D.P. and the N.U.P. into a new party which he called Democratic Unionists.

The politicial scene in the Sudan now became farcical. Sadig's wing could paralyse the Government for it held the balance of power. Mahjoub, who believed that Sadig was only waiting for a suitable opportunity to destroy the Government., moved with speed and dissolved Parliament. The result was uproar and confusion for the majority of members refused to accept the dissolution. The consequence was that two Governments were in being—one meeting inside the building, the other outside on the lawn. In view of this ridiculous situation the Commanding Officer of the Army appealed to the Supreme Court for a ruling as to which had the authority. After much discussion the Supreme Court decided that Mahjoub was the legitimate head of Government and ordered new elections in April 1968.

At these elections the D.U.P. emerged with one hundred and one of the two hundred and eighteen seats. The traditionalist Umma group took thirty six seats while Sadig's wing only had thirty and indeed Sadig himself lost his seat to an Umma traditionalist, a supporter of El Hadi. Twenty five seats went to SANU and the S.F. and one seat was won by the S.C.P. which in the changed circumstances had been permitted to contest the election. Polling was much higher, and elections were held in most of the Southern Provinces for the fist time since 1958. During the elections Deng was assassinated, but SANU continued to be active. However, increasingly the dissidents and exiles broke away and joined the Anya Nya Liberation Front in Uganda.

The D.U.P. had almost a majority of seats in the Parliament (only nine short) but El Hadi demanded and obtained from Azhari the post of PM for Mahjoub and four other Cabinet posts; while the lone Communist Abdel Khalig Mahjoub (Secretary General of the SCP) was made Minister of Health. Politics makes strange bedfellows. Certainly the Government appeared to be strong and had a positive programme for the economy, for government re-organisation, especially in the South and for improving relations with the Arab world and the USSR. Sadig and his supporters were in opposition.

There were, however, serious tensions arising in Mahjoub's administration by the Autumn of 1968, and his Government was dependent on various factions. Sir-el-Khatim el Khalifa, the Sudanese Ambassador in London came to lunch with us and it was obvious from his comments that Sadig and some of the Umma Party had grave differences of opinion with his uncle, the Imam el Hadi, the head of the Ansar.

On the twenty sixth of November, 1968 the Prime Minister suffered a severe stroke and was subsequently flown to the Hospital for Nervous Diseases in London. Later, as he slowly recovered, Ismay and I went to see him several times in December. He was much concerned about the economic problems facing his country. Early in January 1969 he asked us to go to see him at the Dorchester where he was convalescing. He begged us to go to see the British Foreign Secretary on his behalf, as he knew we had known Michael Stewart for many years. He said that the Sudanese Ambassador had endeavoured to obtain economic help from Her Majesty's Government but none had been forthcoming. Mahjoub told us that he needed a ten million pound sterling loan immediately as well as needing the easing of credit restrictions in order to initiate small industrial schemes throughout the Sudan. He was especially concerned to develop small pump schemes for agriculture. We saw the Foreign Secretary on January the twenty-sixth in his room at the House of Commons. There was tight security at the time and we were both thoroughly searched by an apologetic policeman in plain clothes before being allowed in. Michael Stewart was sympathetic but non-committal. He did, however, promise to review the situation. I repeated to him the message Mahjoub had asked me to give the British Government, that unless the Sudan had immediate help there would be a "military coup within six weeks". This was prophetic—he was correct about the coup—wrong as to the timing. He also wanted to warn the British Government that the consequences of such a coup would be appalling. In this, too, he was correct.

Mahjoub left London to continue his recovery as the guest of King Hassan II of Morocco who was a cordial

admirer of Mahjoub's poetic talent as well as his political
acumen and a month later he returned to the Sudan where
he was welcomed back by President Azhari.[8]

During his absence attempts had been made to reconcile
the conflicting factions within the two wings of the Umma
Party. Meanwhile the Foreign Office was still "reviewing
the situation". I renewed my appeal to Michael Stewart
when I met him at the Egyptian Embassy in March and he
did hold out some hope. In the event credit restrictions
were relaxed but the £10 million loan was refused. Even
this small concession came too late.

As the heat of the sun increased in the Sudan in April so
did pressures for reconciliation between the Imam el Hadi
and his nephew Sadig, and it was agreed that the Imam
should become President and Sadig the Prime Minister.
Mahjoub was incensed and threatened resignation, but was
persuaded by Azhari and the Imam el Hadi to stay his hand.
It was about this time that Azhari suggested to Sadig el
Mahdi that he should eventually succeed him as President
and that he would support him. Sadig told me later that
Azhari thought that this would be in the "best interests of
the Country but it was a mantle I could not wear".[9] Talks
had been continuing between the major parties on the
replacement of the Transitional Constitution (dating from
1956) by a permanent one. On May the twenty third the
parties issued an agreed statement that the new constitution
should be Islamic, Republican, and Presidential. Two days
later the Transitional Constitution was abrogated and an
obscure Colonel Jaffar Muhammed Numieri, with a group of
young officers and supported by the communists seized
power.

---

[8]Mahjoub. Democracy on Trial, p. 224.
[9]Conversations with Sayed Sadig el Mahdi.

There was no bloodshed. The Sudanese not only acquiesced but welcomed the Revolution for they had grown weary of the constant bickering among the old parties. Democracy had failed once again and the second military dictatorship had begun. It was to last for sixteen years and to bring the once tolerant, relatively efficient, and self-supporting country to the abyss of total destruction and humiliation. The continued differences between the factions in the Umma Party and the lack of decisive Government had paved the way to a period of Sudan history which was to be marked by more corruption, instability, and bloodshed than the country had known since the days of the Turco-Egyptian rule.

CHAPTER V

NUMIERI—THE STRUGGLE
FOR SUPREMACY

'Tyrants seldom want pretexts'

Burke

The military coup of May the twenty fifth, 1969 had been precipitated by the political infighting of the parties, and Numieri immediately established a Revolutionary Council consisting of himself and nine other Officers with a Prime Minister, "ex officio". The Council dutifully elected Numieri as President and appointed him as Commander-in-Chief of the Armed Forces, promoting him to the rank of Major-General. Thus began the modern tragedy of the Sudan and indeed the sixteen years of Numieri's ever increasing tyranny is a classic example of the insidious corruption of power.

Judge Babiker Awadallah was appointed as Prime Minister and a Government of twenty one Ministers, mostly civilians, was sworn in to office. Babiker had been Registrar of Trades Unions when I was in the Sudan Government Service in he Labour Department, and later he had become a Judge and Chief Justice. He had always held left wing views and was sympathetic to the workers and to the Trades Union Movement. Babiker was a socialist and although his opponents accused him of being a communist, I always doubted this. He was well read and had wide cultural interests. There can be no doubt that he had a basic political philosophy but it was not "scientific marxism" as understood in Russia or the West. Although intellectually limited, he was superior to most of the Army Officers. He immediately declared to the nation that it was to be the policy of the new regime to place

> 'entire authority in the hands of . . . workers, farmers, soldiers and intellectuals".[1]

However, in effect, by Presidential decree, absolute power was invested in the Revolutionary Council with Numieri as its Chairman. The Council proclaimed a 'Democratic Republic'[2] advocating 'Sudanese Socialism'. They suspended the Interim constitution, abolished all previous Government Institutions and banned all political parties. These were denounced by Numieri as the 'Satellites of Imperialism'. Principal industries were nationalised and the economy controlled. The enormously successful Gezira Cotton Scheme and all private banks were placed under the control of the regime.

The new Administration was supported initially by the Sudanese Communist Party, Arab Nationalists, Conservatives, and some religious groups. Muhammed Ahmed Mahjoub was promptly put under house arrest and within a few days sixty-three other leading Sudanese were placed in protective custody. Two days later I heard that Mahjoub was safe. Attempts were made to persuade Sadig el Mahdi to join, or at least support the new régime, but he absolutely refused to have anything to do with a Military Dictatorship and he was arrested on the fifth of June 1969. Ismael el Azhari had already been detained.

One of the first acts of the new Government was to recognise the Communist Government of East Germany,[3]

---

[1]Mahjoub. Democracy on Trial, p. 227.
[2]Ibid, p. 228.
[3]Mahjoub. Democracy on Trial, p. 227.

and it was obvious that the policy of the Revolutionary Council would be anti-Western and pro-Russian. Mahjoub was convinced that the May coup in the Sudan "was certainly fostered by Egypt". Indeed Numieri had an almost idolatrous worship of President Nasser, on whom he modelled himself, and at this time the Russians were in the ascendancy in Egypt. Certainly, the powers in Cairo were filled with horror at the possibility that the Ansar, their traditional enemies, were about to come to power, especially since the recent divisions in the Umma Party were healed. Ismay and I attended a function at the Egyptian Embassy on the twenty sixth of June and Dr. Kamal Hagras, the Minister in London, declared to us that "the Russians are not helping the new Sudan Government but the Syrians were heavily involved".[4]

Sir-el-Khatim el Khalifa, the Sudanese Ambassador, was swiftly dismissed and asked for political asylum in London which was granted. His place was taken by Jamal Muhammed Ahmed who was one of the Sudanese leading intellectuals. In our days he had been warden of the Cultural Centre in Khartoum and inevitably was of left wing persuasion. The new Ambassador assured me that "Sadig would soon come to terms, but that his uncle the Imam el Hadi would be much more intractable".[5] I told him, emphatically, that the Revolutionary Council would have to move a long way before such a regime would be acceptable to Sadig. Ali, the brother of Sadig, who was in the United Kingdom, told me that his uncle, Ahmed Abdel Rahman el Mahdi, had been arrested.

A Peoples' Court was set up to try former Ministers and for the first time the penal law was given retroactive effect. However, the Government was unsure of itself for when Ismael el Azhari's brother died on the twentieth of August;

---

[4]G F Thomas. Mss Diary, Vol. I, p. 302.
[5]G F Thomas. Mss Diary, Vol. I, p. 310.

they hesitated whether he should be allowed to attend the funeral but decided that he could do so. On his return to his home, he suffered a heart attack and was rushed to Khartoum Hospital where he died six days later. His death was announced on Radio Omdurman as "Ismael el Azhari died this morning. He was a teacher in Sudanese schools".[6] No mention was made of his political career and of the high offices of state held by him. He had for thirty years been at the centre of Sudanese politics, as leader of the Graduate's Congress; the first Prime Minister of the Independent Sudan, and first Permanent President of the Supreme Council. The Government did all it could to prevent the Sudanese showing their respect at his funeral, but even halting the trains outside Khartoum and controlling the movement of lorries and buses did not inhibit half a million people travelling, mainly on the ubiquitous donkey, to the obsequies of Ismael el Azhari.

We went as usual to the Labour Party Conference which, that year, was at Brighton and met Michael Stewart, still Foreign Secretary. We also spent time with Ahmed el Fekki, the Egyptian Ambassador.[7] He was quite outstanding as representative of his country and worked unceasingly for its good, for it was a most difficult time as Nasser was wholly committed to the Russians.

A few days later Babiker Awadallah arrived in London on his way home to the Sudan from the United States. He had aged considerably and was exhausted both physically and mentally. He invited me to visit the Sudan, and Jamal Muhammed Ahmed assured me that it would be arranged. The state of the Sudan Government was such that on the 3rd December, only five weeks after presenting his credentials to the Queen, Jamal was sacked as Ambassador.

---

[6]Mansour Khaled. Numiery and the Revolution of Dismay, p. 7.
[7]G F Thomas, Vol. I, p. 336.

For six months Babiker had worked tirelessly to lay the foundations of a Sudanese Socialist State. He had made provocative radical speeches, and made an obvious bid for popularity which alarmed Numieri, who seized the opportunity offered by Babiker's exhaustion, to demote him and himself took over the post of Prime Minister as well as that of President. He appointed Babiker to be Deputy Chairman of the Revolutionary Council and Minister of Foreign Affairs. Numieri did not feel himself to be strong enough to break completely with the left and needed Babiker as a link. He was starting on his policy (although few realised it at the time, or for that matter even later) of removing any possible opponents and was ruthlessly to pursue that policy to the end. It is remarkable that very few Sudanese recognised this trait in Numieri's character for many went on accepting posts, being transferred, or demoted with little or no protest at all. But, as one senior Sudanese said to me at almost the end of Numieri's regime in 1984 when he had accepted a post, "You don't refuse a Dictator's order when he has a revolver to your head".

Ismay and I were in Egypt in March 1970 when we heard of the terrible massacre of Gezira Aba and the assassination of Imam el Hadi. With Mahjoub and Sadig in prison Imam el Hadi had been left with no responsible advisers. In fact, the opposite was the case—for he had been influenced very strongly by religious bigots, devoutly zealous but misguided, who persuaded him that he was to be the new Mahdi, the liberator of his country. Imam el Hadi displayed his lack of political flair and his inflexibility as he was without the worldly judgement and the acumen shown by his father, Sayed Abdel Rahman, or the adroitness of his brother Siddig, who had been his predecessor as Imam. Neither Abdel Rahman nor Siddig ever became involved in direct confrontations for they were always able to extricate themselves with dignity and honour.

The communists, in particular, realised the strong influence of the Ansar and that they were as dedicated in their faith as the Marxists. Numieri said later that it was the communists who had persuaded him to launch his attack on what he saw as a state within a state. There was certainly no other strong opposition, as the other traditional party the Khatmiyya, led by the Mirghani family, were no threat for they had to a degree welcomed the new regime.

Imam el Hadi had withdrawn to Gezira Aba in the White Nile where the Mahdi in 1882 had proclaimed his campaign which had led to the overthrow of the Turco-Egyptian administration and the death of General Gordon in 1885. Numieri decided upon a showdown. He made a visit to Kosti in what he said was an attempt to talk with the Imam. He was met by a large and hostile host of Ansars and scuffles broke out. Numieri hastily returned to Khartoum declaring he had been attacked by armed forces loyal to the Imam and he alleged he had nearly been killed. The Ansars were unarmed except with sticks and some old spears and no match for the trained forces accompanying Numieri. He ordered the Imam to return to Khartoum and the Ansar to surrender which echoed the demands of the Turco-Egyptian Government in 1882. El Hadi (like his illustrious grandfather the Mahdi) refused to go and the Ansar would not submit. Numieri seized his opportunity and the massacre of Gezira Aba took place. The Commander-in-Chief ordered the Army to invade the island and at least twenty thousand Ansar were killed. The island was bombed by the Egyptian air force, the then head of which was Hosni Mubarak, later to succeed Sadat as President of Egypt.

Imam el Hadi, realising that resistance by the virtually unarmed Ansar was hopeless, fled by road towards the Ethiopian border in the hope that he could escape, but his car was ambushed and he was killed. His young son, Fadl, was with him; but he was allowed to live, ever after to be

haunted by the brutal death of his father. The whole episode
was clouded in mystery and the Ansar did not know where
their Imam had been buried. This meant that no Fat'ah
(blessing) could be said over the grave; which is a grievous
sorrow to Muslims.* Sadig el Mahdi, already detained in
prison, was sent to Egypt where he was illegally confined in
the Abbasiya Prison in Cairo. The Egyptian President,
Nasser, always asserted that he had taken the step in order
to prevent the assassination of Sadig, and certainly he was
well treated while in Egypt.[8]

The Russians had not been particularly helpful to the
Sudan regime, taking the whole cotton crop and offering
only barter in exchange which did not help the economy,
now strangled by nationalisation and incompetence.
Numieri took the action of severing ties with Russia. He
was aided by the divisions between the orthodox Communists in the Sudan led by Abdel Khalig Mahjoub
(Secretary-General of the Sudanese Communist Party), and
the 'nationalist' Communists who favoured co-operating
with Egypt and therefore supported the Sudanese Socialist
Union. Numieri considered that he was now strong enough
to deport Abdel Khalig Mahjoub who had remained abroad
for several months and later returned only to be placed
under house arrest. All sections of the Communist Party
became alarmed by Numieri's move to the right and almost
all of them had rallied behind the Secretary-General.

In November 1970 Numieri, in a further attempt to
consolidate his power, took over the Foreign Ministry as
well as keeping all his other posts. He also dismissed three
of his original Council of nine on the alleged grounds that
they were Communists, and had been leaking information to
Abdel Khalig Mahjoub, who was arrested and imprisoned

---

*NB. The Imam's body was eventually located and was buried in the Gubba beside his
grandfather, his father, and his brother.

[8]G F Thomas. Mss Diary, Vol. II, p. 212.

until he escaped in June, 1971. Numieri ruthlessly purged the key areas in the Army, the Police, and the Ministry of the Interior, of known Communists. In February 1971 I heard a report that Numieri was about to move against all the Communists throughout the Sudan and dissolve the party. The gossip from Egypt was that all was not well there and that Sadat had had to move against left wing elements in Cairo.

Meanwhile, the three dismissed officers, Colonel Babiker el Nour, Major Farouk Hamad'allah, and Major Hashim al Ata, were plotting to overthrow Numieri and by July the nineteenth Hashim al Ata surrounded the Presidential Palace where Numieri was holding a meeting with some of his Ministers. Within twenty minutes all was over. Al Ata arrested all the Revolutionary Council Members, released the Communists and abolished all the organisations inaugurated by Numieri. Finally he announced that (the now) Lt General Babiker el Nour was leader, with himself as second in command. By chance el Nour and Hamad'allah were in London on the day of the coup.[9]

A young Egyptian, whom we later befriended, by a strange quirk of fate, was told by an uncle to watch the place where the two Sudanese were staying and to report to the Libyan Embassy when they left. This he did. Al Ata issued his political creed which blamed Numieri for being a Dictator, and he promised a new political system. Iraq immediately recognised the new regime but Egypt and Libya remained silent. Al Nour and Hamad'allah left for the Sudan on a BOAC VC10 on the twenty-first of July. Strange events followed. Gaddafi forced down the plane as it was overflying Libya, took off the two Sudanese and forced the plane to return to London. Meanwhile on the same day (July the twenty-second) an Iraqi plane carrying a

---

[9]Mahjoub. Democracy on Trial, p. 241.

high level delegation to Al Ata crashed north-west of Jeddah killing ten and injuring six. No explanation has ever been given of the accident. Cairo made it plain that it opposed the coup. Al Ata's troops inexplicably burst into an official guesthouse and brutally murdered thirty two officers without any reason. Up to then the insurrection had been bloodless. By another strange chance Al Ata gave priority to a left wing rally in Khartoum instead of carrying on with his intention to shoot Numieri and the others.[10] General Muhammed el Baghir, later the Vice-President told me that he had rallied some troops, mainly N.C.O.s and men, and successfully stormed the Presidential Palace. After an imprisonment of two and a half days Numieri was back in power. Time and time again Numieri survived such episodes. Dr. Khalil Osman said to me, "He was the luckiest Sudanese alive".

Blood continued to flow. Al Ata and three others were court-martialled and shot. Gaddafi returned Al Nour and Hamad'allah to Numieri and they were shot on the twenty sixth and Al Shafiee Ahmed el Sheikh, the Secretary General of the T.U.C., who had shared in the Lenin Peace Prize with the Egyptian Khaled Mohieddin, was executed as was the Southern Communist Joseph Garang. The Russians asked Sadat to put pressure on Numieri to exercise clemency for Shafiee but Sadat was told "It is too late, he has just been hanged". Sadat then asked about Mahjoub and received the same answer although some reports suggested that the hanging did not take place until several days later.[11] Other reports said that having been recaptured he, Mahjoub was sentenced at midnight and hanged at dawn, in spite of denying all complicity. He was an honourable man, a Marxist, but primarily a Sudanese. This continued bloodshed was a sad deterioration. Numieri, by now, had purged

---

[10]Ibid, p. 242.
[11]Heikel. Road to Ramadan, pp. 142–3.

all the Communists except one, Ahmed Sulieman, who it
was alleged had alerted him about the coup. I appealed to
Denis Healey to express displeasure at the barbaric executions of trades unionists and politicians of the left, and he
said that he was going to try to make contact.

Numieri when threatened always reacted by removing
from influence anyone he feared and this pattern was to be
repeated again and again until the end of his regime. He was
particularly bitter about the Soviet Block countries who had
quickly recognised the Al Ata Coup. In his predictably
volatile riposte he broke with his former allies.

The Ansar had been suppressed, the left annihilated, and
the country was now firmly under his control, so in August
1971 Numieri decided to issue a new provisional constitution, declaring the Sudan was a "Socialist Democracy".
Also the system of government was to be presidential
instead of the Revolutionary Command Council. Before the
Sudan could get its breath back, a plebiscite was held and
Numieri was elected President (for six years). The first
period of struggle for power was over.

In July 1971 Numieri had appointed Mansour Khaled to
be his Foreign Minister. The appointment and the timing
was felicitous for Mansour was an extremely able and intellectual Sudanese. He was one of a group of young Sudanese
who had frequently come to our house in Omdurman.
Among the others were Mubarak Zarroug (a previous
Foreign Minister), Kamil Shawki (later head of the F.A.O. for
North Africa, and Commissioner for Refugees and Rehabili-
tation in 1986), Muhammed Tewfig Ahmed, (who became
Foreign Minister in 1987), and Kamal el Jack (Head of
Unesco in West Africa). These and others were highly
intelligent and exceedingly able as their subsequent careers
have proved. Mansour was certainly outstanding. He had a
distinguished academic career, eventually gaining a Doc-
torate at the University of the Sorbonne in Paris. He was a

Dr Abdel Kader Hatem in Cairo

fluent linguist in Arabic, English and French, and practised as a barrister in the Sudan before serving in the Legal Department of the U.N. and UNESCO. Mansour's tastes were esoteric for a Sudanese, with a passion for classical music and literature. It is an interesting facet of Numieri's character that he always had to have around him one or two people who were his intellectual superiors. Mansour was, and still is, an urbane and sophisticated person and at that time he was attracted to the new regime, serving shortly after the Revolution in the cabinet as Minister of Youth and Social Affairs before becoming the Ambassador to the United Nations. With such a background the timing of his appointment as Foreign Minister was auspicious, coinciding, as it did, with Numieri's break with Russia and his turning more towards the Western Powers.

Mansour Khaled was exactly the right person to reassure the West. He was essentially a Westernised Sudanese and understood the corridors of power and influence in the U.N.. The focus of the regime while veering more towards the West was, however, not a united one, as within the Sudan Socialist Union which had been instituted to promote cohesion, there was a split between left and right with everyone manoeuvring for position.

The new Ambassador of the Sudan to the Court of St James was Abdullahi el Hassan who at the time was most cordial and in the next few months there was much contact between us, the Sudanese, and the Egyptians in London culminating in a large reception given by Ismay and me on the twenty-eighth of February, 1972. Almost immediately after this, Babiker Awadallah, now first Vice-President, renewed his invitation to me to visit the Sudan.

In March 1972 an old Egyptian friend, Dr. Abdel Kader Hatem, Egyptian Deputy Prime Minister and Minister of Culture and Information, came to London for the opening of the Tutankhamun Exhibition. The magnificent reception at Lancaster House provided an excellent opportunity for political talk about the Sudan with Ministers and Foreign Office Officials; the F.C.O. was well represented with James Craig, Anthony Parsons, and Norman Reddaway.[12]

Immediately I received the invitation to visit the Sudan I felt that I must consult the Foreign Office. They strongly approved, pointing out that since the Revolution relations had been "cold', to put it at its mildest. There was virtually no contact between the British Ambassador in Khartoum and President Numieri, nor between the Embassy and the Foreign Ministry, while the Sudan Government had been extremely difficult about issuing visas for replacement Embassy staff. It had been agreed that I take a letter of goodwill from the Rt. Hon. Harold Wilson MP to President Numieri as it was thought that perhaps a gesture coming from a Labour ex-Prime Minister would be more appropriate and acceptable than one from a 'Tory Imperialist'. This seemed to fit with Numieri's past preferences for left wing and Communist governments.

On the thirtieth of March 1972 I flew to Africa, spending some time in Egypt meeting Hatem (the acting Deputy Prime Minister, as Sadat was concentrating on the effort which was to lead to the 'Yom Kippur' war in the following year). After meeting with other Egyptian ministers and leaders I was appalled at the almost complete breakdown in relations between Egypt and the Sudan. Numieri had idolised Nasser, but at this time was contemptuous of Sadat. As one Egyptian Minister said to me—

"What can we do with the walad? (boy)"

Eventually my son Radwan and I flew on by Sudan Airways to Khartoum where we were given full V.I.P. treatment, seated in the section reserved for the President and Vice-President, being hospitably entertained, with

---

[12]G F Thomas. Mss Diary, Vol. II, p. 321.

champagne (strange to think about when hardly a decade later Numieri was giving forty lashes to anyone caught drinking). My astonishment was tremendous for, as we landed in Khartoum some two hours later, the red carpet was laid, lights blazed and cine cameras whirled as television and radio commentators announced our arrival. Amir el Sawi, then the Senior Civil Servant (later to be a highly successful Ambassador to London), the Head of Protocol, and the Sudanese Commissioner of Labour were there to greet me and escort me to my hotel.

Numieri was away from Khartoum in the South when I arrived, so I took the opportunity of going to the Mahdi's Tomb (the Gubba) in Omdurman. The protocol officer accompanying me, Nadeem Adawi, was very dubious about the advisability of the visit, as the Gubba had been closed and guards posted by Numieri to prevent entry. He indicated that the President would not approve. However, I persisted, so the guards were ultimately persuaded to open the gates and I was able to speak to the very old Ansari Ghaffir (guardian) who had been there for decades. He was almost blind and very frail. I told him that I was a very old friend of 'Seedi' (the family and personal name for Sayed Abdel Rahman el Mahdi), and wished to pay my respects. Eventually a flicker of recognition came over his face and he unlocked the door to the Gubba for me. As I entered I was deeply moved for the place was uncared for—dust and sand enveloped the flags, banners, mementoes and the tombs of Imam Sayed Abdel Rahman and his son, Imam Siddig. I said a prayer, then signed my name in the visitors Book. It was open but no signatures had been added since the May revolution of 1969. Leaving the Gubba I called on Sayed Siddig's widow, Sayeda Rahma, who was still living in the family house, once a gleaming palace, now dilapidated with peeling paint, broken windows and shabby furnishings. She was caring for all the family children as most of the women as well as all the men were imprisoned. She had great dignity as became a grand-daughter of the Mahdi, and as she said to my wife a year later, "I was born an Arab, (a Bedw)—our needs are few—I am still a nomad—we will survive". The driver of the car which had been put at my disposal by the government said quietly to me, "The President is a good man but my grandfather was an Ansar, my father is an Ansar and I am an Ansar. Sayed Sadig is my leader".

During the next few days I saw the Vice-President and many of the Ministers, of whom five had been my pupils in the Ahlia School in Omdurman in 1951. Then, on the President's return, I was summoned to the Palace on April the twentieth. A motorcade accompanied me, complete with motor-cycle outriders and screeching sirens. We sped along the Nile Corniche to what had been the site of Gordon's Palace, rebuilt by Lord Kitchener in a style evocative of the Raj and British Imperialism. It gleamed like a white wedding cake in the tropical sunshine, as we alighted to the ceremonial presenting of arms and were swept through the magnificent armoury (all relics of the Mahdiya and the Battle of Omdurman) and up to the President's office.

Numieri, in Army battle-dress with rows of medals, was a short, stocky figure who exuded physical force. After greetings, I presented him with Wilson's letter (they had met in London in 1968) which gave him much pleasure.[13] It read:

> 'I am taking the opportunity of Graham Thomas's visit to the Sudan to extend to you my personal good wishes as leader of the Labour Party, and also to express friendship and the desire for close relations with you and your people.'

The President then asked what I had been doing and had I seen old friends adding, to my astonishment, "I am afraid

---

[13]G F Thomas. Mss Diary, Vol. II, p. 324.

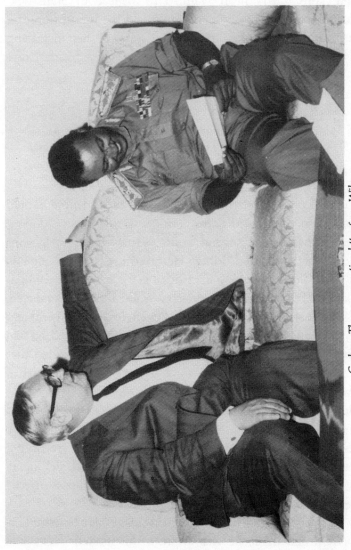

Graham Thomas presenting letter from Wilson

you will find our standards have gone down. The Sudan is not as efficiently and competently run as when you British were here."[14] My heart warmed to a Head of State who could make such a statement and it laid the foundation of a friendship which was to last, in spite of his increasing deterioration, until he introduced the so-called 'Sharia Laws' in 1983 when amputations were introduced.

Emboldened by his frankness, I said:

"Mr. President, I should like you to know, before your security people tell you, that my first act was to go to the Mahdi's Tomb and pay my respects to two dear and respected friends Imam Abdel Rahman and Imam Siddig."

His reply was to the effect that all Sudanese would appreciate what I had done.

We then spent several hours discussing the problems facing the Sudan and Britain. He asked me to speak frankly, which I did, particularly in criticising the excessive nationalisation of commerce and industry which he had introduced. I said that as a socialist, I believed in the Government controlling the economy but that what I considered he had done was to kill the cow that gave the milk. I added that the state had a right to some of the milk but that if everything was taken away the entrepreneur would not work. I told him that in my opinion the Sudan needed entrepreneurs. At this, he laughed and admitted that they had made many mistakes but were taking rectifying measures and wanted Britain's help. He repeated, yet again, "Our standards have gone down, our economy needs help".[15]

At that time, I found the President simple, straightforward and frank; he was aware of his limited intellectual capabilities but was hard working and 'street-wise' (shrewd).

[14]G F Thomas. Mss notes.
[15]G F Thomas. Mss notes.

In this he contrasted with his First Vice-President who was a devious politician but with a narrow, if astute, brain. Babiker Awadallah was a man of some charm, but he was bigoted and fanatical so it was difficult to warm to him. Certainly, in comparison to most of the other Ministers, he was intelligent. I had a strong impression that his influence was weakened and suspected that his 'days were numbered'. Indeed, a few months later he resigned as Vice-President and from the Politburo.

The President complained that Her Majesty's Ambassador, Gordon Etherington-Smith, acting on British Government instructions, would only talk about the twenty-eight million pounds due in compensation to the British concerns which had been nationalised.[16] This theme was repeated by other Ministers and it was obviously deeply resented. As one said to me, "We would like to compensate, but we literally haven't the money". I think this was true. Perhaps the Ambassador had pressed the point too hard, but he could have been acting under instruction from the Foreign Office. His Excellency and his charming wife were very kind and hospitable. Indeed, he warmly welcomed my visit and was instrumental in arranging another visit the following year. He had been appointed to Khartoum unfortunately in the fateful year of 1969, after a long and distinguished career in the Far East and had no experience of Arab, Middle East, or Sudanese politics. Before my visit he had rarely been out of the Embassy to see any of the leading figures. He had presented his credentials but despite subsequent repeated requests had failed to see the President or the Foreign Minister. I tried to assure him that he should go ahead and call and that it was totally against the tradition and culture of the Sudan for him to be refused entry, and said that "there may not be much serious political

---

[16]G F Thomas. Mss notes.

discussion but the courtesies would be upheld with coffee offered." However, he persisted in believing that if he went in person and was not received this would be an insult to the Queen and a 'diplomatic incident' would ensue. I did persuade His Excellency to join me when I 'popped in' to the Foreign Minister Khaled's house. He was listening to classical records and we were welcomed and spent an enjoyable evening.

In the ten days or so I was in Khartoum, I had interviews with over a hundred people, ministers and officials, as well as professional people and the remnants of the entre- preneurs. The hospitality was overwhelming. In addition I was interviewed by radio Omdurman and given daily press coverage. While I was there Numieri decided to make a gesture towards the private sector and established a committee under the Chairmanship of Abdel Salam Aboul Ela to evaluate the value of the confiscated property and to reach a settlement with some of the Sudanese claimants. The President took another decision in April to reinstate dismissed officers, to restore pensions to those compulsorily retired, and to give pensions to the widows or families of those officers shot in the abortive coup of 1971. Numieri was being subjected to pressure because of the War in the South and the state of the economy, and for these reasons he was attempting to achieve some national unity.

In addition, the president permitted visits to Sadig el Mahdi who had been returned to the Sudan by Sadat, but who was still being detained. Sadig was a great embarrass- ment to Numieri, and I was assured that he (the President) would welcome an understanding with Sadig but that this was bitterly opposed by most of the leaders of the S.S.U. At this time the Government seemed genuinely convinced that sectarianism had been abolished but while Numieri was personally popular at this time, his administration had no real basis of appeal. I did not believe that the Sudanese, who are very conservative and loyal people, had reneged on their religious leaders. There was much evidence to support this. Despite the oppression and suppression, scores of Ansar went daily to pray outside the Mahdi's Tomb.

I returned to England via Cairo, where I had a number of meetings with Ministers and was interviewed on Cairo television by Samir Sabri (the David Frost of the Middle East). In this interview I frankly expressed my opinion that war was an "obscene luxury which no country could afford." I thought it would be deleted before transmission but surprisingly this was not done.

Within a few weeks of coming home, His Excellency Gordon Etherington-Smith was pressing for my return visit and it was suggested that Gwyn Morgan, Deputy General Secretary of the Labour Party, should accompany me. He was unable to do so and Sir Harry Nicholas was proposed but Norman Reddaway, then at the North Africa Desk at the Foreign Office, telephoned to say that he was not acceptable.[17] I gathered that he was considered to be too old and that I was the only person acceptable to all parties. I was asked whether I would go alone. Later I saw Etherington-Smith who expressed his appreciation of my last visit which he said had helped him a great deal.

In November General Muhammed el Baghir (the first Vice-President) and Philip O'Bang, who was Minister in London came to lunch.[18] General Baghir was a much-respected soldier, honest, straightforward, and incorruptable. He was liked by all groups. More than once he had come to Numieri's rescue when the latter had been cornered in attempted coups. The Vice-President thought that Numieri's position was much stronger; that normality had returned to the Sudan, although relations with Egypt were extremely bad. He asserted that Sadat always decided what

---

[17]G F Thomas. Mss Diary, Vol. III, pp. 11–12.
[18]Ibid, pp. 13–14.

Graham Thomas with General Muhammed el Baghir, Vice President

he would do and would only then tell the Sudanese President. To this Numieri had reacted very strongly and informed Sadat that the Sudan would pursue its own policy and that they were prepared "to be consulted" but before decisions were made. General Baghir was convinced that Babiker Awadallah, who had gone into exile in Cairo, was disillusioned with the Egyptians and that he expected him to return to the Sudan (this he did not, in fact, do). Baghir also revealed that he had sent someone (name unspecified) to Port Sudan to talk to Sadig el Mahdi who was imprisoned there and alleged that Sadig was in good health and approved of what the government was doing. Neither of these facts were credible as I had heard that Sadig was unwell and needed an operation for a hernia.[19]

I raised the question of the Imamship of the Ansar (Mahdists). Philip O'Bang said that some of the Ansar wanted Wali Eldin, the son of the assassinated Imam el Hadi to succeed him, but that difficulties had arisen because Sadig was not agreeable. It had also been suggested that Ahmed Abdel Rahman was possible and Numieri favoured this course, but the idea was unacceptable to the majority of the Ansar.[20]

After discussions lasting several hours they left, but before that I raised the question of the release from prison of Souad, the daughter of Ibrahim Ahmed, who had been detained as a dedicated Communist. I begged for her to be released on the grounds of the distinguished service that Ibrahim Ahmed had given to the Sudan and because of his age. Baghir laughed and said that Souad was worse than any man and refusing to give any ground. She was completely adamant.[21] I also vigorously attacked him for the executions of the Communists after the last abortive coup;

---

[19]G F Thomas. Mss Diary, Vol. III, p. 14.
[20]Ibid, p. 15.
[21]Ibid, p. 14.

suggesting that it was counter-productive. The argument was heated and he made no excuses but asserted that after the massacre of loyal officers by the Communists at the Government Rest House, no other action was conceivable. He was firm in his opinion that such a policy was the only possible deterrent which would keep young soldiers from attempting yet another coup.[22] I also asked him to consider giving a grant without any condition to Wali Eldin el Hadi who was suffering great hardship financially, doing manual and menial jobs in the United Kingdom but I regret nothing came of it.[23]

General el Baghir invited Ismay and me to visit the Sudan, to which I agreed, as I liked him and thought him strong and straightforward. He was essentially a soldier and at that time was completely loyal to Numieri. It was decided that we go to the Sudan and Egypt in the New Year. Gordon Etherington-Smith revealed to Sir James Robertson and me at a lunch in December that Numieri was fast reaching the end of his patience with Sadat and the Egyptians. It seemed that Omar el Haj Moussa, the Minister of Information had been saying quite openly that if the Egyptians continued to treat the Sudanese as 'awlad' (boys), and supporting subversive groups in the Sudan, then the Sudan Government would have to consider the whole question of the Nile Waters Allocation.[24] This was wild and dangerous talk as Egypt could and would not allow any interference with the Nile Waters, the very lifeblood of the country. Later Dr. Ahmed Anis, Director of the Arab League in London, and his friend Kamil George (formerly translator to Nasser), confirmed that the relations were very bad between the two countries, adding that Sadat had made some very disparaging remarks about Numieri which had

---

[22] Ibid, p. 16.
[23] Ibid, p. 16.
[24] G F Thomas, Diary, Vol. III, pp. 16–21.

been conveyed to the Sudanese President and were bitterly resented by him. Anis was surprised that the Arab League had not attempted a reconciliation, but presumably it was because Sadat was not prepared to take the initiative.

The Ambassador revealed the relations between Britain and the Sudan had eased so much that it was proposed that H.R.H. the Princess Anne should visit Khartoum at the end of February. I immediately suggested that H.R.H. might visit the Ahfad College in Omdurman where the Bedri family had pioneered girls' education. He liked the idea and then and there telephoned the Foreign Office to ask that it should be included in the programme.[25]

The year drew to an end with the arrival of tickets to go to Khartoum. Before doing so we gave a party for Gwyn Morgan, former Deputy General Secretary of the Labour Party and then Chef-de-Cabinet to the Rt. Hon. Roy Jenkins in the E.E.C. at Brussels. Also among the guests was Nefissa el Amin, a Minister in the Sudan responsible for women's affairs and the only woman member of the Politburo. She had trained as a teacher and had developed into a formidable figure, certainly well to the left in Sudanese politics. Nefissa was a charming and attractive woman whose frail looks belied the tough and highly intelligent politician.[26] She had recently been widowed. She was accompanied by Philip O'Bang, a huge man from the Dinka Tribe who impressed me more each time we met. He had been educated at Richmond College.

On 19th January, 1973, Ismay and I flew from Heathrow to Khartoum by VC10. We could hardly help comparing the six-and-a-half-hour smooth flight with our first journey to Khartoum in 1950 which was by Viking and took three days. What had not changed was the glorious technicolor

[25]Ibid, Vol. III, p. 16a.
[26]G F Thomas. Diary, Vol. III, p. 19.

dawn breaking over the Nubian desert, the unbelievable colour combinations are awe-inspiring and never pall.

Our arrival coincided with yet another attempted coup, which meant that we were unable to see Numieri as he had withdrawn from public view for security reasons.[27] I suspected that each coup wounded his vanity. However, it was the usual round of generous Sudanese hospitality during which we saw a great deal of the first Vice-President, General Baghir, who gave a supper party for us in his lovely Khartoum garden. As we got into our car on leaving, we noticed a sub-machine gun lying unattended on the driving seat, which prompted me to remark how vulnerable was the situation. One hand grenade lobbed over the fence would have removed most of the Sudan Government and the leaders of the S.S.U. Little did we realise that tragedy was not far into the future. Nefissa el Amin entertained us as did the British Ambassador at a buffet party for some one hundred people. Perhaps the most enjoyable was a late dinner party with our old friend Muhammed Tewfig Ahmed, where a whole sheep was roasted Lebanese-style, and a galaxy of artists, writers and academics was invited. Most of the conversation was political but a certain reservation was evident and it seemed that the Dictatorship was strengthening its grip on the country.[28]

I argued strenuously with Baghir and Mansour Khaled to release Sadig el Mahdi, pointing out that his continued detention without charges or trial only served to increase his stature. I urged them to give him a small pension and let him go to Europe. I really feared for his life at this time as Numieri was becoming more and more unpredictable.[29] During the visit I gave a lecture to the Department of Social

---

[27]Ibid, p. 30.

[28]G F Thomas. Mss Report, 1973.

[29]G F Thomas. Report on Visit.

Affairs of Khartoum University which was attended by His Excellency the British Ambassador, some Ministers, and old friends, as well as by students.[30]

Ismay flew directly to the U.K., but I returned to Cairo travelling with the Egyptian Minister of Agriculture, Mustafa Gabaley with whom I had a long discussion, during which he spoke most critically of Numieri.[31] Just as we touched down at Cairo our air hostess told us that an Egyptian aeroplane had crashed the day before in Cyprus. I had always had misgivings about Egypt Air, so I was relieved when touch-down was complete. Mahmoud Fahim and his son met me and I stayed with them before flying on to London.

Within a fortnight of my return, on the first of March, a party was held at the Saudi Arabian Embassy in Khartoum when a group calling themselves Palestinian Black September attacked the Embassy, seizing Cleo Noel, the U.S. Ambassador, George Moore, the U.S. Chargé d'Affaires, the Belgian Ambassador and the Saudi Ambassador. The British Ambassador escaped by leaping over a wall and among others who escaped was General Baghir, who was devastated, as security was his responsibility. Black September demanded the release of Sirhan Sirhan (who had assassinated Bobby Kennedy), and some other Palestinian prisoners. Moore I knew quite well; I had met him on several occasions and I had met and talked with both on my last visit. Noel had told me, at a party at the Atabani family house, that he had actually cried as he presented his credentials to the President and the band played the 'Stars and Stripes'. He had been in Khartoum earlier, before relations had been severed and both he and George Moore were very pro-Arab. On the second of March it was

[30]Ibid.
[31]G F Thomas. Mss Diary, Vol. III, p. 31.

announced that both Noel and Moore had been killed. It was a great tragedy.[32]

Great courage was shown by Souad, wife of old friend Saad aboul Ela. She was a doctor and during the seige she had gone boldly through the garden, although in great danger of being killed by the terrorists, to demand the release of the Saudi Ambassador's wife and children. Souad was unable to persuade the Ambassador's wife to leave but she brought the children out safely after berating the terrorists for making war on women and children "which no good Muslim would do". It was an act of great humanity and demanded great courage. Four days later the Black Septemberists surrendered and, although Numieri declared his intention to put the perpetrators on trial, he never did and subsequently released and expelled them. It could easily have happened a few weeks earlier at any of the parties we attended for most of the people at the Saudi Embassy were at the party in our honour, including Noel and Moore.

By the end of March Numieri was in London on an official visit. The reconciliation between Britain and the Sudan was receiving its official recognition. The Anglo-Sudanese Association (a moribund body) stirred itself and gave a reception for the President under the chairmanship of Sir Angus Gillan, who initially had gone to the Sudan in 1909 and was Civil Secretary from 1934 to 1939. Most of the 'old guard' were there, including Sir James Robertson, Sir Arthur Gaitskell (Gezira Board), and Sir Eric Priddie, the doyen of Colonial Medical Administrators. The Foreign Office was represented by James Craig (later Ambassador to Saudi Arabia) and Michael Holding. Numieri was in a very jovial mood and asked about our son Radwan. Mansour Khaled as Foreign Minister was in attendance.[33]

---

[32]Ibid, pp. 34–35.
[33]G F Thomas, Vol. III, p. 42.

The British Prime Minister, the Rt. Hon. Edward Heath, gave a dinner at 10 Downing Street for President Numieri and Madame Buthayna. Besides the Sudanese Delegation there were also present Sir Alec and Lady Douglas Home, the Rt. Hon. the Speaker, Sir Geoffrey Howe MP, Edward du Cann MP (later Sir Edward), Sir Kenneth Younger MP, John Stonehouse MP, Sir Denis Greenhill (Head of the Foreign Office), Sir Dingle Foot, Christopher Mayhew MP, Dennis Walters MP, and Lord Bridges (Private Secretary to the Prime Minister). The dinner was superb—for once I did not grudge my income tax! The Prime Minister took the President around introducing the other guests to him. When he came to Ismay and me, Numieri greeted us in Arabic, turning to Edward Heath and saying, "We are not talking Chinese, you know.'[34]

The Prime Minister made an elegant speech of welcome wittily knocking at his own backbenchers, and singling out for special mention Sir Arthur Gaitskell for his work on the Sudan Gezira Board, which pleased him and us hugely. Numieri replied in Arabic which was translated by the Sudanese Ambassador, Bukhari. A Highland piper playing his bagpipes then walked around shattering our eardrums with Scottish airs. The Prime Minister (as tradition demands) gave the Piper a bumper whisky which he sank in one gulp (as tradition demands).

After dinner we returned to the reception rooms and chatted with some of the guests, including Frank Chapple of the E.T.U.. Gordon Etherington-Smith introduced me to Sir Alec Douglas Home, then Foreign Secretary. Up to then I had had some admiration for Sir Alec, but I was horrified at his views. My diary comment the following morning contains the words, "He reeked with aristocratic hauteur". I was completely unprepared for his attitude and was so

---

[34]G F Thomas. Mss Diary, Vol. III, p. 44.

shocked that I made notes immediately afterwards. I quote
them for I think they are very revealing of the man:

> I do not believe in Democracy, I never have.

> If only they (foreigners) would behave like gentlemen,
> we could resolve matters.

> Look where democracy has brought this country.

> I hope Numieri does not make the mistake of consulting
> the Sudanese too often.[35]

I felt I was listening to a Bourbon. His whole speech had
an air of unreality, although his mind was keen and alert and
he questioned me very shrewdly about Numieri and the
Sudan. I said that in my view, if the President did not
receive the equipment he was asking Her Majesty's Government to supply, then there could be bloodshed and chaos,
adding that I thought that the Sudan was one heartbeat
from disaster. Sir Alec's reply was, "If that is true, I don't
think it's worth giving them anything". The Foreign
Secretary stated quite clearly that he was very much against
selling the Sudanese too many weapons and added that he
hoped their lists were not too long, as, if they were, they
would not get them. I had the distinct impression that the
Foreign Office did not favour the revolutionary flavour of
Numieri's Government.

Etherington-Smith commented that the Americans were
giving Numieri the equivalent of twenty million pounds, to
which the Foreign Secretary tartly retorted, "They can
afford to". He pointed out that Britain was already giving
one hundred million pounds in overseas aid which "was a
lot of money".* Further remarks were made about democracy and feudalism and the discussion became "warm". Sir

---

[35]Ibid, pp. 47–49.

*NB. The Chancellor of the Exchequer had just removed one hundred and ten million
pounds tax from sweets and crisps.

Alec then said to me, "Now you are becoming contro-
versial". At this point we were joined by other guests and
the conversation became polite. The Foreign Secretary was
extremely courteous and gentlemanly, but very reactionary.
In contrast, Lt. General John Gibbon, with whom I spoke in
the presence of Mansour Khaled, seemed to indicate that the
military were in favour of supplying the Sudanese with
weaponry. The Prime Minister made an excellent host,
charming, kind and attentive to all. His public image did not
do him justice.[36]

The next day a huge reception was given at the Sudan
Embassy, to which the Prime Minister came (much to
everyone's surprise). The Sudanese President did a superb
public relations exercise, and obviously enjoyed every
minute of his visit. He told me that Abdel Halim Ahmed,
one of his Ministers and a one-time student of mine, had
arrived and that he would send him over to me, which he
did. After the President's visit there was much activity and
a number of Sudanese came to London. Dr. Francis Deng,
Minister of State at the Foreign Office, gave a talk on the
strategy of Sudanese Foreign Policy and his visit was
followed by that of Major General El Fatih Muhammed
Beshir, MVO, who was the Sudanese Deputy Chief of Staff.
At a reception to welcome the new Sudanese Ambassador,
Ahmed Sulieman Muhammed Ahmed, Philip O'Bang told
me that the Norwegians were nominating Numieri for the
Nobel Peace Prize for ending the war in the South and
asked me to support the move. He also said that Numieri
wanted the return of the Khalifa's jibba which was reputed
to be at Sandhurst and also the Mahdi's 'Blue Banner' I
questioned the purpose and the attitude of the President
towards the Mahdists and Philip O'Bang replied that
Numieri wanted to consolidate all. Muhammed Ahmed

---

[36]G F Thomas. Mss Diary, Vol. III, p. 50.

Mahjoub was there but said nothing and was obviously still suffering from the effects of his stroke.[37]

In October 1973 Egypt and Syria attacked Israel in what is now known as the Yom Kippur War. Syria took much of the Golan Heights but were beaten back, while Egypt under the brilliant leadership of General Saad el Shazli crossed the Suez Canal. During this time Sadat concentrated on the war effort while Dr Abdel Kader Hatem was, in effect, Prime Minister. The Egyptians managed to hold on to their bridgehead, and the Israelis were unable to wipe out the Egyptian Air Force. Kissinger produced his peace plan which was accepted by both Israel and Egypt, thus strengthening Sadat's position.

In the meantime, Numieri declared the Sudan to be a Socialist Democracy, and that, instead of the Revolutionary Council, there would be a Presidential system of government, thus tightening his hold on the country. He held a plebiscite which endorsed his proposals and was elected President for six years.

---

[37]G F Thomas. Mss Diary, p. 51.

CHAPTER VI

ATTEMPTS AT RECONCILIATION

*"Full many a flower is born to blush unseen
And waste its sweetness on the desert air"*

THOMAS GRAY

After a great deal of pressure from a variety of sources Numieri released Sadig el Mahdi from detention, and the Government expected that he would leave Sudan immediately, but this he did not do. However, on Friday 26 April 1974 Ahmed Abdel Rahman, an uncle of Sadig, who was living in London, telephoned me to say that Sadig would be arriving within a fortnight. I thought it very strange that Ahmed had telephoned me, as we had never had much contact, and had only spoken a few times in ten years. He had been arrested for a short time, but had compromised himself with the regime, and Numieri had allowed him to come to England where he was living in some comfort. I had appealed to Ahmed to help Wali Eldin el Hadi, who had been living in penury, having come to England after his father's assassination, but he did not do so, which I thought unfortunate, to say the least. Pat Wogan of the Foreign Office told me that Sadig had arrived on the previous Wednesday and was staying at the Park Lane Hotel, but I could not trace him. It was interesting that the Sudan Embassy was very annoyed with the British Foreign

President Numieri in the London Embassy Official Visit to England 1973

Office which had suggested that a luncheon be arranged for Sadig. Philip O'Bang declared that President Numieri would regard it as an unfriendly act. Late on Saturday night Sadig telephoned and said that he wanted to see me the following day. He came, accompanied by his mother Sayeda Rahma and his daughter Miriam. We talked for seven hours. I did my best to persuade him to come to an understanding with Numieri. Indeed I had already pleaded with Numieri and his ministers for a reconciliation. Sadig had matured and was not at all bitter about his detention first in Egypt, then in the Sudan for nearly five years without trial or even charges being made. As always, he talked intelligently and reasonably. He was convinced that the régime was crumbling, but this I doubted, although I believed that unless a stable and durable Government was achieved bloodshed would not be avoided. Sir James Robertson came over to meet Sadig, and it was interesting to see his favourable reaction as he had always considered Sadig to be "extremist" and even "precipitous".[1] After Sir James had left we were joined by Philip O'Bang. I had been very nervous and anxious as the meeting posed grave risks. However, all went well and we had a warm and generous discussion. They both accepted my suggestion that Philip should endeavour to get the Southerners to act as mediators between Numieri and Sadig. Philip O'Bang expressed the opinion that it was inconsistent and contrary to the principles of revolution that the South should have freedom and autonomy while the Mahdists were suppressed and proscribed.[2] As I took Sadig to the station he asked me to do what I could with General el Baghir when he came the following month.[3]

That summer a number of Sudanese came to London, and

---

[1] Sir James Robertson. Mss letter.
[2] G F Thomas. Mss Diary, Vol. III, pp. 152–53.
[3] Ibid, p. 154.

visited us. There could be no doubt that the younger
Sudanese were becoming militant. Dr Ghassim Bedri, whose
father Yusif had been a close friend since 1950 was
representative of the general viewpoint. He was intensely
Ansari and pro-Sadig, bluntly saying that he wanted
Numieri out of the way; by assassination if need be. He was
firmly of the opinion that blood would have to be shed
before the régime was toppled.[4] Most of our visitors
expressed their horror and bitterness at the appalling
growth of corruption emanating from the Government, and
without exception they were contemptuous of Mansour
Khaled, once an Ansari supporter, but now vigorously allied
to Numieri. Mansour Khalid's life epitomises much of the
tragedy of the Sudan's intelligent elite. Undoubtedly a
gifted individual, like so many others he was caught up in
the sectarian and religious cross-currents in the country.
Mansour began his political career as a supporter of the
Umma Party and secretary to Abdullah Khalil, but as a
result of the subsequent bickering among senior politicians
of all persuasions, he, (as did so many of his contemporaries)
welcomed the Numieri coup d'etat, eventually serving in his
administration. Mansour was always ambitious, and this is
not necessarily discreditable. He swiftly gained Numieri's
approbation and was promoted to the post of Foreign
Secretary which gave him an international opportunity
which he exploited to his own advantage. Numieri, ever
conscious of any threat to his own personal position and
authority became suspicious of his talented Foreign Minister, and dismissed him from office. Mansour Khalid joined
the staff of the United Nations aspiring to high office
(perhaps the Secretariat) of the United Nations, but had to
be content with relatively minor if useful posts. For a decade
his bitterness against the Sudanese régime increased, and

---

[4]Ibid, p. 155.

finally culminated in his fulmination against Numieri in his book "Numieri and the Revolution of Dis-May".*

Early in October Numieri announced over the radio and television that he had smashed another coup, this time in the army.[5] Discontent was increasing towards Numieri's policies, in particular because of the rising inflation and food shortages. Many Muslims were becoming antagonistic to the southern settlement, and late in 1974 a state of emergency had been declared when crippling strikes had been initiated by left wing workers and students. As a direct result of these pressures, at the beginning of February 1975 Numieri reshuffled his government yet again. This was an activity which he undertook more and more frequently, as he sought to surround himself with 'loyal' people. Mansour Khaled had been transferred to Education as Numieri was annoyed at his 'International Pretensions', and General Baghir was put in charge of Internal Affairs with a remit to tighten up on security. Numieri was beginning to feel threatened and wanted no rivals.

Sadig, at this time was very busy with the formation of a United Front as an opposition to the Sudan régime. He came to visit us in the early summer bringing his wife Sara and seven month old son Muhammed Ahmed (incidentally this was the first time a member of the family had been so named since Muhammed Ahmed the Mahdi). On Sara's return to the Sudan, she was arrested and detained on Numieri's orders, presumably as a warning to Sadig, but by the end of the year news reached us that she was to be released but not allowed to leave the Sudan.[6] Imprisonment for the women political activists, was, in many ways, more unpleasant than for their menfolk as there was no separate

---

*Published in 1985.
[5] G F Thomas. Mss Diary, p. 169, Vol. III.
[6] G F Thomas. Mss. Diary, Vol. III, p. 207.

"political wing" in prison and they were incarcerated with thieves, prostitutes, and murderesses. The Mahdi women made very good use of their time in prison by teaching the criminal detainees simple crafts like sewing, crochet, knitting and basic literacy.

I spent the early part of 1976 in Egypt where I had many discussions with ministers and officials.[7] I warned them that Numieri's Government was not stable, and that there was a real danger that one day Egypt would wake up to find a hostile government in Khartoum. In particular I discussed with Dr Abdel Kader Hatem the possibility of a dialogue with Sadig, who was desirous of making this approach. Dr Hatem commented that Sadat was determined not to become involved anymore outside Egypt, but I argued that there had to be a special relationship between Cairo and Khartoum; so that the Sudan could be considered an exception.

Sadig became more involved with the United National Front in cooperation with Sherif Hussein el Hindi and their aims were expressed in an eight point Charter which was published in a memorandum[8] in August 1976 after yet another, even more bloody, abortive coup. Some two thousand people were killed and, for three days, the outcome was uncertain. Numieri denounced Gaddafi for his intervention and blamed Sadig and Sherif el Hindi. Before the news of the attempted coup had been released, I had a telephone call from someone who refused to identify himself, but said that he had had a message from Baghdad to tell me that Sadig was in the Sudan, and twenty four hours from Khartoum. A few days later the same man told me that the attempt had collapsed and that Sadig had left the Sudan.

---

[7]Ibid, p. 223.
[8]G F Thomas. Mss note.

Sherif Hussein el Hindi

On Sunday 8 July 1976, Sadig and two others came to me at our house in Little Milton and told me frankly what had happened.[9] He accepted responsibility for the coup. He had given the signal for the revolt. Gaddafi had helped, but so had Saudi Arabia and other African and Middle East Countries. The man detailed to lead the coup (no name was given and I did not ask) was instructed by the National Front to

1   Seize the High Command at Wadi Seidna
2   Take Numieri as he landed at Khartoum Airport on his return from France.

---

[9] G F Thomas. Mss Diary, Vol. III, p. 231.

3   Take control of Radio Omdurman and broadcast a message to Sadig who was waiting in Darfur.

4   Release the political prisoners in Kober Prison,* North Khartoum, where there were many imprisoned officers who would take over the Army units.[10]

The attempted coup was doomed from the start, and was a chapter of incompetence. The seizure of the High Command HQ took longer than expected, as resistance was strong. However, Radio Omdurman fell quickly and easily but the technicians were so frightened that they ran away and those who captured the station had no technical skills in broadcasting.[11] The civilians had no idea who was leading the coup, and several Sudanese told me later that they had suspected it was a conflict within the Army, and that had they been aware that it was an attack on Numieri, the streets would have been full of demonstrators and Sadig's supporters. Sadig waited in the West of the Sudan for the radio call which never came. He started for Khartoum after a delay of thirty hours. In the heat of the initial thrust, the man in charge completely forgot about Numieri who was vulnerable, as he was at the airport, although Sadig had sent a message from Paris, saying the President was on his way. Numieri stayed in hiding at the airport for three days, paralysed with fear as he did not know whether he was in control, until General Muhammed el Baghir mounted a counter attack, which led to the restoration of the régime. Yet again Numieri had survived! The final failure had been not to release the political prisoners who could have taken command. Sadig was in sight of Omdurman when he realised that the attempt had failed, and escaped through Libya to England. He told me quite categorically, that

*From Cooper who was a Sudan Government official whose house it originally was. Eventually it became known as Kober.
[10]Ibid, p. 232.
[11]Ibid, p. 232.

although the National Front had received financial support and weapons from Libya and others no foreign troops were involved. It was essentially a revolt by and for the Sudanese. The Communists remained aloof, hoping that the National Front would exhaust itself and then the Sudanese Communist Party could take over.[12] In June 1976 Al Sahafa published ten photographs of political figures wanted for the abortive coup. These included Sadik al-Mahdi, al-Sharief al-Hindi, Ahmed Zein al-Abdein, Muhammad Abdul Jawaad, Omer Nur al-Aiem, Babiker Karrar, Tawfiek Salih Osman Salih, Abdul Daiem Abubaker al-Sanousi, al-Sadik Balla, and Hassan Muhammad Omer Dandash.*[13]

Numieri had demoralised the armed forces, by dismissals, arrests, executions, and forced retirements; consequently there was a real risk of a Communist take over, especially in the technical service of the army.[14]

Ninety-eight people were executed in August for their part in the rebellion and by the end of September Sadig el Mahdi and Sherif el Hindi had been sentenced to death 'in absentia'. Of the other twenty four accused of attempting to overthrow the Régime, seven were sentenced to ten years imprisonment, three for three years and eight acquitted.[15] For the first time the Egyptians realised the gravity of the situation. Their confidence in Numieri was seriously shaken and they were alarmed, but they were still asking what alternative there was to supporting Numieri. I urged them to put pressure on President Numieri (and in the army where they had influence) to widen the basis of government and I told them bluntly that if they continued to support him, they would ultimately, at his downfall, be faced with a

[12]G F Thomas. Mss Diary, Vol. III, p. 234.
*Spellings of names as in "The Times" report.
[13]The Times, 13.10.76.
[14]G F Thomas. Mss Diary, Vol. III, p. 232.
[15]The Financial Times, 1.10.76.

hostile government in Khartoum. The Foreign Office in London became increasingly cool towards me, and relations were virtually non-existent as Numieri had protested about Sadig's presence in Britain, and they reacted in a very pompous fashion. It grieved me that dictators like Idi Amin of Uganda, and Numieri, only had to snap their fingers and the Foreign Office crumbled under the pressure. I was telephoned by someone called G Lawes on August the eighteenth to ask if I knew Sadig's whereabouts. When I replied that he was out of the country Mr G Lawes asked if I would request Sadig to telephone him.[16] I suspected increased pressure from Numieri and telephoned Evan Luard, then Minister of State at the Foreign Office and Member of Parliament for Oxford. We knew him well, and Ismay had stood against him at the Parliamentary Election Selection conference. It was a frank talk and he told me that they (the Foreign Office) wanted certain undertakings from Sadig. I warned Evan Luard that serious threats against Sadig's life were being made publicly by General Abul Ghassim, the Sudanese Vice-President, and added that while I understood that HMG did not want to break relations with the Sudan, he should appreciate that Sadig was a democrat and had done nothing illegal. I was assured that there was no question of deportation, but that certain undertakings were required.[17] Sadig, on his return to England came directly from the airport to see me, after I had sent him a message. I briefed him on the situation, and his immediate reaction was to say that he had no wish to stay in England if he was unwanted. On Monday, Sadig went to the Foreign Office to see Lawes and Urwick, who asked for certain "undertakings". When he asked whether he had done anything illegal, they agreed that he had not but "it was not

---

[16]G F Thomas. Mss Diary, Vol. III, p. 239.
[17]Mss Correspondence with Evan Luard.

a question of legality—they wanted his help, particularly by not talking to the Press".[18]

Sadig asked whether Numieri's Press Censorship was now being applied to Britain, and requested that the conditions be put in writing so that he could consider them carefully. He put his point of view but he declined to "talk politics". Sadig reminded them that his wife and family had been detained for months by Numieri without trial although in no way had they been involved in the attempted coup. Urwick and Lawes said that Sadig had gone most of the way to understand their problems, but they had hoped for a simple answer.[19]

At this time, a good friend of mine, an American in the US Armed Forces in the UK, had discussions with a friend in the US Embassy, John who had met Sadig on several occasions in our house and had been deeply impressed by him, wanted to help. However he did not think much could be done before the American Presidential Elections. He told me that America was convinced that Gaddafi would not last more than six months. He added that secret meetings had been held between Egypt, Sudan, and Saudi Arabia and they had agreed that Gaddafi must go.[20] Sadat was quite determined, particularly after bombing attacks had been made on Cairo and Alexandria. The Americans believed that Sadat was planning military action which could not be resisted effectively by the Libyans. I did not believe that the Egyptian President would lead a direct strike against a fellow Arab state but he might be willing to support a coup and a puppet administration. Assassination was also improbable as the Egyptians would find such an act repugnant. John however was convinced a military strike would be

[18]G F Thomas. Mss Diary, Vol. III, p. 241.
[19]G F Thomas. Mss Diary, Vol. III, p. 242.
[20]Ibid, pp. 240–243.

launched, and no doubt he had reasons for his convictions as he was involved in military intelligence.[21]

I had been horrified by the bloodshed of the abortive coup in the Sudan, and had warned Sadig against the "Hawks" around him as I believed it folly to think that virtually unarmed civilians could take on the Armed Forces with modern tanks and weaponry. I said that "it is very difficult to argue with the barrel of a gun, and it is only when the army itself becomes disenchanted by a corrupt dictatorship that a revolution becomes possible". Close to Sadig at this time were Mahmoud Salih, Sherif Touhami, and Dr Abdel Hamid Saleh, who, after the May Revolution in 1969, had attached himself to Imam el Hadi on whom he had had a disastrous influence. He was among those who had counselled confrontation with the President which ultimately led to the massacre of Gezira Aba and the assassination of the Imam el Hadi.

Another coup was attempted in September and yet again failed. Dr Abdel Hamid was sentenced 'in absentia' to ten years imprisonment and had all his property confiscated, although he was in Cairo at the time and had nothing to do with it. Sadig had been sentenced to death 'in absentia' previously and Sara was still arbitrarily imprisoned. Numieri was continually pressurising HMG, sending Mansour Khaled to the British Prime Minister to request him not to give asylum to Sadig. I was deeply worried for Sadig's safety and when he came on Sunday the seventeenth of October 1976 I gave him the key of our house so that if he felt in danger he could come immediately. He then told me a very strange story. He had been in a bookshop in London when the woman who was serving him, had told him she was a clairvoyant and asked to read his hand. When he agreed she had said to him "You have a Welsh friend who

---

[21]Ibid, p. 244.

is very anxious about you and he will give you something shortly. You also have some tragic connection with Germany but this will turn to your advantage". It was only days after this, that I had given him the key and he also said he had heard from Germany, but only said that the man who had headed the coup in Khartoum and who had been shot by Numieri had been married to a German girl. It was indeed a strange story.

Pressure continued on Sadig from the Foreign Office, and I was so concerned that Ismay and I went up to No 10 Downing Street to see Tom McNally, an old friend, and now political adviser to Jim Callaghan, about Sadig and Tom confirmed that Mansour Khaled had raised the matter with the Prime Minister.[22] I gave him a memorandum which Sadig had prepared for Jim Callaghan and, as we left, Tom promised that he would discuss the whole matter with the Prime Minister adding that he was sure Sadig would not be deported.

The abortive Coup of 1976 seemed to clarify a number of minds. Numieri came to the realisation that his security forces could not guard all eight borders with his neighbour countries, and at the same time police the Sudan internally. The Egyptians were forced to accept that the Sudan regime was unstable. The National Front, and Sadig in particular, admitted that the dictatorship would not be overthrown by force. The Saudi Arabians and the west were concerned about the destabilisation of the whole of the area, the horn of Africa.

Sadig had returned to England at Christmas time (1976), and on Boxing Day we had a large gathering of the Mahdi family and friends, eighteen of them including Dr Khalil Osman[23] who had just bought Rod Stewart's house at

---

[22]G F Thomas. Mss Diary, Vol. III, p. 248.
[23]G F Thomas. Mss Diary, Vol. III, pp. 255-256.

Windsor for three hundred and fifty thousand pounds. Khalil
Osman, who had joined the 'doves' and like myself wanted
a reconciliation between Sadig and Numieri, appealed to me
for support. He had been to Washington to see some
officials and was meeting a Senator and a State Department
Official in London on the first and second of March. Khalil's
plan was for the Americans to lean on the Saudi's, the
Saudi's to pressurise the Egyptians and the latter to
approach Numieri directly. Another Sudanese businessman
Fatah el Rahman el Beshir was also involved, and had a
close connection with Numieri. Sadig and I had a long
session in private and he accepted my initial suggestion for
discussion points with the President, which included, first
and foremost, an amnesty for all; an interim National
Council for two to three years followed by free elections.
Dr Abdel Hamid Saleh was called in and it was agreed that
I should give Khalil the go-ahead on these lines. Sadig
wanted a 'Third Force' to act on the reconciliation but I was
not certain who this force would be or from where it would
come.[24] Shortly afterwards I received a charming letter from
Sadig.

> "Your activity has been highly beneficial to the image
> of the Sudan in general, and to our cause in particular.
> Even when you have disagreed with us your opinions
> were well received".[25]

A large number of the Mahdists (Ansari) were gathering
in London and there was some talk of setting up an
'opposition centre in London'. News was then received by
Dr Abdel Hamid Saleh that a Colonel Osman and two
Sergeants from the Sudanese Army (Seif-el-Din Abdullah
and Awad Jahia) were being sent to the United Kingdom to
'liquidate' Sadig and others.[26] It was confirmed by Mansour

---

[24]Ibid, p. 255–256.
[25]Ibid, 257.
[26]Ibid, 259.

Khaled[27] that Numieri had ordered a 'hit squad' to be sent. I hesitated about telling the Foreign Office, as I thought they might use it to prevent Sadig from coming, and I was certain that he was less at risk in England than elsewhere. After a few days I tipped off the media, and they made use of the information. Despite the despatch of the 'hitmen' it appeared that some moves were being made towards reconciliation; for I was invited to a reception (after a lapse of several years) by the Sudanese Ambassador Amir el Sawi.[28] Outside there was a considerable demonstration by the Ansars including members of the Mahdi family against the régime.

Sadig was regarded with suspicion by members of the old Sudan Government Service, of whom Sir James Robertson remained the outstanding figure. He wrote to me "I quite see your point about Numieri and Sadig and I am sure if you could engineer some reconciliation between them it would be a good thing all round. But so long as they are so obviously in opposition and Sadig still seems to wish to overthrow Numieri by another armed coup d'etat, I should not want to be thought friendly with Sadig". He also wrote that he was concerned that if Numieri was overthrown his work in the South . . . "might be lost as he is much respected by the Southerners and the previous civilian Governments were responsible for much of the troubles and were worse under Mahjoub's Government while the Sadig Government was not much better".[29]

In the Summer of 1977 there was much activity, with comings and goings, and many claiming that they were the originators of the reconciliation. Ismay and I embarked on a campaign to introduce Sadig to as many leaders of opinion as we could in order to prove that he was not a 'Wild Man'.

---

[27]Mansour Khaled. Revolution of Dis-May, p. 170.
[28]G F Thomas. Mss Diary, Vol. III, p. 261–262.
[29]Sir James Robertson. Mss letter, 12.6.77.

In June Michael Roberts MP, a Tory Whip, (who had once been secretary of the Union Debating House when I was President) gave a luncheon for him at the House of Commons, attended by Barney Hayhoe MP, Richard Luce MP (later Minister of State FCO and Minister of the Arts) Christopher Brocklebank-Fowler MP, Dr Abdul Hamid Saleh and David Crouch MP.[30]

All shades of political opinion in Britain were approached. Jeremy Thorpe was most helpful, asking a Parliamentary Question on July the Seventh about the secondment of personnel to the Sudan armed forces and being especially concerned about the special branch who had been sent to help the régime. Members of the Middle East Committee of the Labour Party including David Watkins MP (later director of CAABU), Ron Hayward, Secretary of the Labour Party, and Gwyn Morgan (later to be Chef-de-Cabinet to Roy Jenkins at the EEC) as well as many journalists from press and media were invited to meet Sadig. One of the most interesting meetings was that with the Rt Hon John Davies[31] who had been brought into politics from industry and was the Conservative spokesman for Foreign affairs. He was surprisingly sympathetic, courteous, and charming. He talked of the tyrannies of the Middle East all despotic and none democratic. Sadig did not warm to him, so I deflected the conversation into the problems of intellectual life in the Sudan. John Davies did promise to try to arrange a meeting between Sadig and Mrs Thatcher. Just prior to this meeting Sadig told me that negotiations had been proceeding with Numieri and had reached such a stage that he felt he ought to return to the Sudan.

He thought that the pressures which had persuaded Numieri towards reconciliation were Kuwaiti and Saudi Arabian influence; and also the fact that the high salaries in

[30]G F Thomas. Mss Diary, Vol. III, p. 263.
[31]G F Thomas. Mss Diary, Vol. III, p. 263.

other areas of the Middle East were enticing the elite Sudanese away from the Sudan thus leaving the administration bereft of talent. The discipline also in the army had been weakened by the President's constant changes in the military hierarchy, and the necessity for constant vigilance of Libya, Ethiopia and Eritrea; coupled with the ever present fear of yet more coups had compelled Numieri to open talks. After thinking it over carefully, I said that I was unhappy about Sadig going to the Sudan, as I felt that if he were killed the Opposition would have lost its leader. Sadig was convinced that he should settle the question "once and for all" and was quite phlegmatic about the possibility of assassination. In his view, if Numieri was sincere, a reconciliation would result, while if Sadig were killed then the Sudanese people would know the duplicity of the President. I put up all sorts of objections, but I could see that Sadig had already made up his mind. As the momentum for reconciliation gathered Numieri made several speeches which were conciliatory and in the Sudanese National Assembly he addressed himself to the exiled Sudanese hoping that they would be enabled to "participate in the building of their country".

At this critical time I had to go into hospital in Windsor for an operation; and Sadig came to see me there to discuss the possibilities of a meeting in the near future with Numieri, who had recently made yet another conciliatory appeal. He wanted to take up Numieri's challenge and fly to the Sudan. I was opposed to this, partly as he was still under sentence of death, but mainly as it would be seen as a response to Numieri's initiative. I favoured a meeting in a neutral place, possibly Switzerland, or on a ship and I strongly advocated that a neutral person should be present. Sadig argued that he had to test Numieri's sincerity, and if he suggested an alternative venue or imposed conditions this might give the impression that he was afraid or ambivalent. I did not accept this argument as Sadig's courage was a by-word. I was convinced, when Sadig left me after a long discussion that no absolute decision had been made. At 7.10 am on the sixth of July Dr Abdel Hamid Saleh rang to say that Sadig had left for the Sudan that morning and had taped a speech and instructions in case he did not return. "Sadig had decided that he had better go and have a decision made one way or another". He was concerned that Numieri could be bluffing, and was determined to know the truth as this was best for the the Sudan.[32]

Having flown first to Athens, he proceeded by private plane to Port Sudan. At first it was reported to me that he was going to the Western Sudan, but because of a flare up of ever recurrent violence between the Dinka and Baggara tribes in which three hundred were killed, that was cancelled and the President and Sadig met in Port Sudan. They spent twenty four hours together, mainly talking, before Sadig returned to Athens and from thence to London.

The reconciliation talk covered a number of points. These were:

1   Civil Liberties were to be restored
2   These were to be constitutionally guaranteed
3   Political prisoners were to be freed
4   Property and civil service positions were to be restored
5   There was to be a policy of non-alignment in foreign affairs
6   Reforms in Local Government were to be instituted
7   The membership base and the function of the SSU expanded
8   Areas of devastation were to be rehabilitated; ie Gezira Aba.

---

[32]G F Thomas. Mss notes, 6th and 17th June, 1977.

There was an agreement that Imam el Hadi's body should be given back to the family. In return Sadig gave up multi-party policies and accepted a one party state on the grounds of 'In politics nothing is permanent'. I deeply regretted and was totally opposed to his accepting a one party state. Many in the SSU were opposed to the reconciliation but the Armed Forces were generally in favour.

On 9 July Sadig sent me a note which read—
"My mission was positive but things will take some time to brew. I had to take the plunge, the Sudan, as you know is a unique thing. I shall leave Britain for a short journey tomorrow".[33] Sir James Robertson, who was deeply concerned for the future of the Sudan met Sayed Ibrahim el Nur from the Sudan Embassy at the Gordon Boys School Annual inspection and wrote to me to say that he had been told "Things are improving and conversations are going on between Numieri and Sadig".[34] His comment was that he had not told Ibrahim that he had known of these but that he hoped they would be successful.

Numieri announced the Port Sudan meeting ten days later to an astonished Sudan, and subsequently made another conciliatory speech. Sadig, who had returned to London, Ismay and I drafted an immediate reply in the form of a Press Release. This read as follows—

PRESS RELEASE 12 Noon 4.8.1977

STATEMENT OF THE LEADER OF THE SUDANESE
NATIONAL FRONT (SADIG EL MAHDI)

The Sudanese Opposition welcomes the recent speech of the President Numieri of the Sudan with regard to the reconciliation of the Sudanese, whether inside or outside

---

[33]Mss letter from Sadig el Mahdi, 9.7.77.
[34]Mss letter from Sir James Robertson, 10.7.77.

the Sudan. The Opposition appreciated the initiative taken by President Numieri in inviting Sadig el Mahdi to Port Sudan to review the present Sudanese position. Subsequent to that meeting numerous detainees have been released, other leading figures in the Opposition have met with the President, and the prospect of a general amnesty has been advanced.

The Opposition wish to place on record their unanimous desire for an immediate return to normalcy so that reconciliation can become effective, total national unity established and stability ensured, all of which will contribute to material and moral construction. National reconciliation will consolidate the North—South accord, remove any factors likely to prevent the further development of civilian—military brotherliness; put an end to violence in Sudanese politics and mobilize all efforts to the building of the Nation.[35]

I was unhappy about the Port Sudan meeting, and as I explained to Sadig I felt that he had given away his strongest card by going to the Sudan while Numieri had surrendered nothing, or very little. The President now had only to "sit sahkit" (do nothing) and the opposition would fall apart and be picked off piecemeal. Numieri had been the more skilful politician. Later Sherif Hussein el Hindi who was suspicious of 'the understanding' declared that the aims of the National Front were twofold—free elections for a Legislative Assembly and including curbs on the President's power, and on the other hand the possibility of reconciliation with Libya and Ethiopia. Sadig admitted that the President had made no promises. "but he is demonstrating good faith".[36]

There were many meetings during the Summer of 1977, most of which took place in our house. After a meeting in August with Sadig, Dr Abdel Hamid Saleh, Sherif Touhami,

[35] The Guardian, 5.8.77.
[36] G F Thomas. Mss note.

and his wife Fatma Abdel Rahman, Dr Khalid Farah, Sara
(Sadig's wife) and Wali Eldin el Hadi, it was decided that Dr
Abdel Hamid Saleh should go to Khartoum to continue the
negotiations, and we saw him off on the twenty second of
August,[37] from Heathrow Airport. On the second of
September a Ramadan breakfast was held at the Dorchester
Hotel for all the Members of the Mahdi family and others
including Dr Abdel Hamid Saleh who had returned from a
successful meeting with Numieri, it was a joyous occasion,
as all were hopeful that a genuine reconciliation meant that
the exiles could return to the Sudan. While the jollification
continued Sadig and I went next door to his flat in Park
Lane where General Joseph Lagu, who was head of Anya
Nya, and third in the Sudan Army hierarchy being the
effective leader of the South, was summoned for a meeting.
He arrived at about ten pm, and we talked for about an hour
and a half. This meeting was followed the next day, by a
surprise visit to our house in Buckinghamshire of Sadig,
Lagu, and Dr Abdel Hamid at ten pm, the discussions
continuing for four hours. General Lagu left me in no doubt
that if and when Sadig returned to the Sudan he would give
him full support. He was a short rotund figure, very black in
complexion, and had a quick and alert mind. His reputation
as a guerilla fighter was out- standing.[38]

During this period the political temperature continued to
rise and it appeared that developments were continuing
satisfactorily and with some speed in Khartoum.
Muhammed Abdel Rahman Nugdallah, the Secretary
General of the Umma Party, arrived to join in the
discussions, but he was obviously a very sick man. Sadig
then flew to Libya to explain the situation to Gaddafi and
to the thousands of Ansari still in camps there and to meet

[37]G F Thomas. Mss Diary, Vol. III, p. 265.
[38]G F Thomas. Mss Diary, Vol. III, p. 266.

General Joseph Lagu, Vice President South under Numieri

with Sherif Hussein el Hindi and the other National Front
leaders who had remained there.[39] It had been agreed that he
should fly to Khartoum to make a public return, but
alarming reports had been received from the Sudan, that
security was very bad (as the messenger Amin el Tom told
Sara, Sadig's wife that Sadig's life could well be in danger.)
So Sadig returned to England, and telephoned me from
Gatwick (he had no re-entry visa for Britain) and insisted
that he had given his word to go, and whatever happened
he would keep his word. He added "If it is Allah's will that

---

[39]Ibid, p. 266.

I am killed it might as well be in my own country as in London or Paris".[40]

There was a very long delay at Gatwick and he suspected that it was a plot by the Foreign Office to keep him in the UK, but as there was a Civil Aviation strike I was convinced that this was the cause of the delay. I telephoned the Foreign Office, and they assured me that they were doing all they could, and clearance was given for 12.30 pm.

The reception of Sadig at Khartoum airport was fantastic. The official welcoming group was four hundred who each had to have a handshake. After eight years of dictatorship the euphoria was unbelievable. The drive of ten miles from the airport to The Gubba took nearly five hours so dense were the crowds. At one stage the car was physically lifted and carried along. The crowds waiting at The Gubba were so vast that he was unable to speak to them until nearly two am. He telephoned Sara, who remained in England, at half past three in the morning saying that his feet had not touched the ground. He was literally carried everywhere. There was one sour note. Sayed Ahmed Abdel Rahman, uncle of Sadig, did not go to the airport to greet his nephew, but went to the house on the following morning. The Ansari still crowding around the house would not let him in as they disapproved of his ambivalent attitude towards Numieri, so Sadig had to personally go out and fetch him, but he would not join Sadig and the men, but sat with his sister-in-law, Sayeda Rahma. Later in the day Numieri received Sadig in the Peoples' Palace and for the next few weeks they met regularly. "In an atmosphere both cordial and friendly. It is understood that the negotiations, will of necessity take some time because of the complexities of the problems".[41]

---

[40]G F Thomas. Mss notes.
[41]Voice, Vol. 16, 20.11.77.

Our 1977 Christmas visit to Khartoum was most enjoyable, allowing us to renew old friendships and to assess the situation at first hand. The usual round of social events was exhausting but valuable, as our old friends welcomed us. Beshir Muhammed Said, the doyen of Sudanese journalists with an international reputation, gave a dinner at which we met one of Numieri's close friends, Azzadin el Sayed and learned the views of the régime. It was fascinating then to enjoy the hospitality of Bill Carden, HM's Ambassador, who had been an old Sudan Government Official and whose appointment had been welcomed by the Sudanese as he had a deep affection for the Sudan, being a kindly yet shrewd man, at a working breakfast. We were joined by his Head of Chancery, Richard Palmer, an extremely bright and quick witted young man. The Ambassador was glad that the reconciliation was happening and wished it well.

Not at all in favour of the news was Bona Malwal, Minister of Information, with whom I had a long talk. He was one of the emergent Dinka Tribe; a huge, impressive man with a considerable intellect. Highly educated and with pronounced political views he reminded me of a younger version of Muhammed Ahmed Mahjoub. He was violently anti-reconciliation; openly hostile to Sadig el Mahdi whom he considered to be a religious reactionary. I was also able to assess the Egyptian attitude to the negotiations at a delightful family lunch given by H E Fatatry, the Egyptian Ambassador to Khartoum. Before being summoned to see President Numieri we also had long chats with Fatah el Rahman el Beshir who had played a significant role in the opening of negotiations between Numieri and Sadig el Mahdi.

On December the twenty eighth, accompanied by our daughter, Rhiannon we were escorted to the Palace. After introductions she was whisked away for a tour of the Palace by the Sudanese ADC while Ismay and I talked with the President. It was free of formality and very frank, as indeed my talks with Numieri had always been. On the subject of the reconciliation the President praised Sadig saying that he was very impressed by him. He said that he did not want Sadig to take office but "needed his help". Numieri had considerable charm and was very good at personal relations, having the ability to flatter when he wished to do so. That morning he called me "Brother of the Sudan" and proceeded to discuss the country's problems. He emphasised that the greatest problem was the balance of payments, openly admitting that the country was bankrupt and that inflation was ruining development. He poured out a list of what he called the "woes" of the regime.

The President was deeply concerned about 'The Horn of Africa' and wanted a non-aligned policy. In this he thought the British Government could help by indicating its support. He also questioned why he had heard nothing more about the million pound loan promised by HM Government. The President was emphatic that the Sudan had no wish to see the Red Sea really "red" and feared attacks from Ethiopia on Juba, particularly as the twelve MIGs grounded there were useless without spare parts. Numieri expressed great bitterness at the failure of the US Government to give him the twelve fighters which he had requested and he asserted that without these and in spite of the six American fighter planes given him by Saudi Arabia, both Atbara and Juba were vulnerable. Ismay and I left after an hour and fifteen minutes of this open discussion.[42]

It was quite a contrast to go directly to a huge informal lunch at the house of Joseph Kronfli, a member of one of the families of Syrian and Lebanese origin who had settled in the Sudan even before General Gordon's time. Joseph was a

---

[42]G F Thomas. Mss Diary, Vol. III, pp. 272–274.

friend of some twenty-five years, and he like all those present, was of the second or third generations of Levantines and Greeks, who had contributed considerably to the development of the Sudan. With their capacity for hard work and their entrepreneurial skills they had become wealthy and had a high standard of living, but they had strong social consciences. The families of Morhig, Vanian, Contomichalos and Haggar as well as Kronfli had generously supported schools, colleges, medical, and other charitable services. Joseph for years had been the only pharmacist in the town, and was highly respected. It had long been his practice to charge the rich in order to give medicines to the poor. This community had suffered much under the Numieri régime when all their businesses were confiscated in the 1969–1970 period. 'Dr Jo' as he was affectionately addressed, himself had arrived at the Pharmacy one morning to find a soldier on guard and a notice on the door stating that it was 'Now under the Control of the Revolutionary Council'. Joseph returned home, and two days later a young army officer had come to his house and ordered him to open up the chemist's shop. He refused saying that he no longer had a shop, as it was now the Revolutionary Council's responsibility. A second visit was responded to in the same way, but finally (I understand the President needed some medication) the Vice-President Babiker Awadallah had the offending notice removed and Joseph Kronfli resumed his ministrations to the sick. We were interested to hear the non-Sudanese views on the reconciliation, which they looked forward to in the hope that there would be some improvement in their circumstances. The day ended with dinner at the home of Francis and Dorothy Deng. He was then the Minister of Foreign Affairs. A distinguished anthropologist, Francis was also (like Bona Malwal) a member of the Dinka tribe—in fact a member of the leading family. He had married an American girl, and had had wide experience, which stood him in good stead in his post in the Foreign Ministry. I was much intrigued as he 'probed', or rather 'fished' for information about my visit to the President. I thought it strange that the relationship between the Head of State and his Minister of Foreign Affairs should necessitate such probing and felt it revealed just how much Numieri kept matters in his own hands.

The round of Sudanese hospitality continued unabated, Fadl el Abdullahi, Yusif Bedri, Muhammed Tewfig Ahmed, Abdel Gadir Yusef (my old chief), Amin Hassoun and the Shawki family were among the many who entertained us lavishly. Perhaps the greatest pleasure was in meeting once again our first Sudanese friend Abdel Rahman Abdoun who was in his eighty-fifth year, having been born during the Khalifa Abdullahi's rule, and Dr Ali Bedri, the doyen of Sudanese doctors.

Soon after our return from the Sudan, events once more saw my involvement. In February Dr Abdel Kader Hatem telephoned from Cairo asking me to arrange for Sadig el Mahdi to meet him in London preferably at the end of February. He stipulated absolute secrecy to which Sadig agreed.[43] I was delighted, as it seemed as though all the years of work trying to bring Sadig and the Egyptians together was about to be achieved. Alas, there was to be another delay, as Sadig rang to tell me that he had to go urgently to the Sudan, and would Dr Hatem agree to a delay. In the event, it was to be several weeks later that the meeting took place. I had a telephone call at the beginning of April to say that Sadig would be arriving that Sunday. Unfortunately I had to be rushed into hospital for yet another operation so that when Hatem arrived in London on 5 April we met in my room at the King Edward VII

---

[43]G F Thomas. Mss Diary, Vol. III, p. 276–277.

Hospital, Windsor. He told me that he had discussed the whole matter with Sadat who had told him "to come to London and talk to Sadig". Hatem asked my opinion on what Sadig wanted of Egypt, to which I replied "nothing but good relations and non-interference". He was concerned at Sadig's absence but, by 7 April, Sadig had returned to London and Ismay arranged for them to meet at the Carlton Towers Hotel where Hatem was staying. I regretted that I could not be with them, but all went well, and the next day Hatem spoke to me saying that "all you told me about Sadig is true".

Hatem was very deeply impressed with Sadig's intellect and personality. He was convinced that he (Sadig) was "straight and honest", and considered that the visit was well worthwhile. He was grateful to me for arranging it and offered to pay any expenses involved,telephone calls to Khartoum,maybe Sadig's air fare. I thanked him kindly, but had no wish to become financially involved with the Egyptians. Sadig, too, was delighted with the way the meeting had gone. It was clear that there was a rapport between the two men, each respecting the other's intellectual abilities, and integrity. He said that he had put clear propositions to Hatem who was going to convey these to Sadat.[44]

Sadig came to see me, bringing with him the much respected Judge Abdel Rahman, an old and close friend of Sayed Abdel Rahman el Mahdi. At this time I was becoming increasingly worried about Sadig's isolation from both his own people and the other opposition groups. The stresses which I had feared after the Port Sudan conferences were appearing. Numieri wanted Sadig to commit himself more to the regime, while Sadig was reluctant to do so. Our discussion was strong and vigorous. Sadig rejected the idea

---

[44]G F Thomas. Mss Diary, Vol. III, pp. 279–280.

Hassan el Turabi, Leader National Islamic Front

of taking over the SSU or of joining the Government as he was utterly convinced of the corruption within. I had a feeling at this time that Numieri would have been relieved if Sadig had taken over at this point as long as he continued as titular Head of State, but further reflection leads me to reject this as I cannot believe he would voluntarily give up ultimate power. Hassan el Turabi a leader of the Muslim Brothers had seized his opportunity and had joined the Politbureau. On the other hand Sadig believed strongly that he had a majority of support in the country, and that the whole regime was collapsing. With the extension of corruption which was rife, Sadig felt that he had to maintain his own "personal and political standards". He also argued that he could "go no further than his followers would follow". This was a valid argument, as thousands of Ansar could not and would not forgive Numieri for the massacre at Gezira Aba as well as the assassination of Iman el Hadi and the subsequent repression. Foremost among these were Sadig's mother, Sayeda Rahma, and his wife, Sara, both of whom had great influence on him. Nevertheless, I felt that his attitude would be interpreted, as indeed it was, as being arrogant and intransigent.

Numieri had detached Hassan el Turabi and the Muslim Brothers and now set about building a wedge between Sadig and Sherif Hussein el Hindi, who had been consistently remarkably suspicious of the President's motives. The Sudan Embassy, on the twelfth of April 1978, gave a press conference which was reported both on radio and television in which Sherif Hussein el Hindi was urged to return to the fold. Sadig, at this time, was still asserting that there were no major differences between him and Numieri, and told me that he had even told the President of the meeting with Dr Hatem.[45] Rumours abounded but, publicly,

---

[45]G F Thomas. Mss Diary, Vol. III, pp. 281–282.

all seemed sweetness and light. It was said that Sadig would join the Government and become Prime Minister. We accompanied Sadig to the Sudan Embassy for the May twenty sixth Anniversary, where everyone was "all smiles and insincerity". We left together and as we bade farewell to the Ambassador Amir el Sawi I said "Don't worry, I'll look after him". The swift reply was "Well, you always have". We lunched at the Lowndes Hotel and reviewed the situation.[46]

By June, Sadig was still coy about joining the Government and I was unhappy about the total lack of developments. Dr Ahmed Abdel Aziz Yacoub (then Director of the Khartoum Hospital), who was in London, and I spent a long while arguing with Sadig who was inclined to favour the one-party state. We pointed out that if he advocated a multi-party state all groups other than the SSU and Numieri would support him and he would thus "outbid" Numieri. He seemed to be "waiting for the call" which he wanted to come from the people, and totally rejected accepting office on the President's initiative, yet he accepted the idea of a one-party state.

James Buxton of the Financial Times, who visited the Sudan at this time, told me that he was quite confused about the situation in Khartoum. The general analysis from Richard Palmer and the British Embassy indicated that Numieri had succeeded in dividing the opposition and was now playing one off against the other (his normal policy). It was felt that even the Ansar were divided and that the sons of Imam el Hadi, Wali Eldin and Nasr Eldin were opposing Sadig (certainly it was not true as far as Nasr Eldin was concerned). The IMF were providing funds after devaluation so that what was described as a 'mini boom' was taking place. Numieri had no intention of taking any action, and

---

[46]Ibid, p. 286.

Sadig's withdrawal and ambivalent attitude was losing him support. Dr Yusif Bedri, who called in on his way to the States told me that he was concerned about Sadig's position and was curious to know why Wali Eldin and Nasr Eldin had gone to see Numieri. Yusif thought that it might have been to make an appeal for the return of their father's body, so that it could be buried at the Gubba.[47]

During the summer there was another 'frisson' of anxiety in the Sudan with the Ansar becoming increasingly anxious about Sadig's security. Mubarek el Abdullahi told me that rumours abounded, that the communists were planning a coup and it was reported that Sherif Hussein el Hindi was plotting with the Libyans and the Russians. He asserted that Dr Abdel Hamid Saleh who was in London was exerting much pressure on Sadig, mainly because he wanted to become a Minister again, preferably Prime Minister. Mubarek went on to say that Dr Abdel Hamid Saleh was "imposing himself on Sadig every minute of the day . . . he gets there at 6am". There is no doubt that Abdel Hamid was much disliked by the younger Ansari. Mubarek begged me to use my influence to persuade Sadig to stay in the UK until after the expected coup in July. He feared that he would be assassinated "he is so vulnerable in the Sudan".[48] Early in July, Fatah el Rahman el Beshir asked me to go to see him at his home in Brompton Square, which I did. He had just returned from Khartoum with a message for Sadig from Numieri, begging him to return to Sudan and join the Politburo. Fatah el Rahman said that Numieri had fulfilled everything that Sadig had asked of him, but that the opposition kept adding new items and he "could go no further".

He also commented that the President had been most

---

[47]G F Thomas. Mss Diary, Vol. III, p. 288.
[48]Ibid, pp. 289–290.

generous in his reception of Wali Eldin and Nasr Eldin el
Hadi, and had told the Iman's sons that he and the Imam el
Hadi had had the same aims but they had been "led" by
others into the tragic confrontation at Aba. Fatah el Rahman
was concerned about the plans of Yemen, Ethiopia, and
Libya and begged me to use my influence to get Sadig to
agree to return to Khartoum. He was convinced that
Mubarek el Abdullahi was a bad influence on Sadig as he
was still hankering after a military coup, and had a very low
opinion of Dr Abdel Hamid Saleh as being opportunist and
a place seeker.[49]

He went on to say that Sara had more influence than
anyone but that of the 'non-Sudanese' I was held in much
esteem and was closest to Sadig. I assured Fatah el Rahman,
that, as he already knew, I was in favour of the reconciliation, always had been and that I could try to persuade
Sadig to return to the Sudan. However I was opposed to
Sadig joining the Politburo. His reply was that he, Sadig,
and Hassan el Turabi had gone through the list of members
and of these twenty were pro-Sadig and only four against. I
was amused when Fatah assured me that Colonel Abul
Gassim was for Sadig. I pointed out that if Sadig joined at
Numieri's invitation, he could also be dismissed by a
decision of the President, and quoted the names of those
who had been removed at Numieri's whim,people like
Mansour Khaled, Raschid el Taher (a former PM) Ahmed
Abdel Halim and many more. He refused to accept that this
was comparable as unlike those "Sadig had real political
power". He argued that Sadig did not need to go to every
meeting but that it would enable him to have daily access
to the President which was what Numieri wanted.

After leaving Fatah, we joined Sadig for lunch at Brown's
Hotel (a place much loved by Sayed Abdel Rahman, Sadig's

---

[49] G F Thomas. Mss Diary, Vol. III, p. 291.

grandfather). Sadig was furious about the Presidential recent declaration on devaluation and said that it would lead to the further hoarding of goods to wait for a further period of inflation. I summarised for him the talks with Fatah el Rahman and Sadig said he would return to the Sudan, but Numieri had not fulfilled his promises, and that meant Sadig could not join the Politburo.[50].

Sadig also told me that a new dimension had developed. New events had overtaken them, and the reconciliation. Gaddafi, in Libya was refusing to release the Sudanese in Libyan Camps and was "putting every difficulty" in Sadig's path. At this time Sadig believed that the Sudan was threatened and that both he and Numieri were in grave danger of assassination. There were fifty thousand Ethiopians in the Sudan and the security forces could not contain the situation. He confirmed that both Mubarek el Abdullahi and Sara were strongly opposed to his return but Omar Nur el Diem, who had gone to Libya, would be returning to London within a few hours and, when he had heard Omar's report he would make a final decision. At this stage Dr Abdel Hamid Saleh talked such 'gibberish' that neither Ismay nor I could make much sense of it except that he was insisting that Sadig return to the Sudan immediately and "Take Office". He was talking most excitedly that the country was surrounded and imperilled. It seemed to me to be a Numieri orchestrated piece.

As we left, Sadig asked me rather mysteriously for the key to our country cottage in Oxfordshire—so Ismay immediately gave it to him. He gave no reason, and we asked for none. Apparently he wanted to meet with Omar and Fatah el Rahman to continue negotiations but this proved to be impossible, as Fatah el Rahman was leaving almost immediately for Khartoum. However, they did reach

---

[50]G F Thomas. Mss Diary, Vol. III, p. 293.

some agreement and Sadig left for the Sudan on Wednesday, the fourth of July. Unfortunately we had no opportunity for discussion as Sadig's phone was out of action.

By the end of July 1978 heavy torrential rain had wiped out the town of Wad Medani, and annihilated the cotton crop, including the seedlings for the next year which were swept away in the floods. Five hundred thousand were made homeless and Numieri sent for thirty Western Envoys, begging for their assistance. Her Majesty's Government reacted swiftly and a helicopter was organised from Cyprus with tents and other supplies. At the same time there were increasing reports that a Communist Coup was imminent. Peter Torry of the Sudan Desk at the Foreign Office sent a memorandum to Carden on the matter. Richard Palmer thought that there was some activity and Carden went to see Sadig in Omdurman to seek his opinion which was that there was increased Communist activity, but that he thought a coup unlikely, although the Communists were particularly strong in the Gezira Cotton area and the Blue Nile Province.[51]

It was reported that Sadig had given a press conference at which he had said that he was not entering the Government, that the agreement had not been fulfilled and that he had been unable to secure the return of his people from Ethiopia and Libya. Fatah el Rahman expressed his pleasure at Sadig's broadcast from Radio Omdurman which had been very well received. Numieri went to Sadig's Omdurman home and further negotiations had taken place. It was agreed that Sadig should join the Politburo and he was to have an office next door to the President. When Sadig had taken the oath, the announcement could be made. Fatah el Rahman was certain that by the end of the year

---

[51]G F Thomas. Mss Diary, Vol. III, pp. 300–304.

Sadig would hold high office. When I asked whether he meant Vice-President or Prime-Minister he laughingly replied "Yes, maybe both".[52] The new understanding included the appointment of Dr Abdel Hamid Saleh as Leader of the Opposition (a Government post). Fatah el Rahman was convinced that all had gone well and that both men were happy and satisfied. I made a note in my diary indicating my doubts. Many of the young Ansars were extremely unhappy about the developments, and Abdel Rahman el Siddig (Sadig's half brother) expressed his reservations. He was at that time a student, a young man, charming, good looking, with much of the Mahdi family charisma.

It was not only the Ansar who were uneasy. Many on Numieri's side were bitterly opposed to the reconciliation, these included Bona Malwal, Abul Gassim, Bahaa Eldin, Azzadin el Sayed, and the whole bureaucracy of the Sudan Socialist Union. These were forces exerting pressure to kill the reconciliation. Sayeda Noon Abdel Rahman forwarded me a letter from Sadig in which he justified his joining Numieri, mainly on economic grounds as the country was in an appalling state. In his letter* Sadig wrote:

> "I have agreed with Numieri on a sum up of the reconciliation, and declared the agreement in a comprehensive way. The agreement outlined the shape of things to come and the democratization to be expected. The politics of the situation are encouraging. The economics, thanks to the IMF, and self inflicted damage are in a very bad shape indeed, so bad in fact that they may undo the positive developments in the political field.
>
> I hope we will be able to do something radical to pull out of the present economic developments."

---

[52]Ibid, pp. 301–302.
*Dated 31.7.78.

The Sudan continued to deteriorate throughout the summer. Abdel Rahman el Siddig confirmed what Carden had reported to the Foreign Office. There were prolonged electricity cuts and long queues for bread, sugar, tea and coffee and there had been no petrol. Meat prices rose by five hundred per cent. Just before Abdel Rahman el Siddig had left for England a little petrol had come through and was rationed at four gallons per week. Our son, who had gone to the Sudan to do some teaching at the Ahfad College, was writing home gloomy reports about electricity cuts lasting days, the non-availability of gas for cooking and the almost impossible search for the basic necessities which, if to be found, were extremely expensive. Chicken, eggs, and fish, which had always been plentiful and cheap in Khartoum, were not to be seen.

On the seventh of October, Sadig who had come to England, came alone for breakfast; naturally we discussed the situation. Sadig was insistent that the "Reconciliation must lead to reform, or all is finished". He said that Abul Gassim and the SSU were opposing moves towards reform and he was adamant that Numieri must accept the 'non-aligned' position, to which he and Numieri had agreed at Port Sudan. If Numieri adhered to his support of Sadat and the Camp David Agreement, then Sadig, the Mahdists, and the other members of the opposition who had agreed to reconciliation, would withdraw and go back to square one, thus recreating the opposition to Numieri. He spoke warmly of Dr Abdel Hamid Saleh whom he thought, was doing "a good job as a buffer". I doubted this myself and felt that Abdel Hamid was self-motivated and ran with the hare and hounds, although I was sure he believed he was sincere in his effort. We then talked about the problems of the resettlement of the Ansar, and also of the family. Sadig said that Sayed Abdel Rahman had left his house in Khartoum as well as the Island of Aba to the Ansar, while the house in

Omdurman, (now occupied by Sayed Ahmed Abdel Rahman) was to be used as a hospital. He went on to reveal an exciting new project for settling forty thousand of the Ansar on eleven thousand feddans of land at Gezira Aba. It was to be a gigantic co-operative society, financed initially by the Sudan Government and Libya which was donating a number of heavy duty lorries. The co-operative venture would produce, among other things, fruit and vegetables. There were plans for a further development of another forty thousand feddans in the White Nile area at a later date. It was at this point that I asked Sadig why I had never been invited to Libya (I had always wanted to visit Leptis Magna) and was astonished when he told me that Sherif Hussein el Hindi had told Gaddafi that I was a British Agent.

A few weeks later Bill Carden (HMG's Ambassador to the Sudan) invited me to visit him at his home in Portchester, Hampshire. During our discussions, we agreed that there were seven distinct groups in the Sudan at that time. These were:

1   Numieri and the Army and SSU.
2   Sadig and the Mahdists (I estimated these at 35% of Northern Sudanese)
3   The Old Unionists—Khatmiyya, Idrisi, and other tariqas
4   Joseph Lagu and his Southern supporters, which included the only armed and trained group outside Numieri's own control
5   The Muslim Brothers, which probably commanded a majority in the Universities and other higher academic institutions. Electorally they carried about 5–7% but might reach 10%
6   The Communists, which were a small group but effectively organised and disciplined

7   The businessmen and entrepreneurs such as Fatah el
      Rahman el Beshir, Dr Khalil Osman, Dr Khalid Farah,
      the Aboul Ela family, and the Abdel Moneims who
      "desired stability and peace".

We discussed the external factors which influenced the
internal situation, mainly Egypt. Sadat saw Numieri as
essential to Egypt, and would only withdraw support when
Egypt decided that Numieri was a liability and that
whatever regime replaced him would not be, in any way a
threat to Egypt.[53] There was a Libyan influence on the
opposition especially on Sherif Hussein el Hindi and, to a
lesser extent, on Sadig; as Gaddafi would undoubtedly seek
to isolate Sadat wherever possible. I considered that the nub
of the problem was Numieri himself. As I had told Sadig
after the Port Sudan Agreement, Numieri only needed to
pursue a policy of doing nothing, and the opposition would
fall apart but the President was still on the horns of a
dilemma. He could not break with Egypt and abandon Abul
Gassim and the S.S.U., because his only alternative was to
join Sadig and the Ansar, becoming entirely dependent on
them thus having no power base of his own. It was equally
unthinkable for Sadig to revert to the use of a military coup
although he might use this as a threat. It was possible that
Sadig might quietly accept the status quo and build up the
Ansar financially and economically (which is what he did, in
effect from 1978–1985). Should Sadig give up the idea of a
one-party state (I had always opposed the idea) and
advocate a demand for free and democratic elections, this
would command the respect of, and support from, the Old
Unionists, Communists, probably the Muslim Brothers, the
South, the intelligentsia and the middle class. Thus, at a
stroke, there would be an erosion of support for the regime
and the armed forces would be put on the defensive. This is

---

[53]G F Thomas. Mss note, 7.10.78.

what ultimately happened[54] and, in my opinion, could have occurred earlier if Sadig had been more resolute.

As I had expected, Sadig was constantly assailed in S.S.U. and government circles, behind his back and in the Politburo. Colonel Abul Gassim was extremely hostile and personally insulting. The old guard of the SSU lost no opportunity to denigrate him and he was frustrated at every turn. Numieri was reluctant to jettison his old cronies, and ally himself with Sadig, for he still feared and mistrusted the Ansar, with some justification. Above all, he had no wish to surrender his arbitrary powers. In November, Sadig saw his opportunity to resign from the Politburo,[55] expressing disapproval of Numieri's conditional endorsement of the Egypt/Israeli Peace Treaty and dissatisfaction with the performance of the SSU.

A fortnight later, the Foreign Office in the person of Frank Judd MP, gave a luncheon in honour of His Excellency, Joseph Lagu, President of the High Executive Council of the Southern Sudan. Also with him were L Wolwol and Joseph Tonbra (Minister of Commerce, Roads and Transport), Omar el Sheikh (Chargé d'Affaires), W R Tomkys (Head of the North African Desk), Peter Torry (Sudan Desk), Keith Kyle, James Johnson and four other MPs together with Pearce Wright of "The Times".

I collected Joseph Lagu from the Hyde Park Hotel and took him to my club, where we discussed the whole situation. Lagu was convinced that Sadig had made an error of judgement in resigning from the Politburo. He said that Numieri had set up a Committee to investigate the SSU, but in reality he wanted to deal with Abul Gassim 'who was frightened'. He was convinced that had Sadig not resigned Abul Gassim would have been removed, and probably

---

[54]G F Thomas. Mss note, 18.10.78.
[55]G F Thomas. Mss Diary, Vol. III, p. 312.

posted to the United Nations. General Lagu was very bitter
about the "northern technocrats" as he called them, including Raschid el Taher, Mansour Khaled and Mamoun
Biheiri who he said "deliberately held up things in Khartoum
for the South". Lagu said that he was sure that the President
had the right intentions, but he was deeply worried about
Hassan el Turabi and had urged Sadig to "soften his Islamic
call". He revealed that there was infiltration from Ethiopia
and that Her Majesty's Government was going to send a
squad of Royal Engineers to the South to help build bridges.
Lagu said that he, himself was unwell, had a severe attack of
malaria, and was very tired, but I felt that he was depressed
and unsure of himself and his own position. His last words
were to ask me to use my influence with Sadig to return to
the Sudan, as he had recently come back to England.[56]

As I looked back on 1978, as the year ended, I saw all
the hopes of a reconciliation were ending too and the Sudan
would continue to drift into further decline and anarchy. In
the new year Sadig was quite depressed and thought that
the Reconciliation was quite dead. I suspected that he
thought that the only way to overthrow Numieri would be
by a military coup. He came several times, once with Abdel
Rasoul el Nur.[57] I was not much help to him at this time as
I had serious medical problems. It was indeed a "Winter of
Discontent". At home the country was in the grip of snow
and strikes. The British Government was feeble and vacil-
lating and the Prime Minister Jim Callaghan exasperated
everyone when on his return from the West Indies in reply
to a query he flippantly asked "what crisis?" Abroad, the
Americans had failed to keep their Humpty Dumpty on the
wall, and the Shah in Iran, having only recently celebrated
thousands of years of Imperial Civilization at Persepolis, was

---

[56]G F Thomas. Mss Diary, Vol. III . pp. 314–315.
[57]Ibid, pp. 316–317.

gone, and after much bloodshed and chaos the Ayatollah Khomeini had established an Islamic Republic. Among my visitors at St George's hospital were Sadig, and the Sudanese Ambassador Amir el Sawi, who both wanted me to go to Khartoum for convalescence. Sadig himself was determined to stay away until Numieri had moved towards reform.

In February, Sadig went to Libya for consultations with Gaddafi during which time Gaddafi sent a plane to fetch Sherif Hussein el Hindi so that the two Sudanese opposition leaders could once more co-operate, they had disagreed over the reconciliation and Sherif was taking a hard line. They were actually both in the same house but Sadig refused to meet el Hindi and was adamant that a military solution was not the way forward. Sadig told me that it was a bad seven days but, ultimately, Gaddafi had accepted that Sadig had a better understanding of the internal situation and, calling his sons to join them for a photograph the Libyan leader said, "You have always spoken truthfully and straight to me, you do what you think best". Sadig refused to see Sherif Hussein el Hindi and returned to England, but he was very restive and wanted to go to Baghdad, Damascus and to see Yasser Arafat.[58]

Francis Deng came to London and it was very depressing, for he was not in favour of the reconciliation, he followed the line taken by Bona Malwal. He merely wanted Sadig to come into the government as "one of many". I thought this ridiculous, as Sadig was the leader of thirty to thirty five per cent of the Northern Sudanese but Francis questioned this. I was convinced that he was not in the confidence of Numieri but he indicated the strength of the opposition to the Reconciliation. Later, Sadig met both Francis and Bona Malwal in London, but there was little said

---

[58]G F Thomas. Mss Diary, Vol. III, p. 325–326.

and the meeting was fruitless.[59]

It was at this time that the situation changed drastically, as it was announced that the Egyptians and the Israelis had agreed a Peace Treaty. The repercussions of this were great, not only in the Arab world in general but the Sudan in particular.

In the meantime, Numieri caused a sensation in Khartoum when, in the Assembly, while he was defending the actions of two of his Ministers, he was heckled and jeered at, and broke down in tears. All of this was broadcast live by Radio Omdurman. He was obviously under much strain/and, early in April, he came to Liverpool for consultation with a medical friend.

During his absence it was reported that an attempted coup had been uncovered, involving some of the Nuba Tribe and Sherif Hussein el Hindi's men. Perhaps of more significance was the private meeting between Numieri and Sadig at Chadwick (halfway between Liverpool and London). Once again, an agreement was reached. This was that Sadig would remain aloof from the regime in "Responsible Opposition" (not in "Military Opposition"), until Numieri could move towards some reform of the regime. In return, Sadig would come to the "aid" of Numieri, when required. These words were particularly revealing, especially the phrase "could move" and "aid". It confirmed my conclusion that the old guard of the SSU, together with the young technocrats, were opposed to any move towards Sadig. The two men also agreed that Sadig should distance himself from Gaddafi, while Numieri should take a more neutral stance towards Sadat. Numieri told Sadig that he had instructed the Sudanese Ambassador to Washington not to attend the signing of the Agreement between Sadat, Begin and Carter, which was to take place on 18 September.

---

[59]Ibid, p. 327.

He had already withdrawn the Sudanese Ambassador from Cairo, to avoid his being present when Begin visited Cairo. Sadat had expressed his anger with Numieri and "strong words" had been used but the President told Sadig that he was "fed up" with the Egyptians, who were getting much aid from America and getting nothing for the Sudan. Sadig said that he wanted time to re-establish the Ansar as they had suffered much deprivation and poverty. He assured Numieri that he would not ally himself with either the Communists or Sherif Hussein el Hindi in an irresponsible opposition. I was much relieved at this, as I was convinced that it would do no good. Sadig told me all this in private and, later, I talked to Dr Abdel Hamid Saleh, who had seen Numieri at Liverpool but had not attended the Chadwick meeting, which was between Sadig, Numieri and Fatah el Rahman el Beshir. Even Amir el Sawi, the Ambassador, who drove them to the rendezvous, was not present. Tomkys, of the Foreign Office, told me that they knew of the meeting, as they had been involved in the arrangements, presumably security. During my conversation with Abdel Hamid Saleh, he assured me that the President had declared to him that he was prepared to hand everything over to Sadig, including the Presidency, which fitted with what Numieri had told me during our last visit. Abdel Hamid was convinced he was sincere but Sadig did not make even a hint or a reference to it. Nevertheless, I recorded it in my diary and commented that it would fit in with Sadig sorting out the Ansar, while Numieri carried on for a year or so. I had felt for some time that Numieri was tired, almost certainly ill, and that he might be prepared to go if he was assured of his place in history, his life and a reasonable life style, and this would ensure a peaceful succession but I remained dubious.[60]

---

[60]G F Thomas. Mss Diary, Vol. III, p. 333.

On May 3rd, the Tories were successful in the British General Election and Mrs Thatcher with a comfortable majority, became the first woman Prime Minister. It was all due to rubbish, grave diggers striking, hospital pickets and commuters fed up with one-day stoppages.

Sadig again visited Libya, to try to secure the return of the Ansar, still held in camps. On his return he confirmed that Numieri had talked of an "orderly succession", and had definitely promised reforms. Sadig said that he had made his conditions clear but I had the distinct impression that Sadig had no intention of being 'beholden' to the President or the old regime, with its taint of blood and corruption. I was convinced that he wanted the 'call' to come from the people, but he liked and trusted Numieri at that time.

We had a big family gathering on the ninth of June, to which Sadig brought Hafia and his new son, Bushra, and they were accompanied by Hassan el Turabi (his brother in law) who was still participating in Government and said, frankly, that the Muslim Brothers were gaining strength everywhere and even had "14 different cells in the Army".[61]

Sadig left for a tour of the Arab countries, to Saudi Arabia, Jordan, Iran and Iraq. He was given red carpet treatment by King Khalid and the Saudis. They gave Sadig the impression that they regarded Numieri as dispensable. Sadig declined to talk about internal Sudan affairs and concentrated on external affairs. King Khalid and the Royal Family were genuinely angry with Sadat and Carter. He travelled on to Amman, where his meetings with King Hussein and his brother, Prince Hassan, were cordial. Sadig was most impressed by Prince Hassan and a personal friendship developed, which has given Sadig support in the most difficult days.

His opinions of the Ayatollah and the Iranian leaders

---

[61]Ibid, 336.

were that they had no grasp of world affairs and they were good but provincial men. He thought that Bachie (Secretary-General) and Sadig el Khomeini were the men of the future and that Khomeini's grandson, then aged 22, was "extreme in his views". I was becoming deeply concerned, for Sadig was becoming more exasperated and disillusioned by Numieri and I expected a complete rupture.

In August, Sadig went to the Sudan, unwillingly but, as he said necessarily as the death had occurred of Muhammed Nugdallah, who had been a great stalwart of the Umma Party since the early days and would be much missed. Sadig was convinced that he would either be "discredited or eliminated" by the regime, but that he had to pay his respects to the family of Nugdallah.

Suddenly and inexplicably, Numieri dismissed his senior ministers and the next day appointed a respected soldier, Abdel Magid Khalid, as first Vice-President and Minister of Defence. It was suggested that Sadig might be offered the post of Prime Minister but he had assured me that he would refuse but "might suggest a nominee".[62] Before he left, we devised a code in case of emergencies.

The situation was tense, Amir el Sawi told me that the "regime is in a state of total collapse". Students from the universities rioted in Khartoum and elsewhere and it was reported that two people were killed in Khartoum North. Sadig considered that he needed to stay on in Omdurman to "cool things down".

---

[62]G F Thomas. Mss Diary, Vol. III, p. 341.

CHAPTER VII

ABSOLUTISM AND DISINTEGRATION

'Power tends to corrupt, and absolute power corrupts absolutely"
LORD ACTON

Despite the early enthusiasm, the Reconciliation ran into serious difficulties. Numieri, as I suspected, did not implement his agreement and this led to increased opposition by the leaders of the SSU vigorously led by Colonel Abul Gassim. As a result, Sadig tactically withdrew to England.

I did not see much of him during January 1980 as I was in and out of hospital yet again, but by the end of January he had decided to go to see Khomeini once again, and then on to Washington where he planned to see Secretary of State Vance.[1] The day before his departure a deputation consisting of his uncle Ahmed Abdel Rahman, Dr Abdel Hamid Saleh and Dr Khalid Farah arrived from Khartoum to urge him to return to the Sudan immediately where he was urgently required as problems were getting acute. They discussed this with me, and I counselled that he should go back home for the sake of the Ansar, who were, I knew, feeling leaderless and confused by his absence. Sadig decided to return home, but assured me that he would on no account join the Government, despite a story emanating

---

[1]G F Thomas. Mss Diary, Vol. IV, pp. 1–2.

181

from the Sudan Embassy. Sadig accompanied the deputation back to Khartoum.

On the fourth of February, following Numieri's re-election as President of the SSU in January, there were elections in the SSU; Abul Gassim and the old guard were elected, while Dr Abdel Hamid Saleh and Sherif Touhami, representing the opposition were defeated. Numieri then reversed his stance of neutrality, and openly espoused the cause of Sadat of Egypt. Sadig issued a statement in which he declared that Numieri had not fulfilled his side of the Reconciliation Agreement and in retaliation Numieri, not only declared the Agreement to be dead and that only the SSU members could join the Government but the President created great difficulties for Sadig in obtaining a new diplomatic passport. Sara was convinced that Sadig was being detained.

I had a long talk with James Buxton of the "Financial Times" who had just returned from the Sudan. He reported that, in addition to the usual chaos, petrol was in short supply, and that Sadig had been very impressive in his analysis of the situation at a dinner he gave for the Press in Omdurman. One of his most interesting comments related to the views of Beshir Muhammed Said, who, speaking for the elite middle class had told James that they (the elite) wanted neither Numieri nor Sadig. They considered Numieri to be uneducated and uncouth, and instanced the President's behaviour towards his ministers some of whom he dismissed in an announcement over the radio. In total contrast they admired Sadig's intellectual gifts, but did not want to return to the Sadig leadership of the 1960's. James Buxton was very fearful of what could happen after the hot summer and the rains when commodities would be in very short supply.

From March to September 1980 there were no dramatic developments. The only event of consequence was the issuing of a report of a committee set up by Numieri in

1977 (shortly after the Reconciliation) to propose means of proceeding towards reform, which was published in August. The committee, which was composed of the first Vice-President Abdel Magid Hamid Khalil and General Omer el Tayeb for the Government, and Omar Nur el Diem and Sherif Touhami for Sadig, recommended the dissolution of the SSU and the convening of a National Congress to examine the reforms necessary. Of course, none of their recommendations was implemented or enacted.

During the summer and autumn Sadig embarked on a punishing schedule of writing, lecturing, and travelling including a visit to Russia at the invitation of the Soviets during which he attended an Islamic conference in Tashkent, where with his usual courage he refused to endorse a pro-Russian resolution and substituted an Islamic one calling for the freedom of Muslims to visit Mecca and to support Islam in Russia. Ultimately to the satisfaction of the Soviet Government and the non-Soviet Muslims both resolutions were passed. He was genuinely impressed by the general attitude of the officials, and was surprised how many of the Ulema could both speak and read Arabic. He was greeted enthusiastically and frequently told by Russians that they were first Muslim and then Russian. Just before Sadig returned to England my daughter Rhiannon was married, and to our astonishment, a splendid present arrived from President Numieri. In the light of later events it was a bizarre choice of a full suite of crystal wine glasses. I wondered if it was an olive branch. The Sudan was well represented at the wedding in the persons of Omar el Sheikh the Sudanese Minister in London and Sadig's sister Sha'ma. When Sadig did return he held a press conference in London but it was not very successful as he seemed ill at ease.

The Sudan Government was tottering further out of control. In 1981 even the judges went on strike. Numieri appealed to Egypt for replacements, but neither the Government in Egypt nor individual judges responded. Corruption, incompetence, and inflation were taking their toll of the already tattered economy. Sadig continued to denounce Numieri's fiscal and economic programmes as "faulty and socially destructive". He strenuously campaigned for effective reforms and at the end of February sent a vigorous memorandum of protest to the President. Shortly afterwards Numieri, ever astute, met Sadig to discuss[2] the memo which he 'received in a good spirit' and they reached an agreement on some reforms which 'were to be effective'. In the event they were pure 'window dressing' on the President's part as his policy was the usual one of buying time.

In the South, tensions were rising. General Joseph Lagu had been made President of the Southern Regional Assembly after Abel Alier who had been its President from 1974–1978 had been 'persuaded' by Numieri and the assembly itself to give way, but Lagu had eventually dismissed the entire leadership and replaced them, with his own nominees. The Southern Regional Assembly never met again, ultimately being dissolved by the President who asked Lagu to seek a new mandate. Lagu however, realising his lack of support gave up the contest and Abel Alier was re-elected by sixty seven votes while Samuel Aru had thirty five. There was serious disquiet in the South over the decision by Numieri to declare that Kosti would be chosen as the site of the refinery for the recently discovered oil wells in the south west of the Sudan by the Standard Oil of California under the name of Chevron. The production of oil was seen as being a valuable contribution to the development programme in supplying domestically produced oil and thus freeing both imported fuel and railway freight capacity. There was also talk of changing provincial

---

[2]G F Thomas. Mss notes.

boundaries to bring land now in the Southern Region into the Northern Sudan. This report further irritated the Southerners.

During most of 1981 Sadig was busy trying to settle back into the Sudan refugees who were still in Libya and Ethiopia whence the Ansar had fled. We spent several months in the Sudan during the winter as I had been forced to retire. Sadig gave us a house in Khartoum North and we were able to renew old acquaintances and assess for ourselves what was the situation. Things were very difficult; fish normally plentiful was only available by clandestine visits to the river bank before dawn and at a vastly inflated price. The staple food of the Sudanese, 'dura', had quadrupled in price in eighteen months, while sugar was very scarce. The most visible of the problems was the lack of petrol. Long queues of cars were to be seen at every petrol station sometimes for fourteen hours or even days for only four gallons. The frustration culminated in rioting in the early days of January 1982. School children rioted in Omdurman and Khartoum, cars and buses were overturned and set on fire as were shops and petrol stations. By the fifth of January the army were out in strength determined to quell the disturbances which had spread through the Sudan. Casualty figures emerged, seven at Wad Medani, fourteen at Atbara, nineteen at Port Sudan and many more elsewhere; totalling two hundred and eighteen within one week. The violence continued but the Ansar were not involved as in the absence of Sadig el Mahdi they were confused.

I was in no doubt that the country was one heart-beat away from disaster, and what was even more depressing was the total apathy not only of the people but amongst the ministers, a number of whom I saw at this time. A curious state of inertia seemed to pervade the administration. Constant policy changes, and the regular restructuring of the Assembly, and Government Departments, together with the frequent ministerial changes which had been the tactics of Numieri (in order to prevent any centres of power being developed) had a devastating effect.

In January Ismay and I went to see President Numieri at his office in the Council of Ministers.[3] He had aged considerably since our last meeting and had grave difficulty in recalling the names of people, even world figures. In previous years he had done this deliberately to disparage anyone he wished to belittle, but now he was not pretending. After the usual warm and generous welcome it was soon apparent that he had no desire to discuss the economy or any part of the enormous problems facing his country.

While we were talking, General Omer el Tayeb phoned to say that the Saudi Arabians had been on the telephone asking whether President Numieri would allow the body of Sherif Hussein el Hindi (who had died suddenly in an Athens hotel room a few days before) to be brought home for burial. Muslims are invariably buried within 24 hours but Sherif el Hindi's corpse had been transported in a very unseemly fashion from country to country. The Saudis had no wish for him to be buried there. Numieri quickly agreed but wanted assurances from General Omer el Tayeb that no demonstration would take place and that security would be effective. Omer assured him that the family had agreed to a simple burial devoid of any political overtones. After his conversation he said to us "Sherif el Hindi was no friend of mine. He was an enemy but I would not deny him burial in the Sudan". Thousands attended the funeral but there were no security problems.

I continued to press the President on a number of issues but the only reply I received was "I have a new Minister, it will soon be under control". He was utterly complacent

---

[3]G F Thomas. Mss notes.

about the acute problems in the South saying, when I raised
the matter "Joseph Lagu has things in hand". He then raised
the question of Sadig el Mahdi, revealing considerable
irritation and forcibly expressing his annoyance repeatedly
asking me "Why does he go to that man?" (Gaddafi). He
often did not wait for an answer going on to say "Why
does he not come to me? I am a Sudanese, he is Sudanese I
am an Ansari" and then astonishingly "The Mahdi was my
grandfather".

I said that I thought that Sadig leaned towards Libya to
counter-balance the President's own inclination to Egypt. I
expected an outburst especially in view of his earlier
vehemence, but he became suddenly subdued saying "I am
not always a free agent. Do you realise there are eighteen
thousand Sudanese students in Egypt supported by Sadat.
These could not be absorbed elsewhere. I have asked Saudi
Arabia and others but they have refused". He obviously
feared the return of eighteen thousand disaffected students
to the Sudan should they be expelled from Egypt which
Sadat had intimated would result if there were any
interruption in the relations between Khartoum and Cairo.

We spent nearly two hours together—Ismay and I were
alone with the President and towards the end of our
interview he suddenly said "You know that I am going to
the USA soon with my wife Buthayna. We have never had
any children and it is a great disappointment to us. So we
are going for tests". For nearly half an hour he talked of his
personal problems going into his family circumstances in
great detail such as the number of children some of his
relatives had, and finally saying "while I have none". We
were quite abashed, although we were used to Sudanese and
Arab frankness about personal matters, but we had not
expected it to come from a Head of State. It revealed, I
thought, a terrible confused loneliness.

A bizarre episode occurred less than a week after my talk

with him. He called the first Vice-President Abdel Magid, and twenty-two senior officers to a meeting, told them that things were in disarray, that they had two days in which to discuss frankly these problems without him being present. However without their knowledge he had listened and watched through closed circuit television and at the end of the second day he stormed in and dismissed Abdel Magid and all twenty two of his most senior officers, a savage act, thus decapitating the army in one blow. Once again it appeared to me that the President's sole policy was to survive personally and all the shuffling of ministerial posts was to that end, so that no opposition power base had a chance to materialize. Numieri's lack of cohesive policy was having devastating results.

As well as the probability of interference from any of the Sudan's eight neighbours, the President faced internal secessionist movements and these he had sought to counteract by introducing the de-centralisation of Government. In spite of his recent mass sackings, the armed forces were still to a large degree a coherent force, but with the increasingly appalling state of the economy the threats to his survival were severe.

Events in the outside world were to have an effect on Sudan affairs in 1982. Lebanon flared up again, and the Israelis grasped the opportunity of the focusing of the attention on the Falkland Islands conflict to seize Beirut Airport and the surrounding heights. The Red Cross reported nearly ten thousand dead and twenty thousand injured in an attack seen as a reprisal for the shooting and wounding of the Israeli Ambassador in London. It was at this time that King Khalid of Saudi Arabia died and when I discussed these factors with Sadig el Mahdi who was on a prolonged visit to England, he made some interesting comments. He was convinced that Begin and Khomeini had been sent by Allah to bring the Muslims back to their faith by chastisement. He was reluctant to go to Saudi Arabia at this time as he felt that "The guardianship of the Holy Places had become a mockery"[4] The world was horrified by the appalling massacre at the Sabra and Chatila refugees camps in Beruit and the bloody scenes as recorded on our television screens will long be remembered and have seared the hearts of the Arabs.

We were able, during the year to press many active politicians to become interested in the plight of the Sudan as we addressed a number of meetings, and we followed this up in Egypt where we went on the thirtieth of October. We had a very cordial meeting with General Kamal Hassan Ali the Foreign Minister.[5] We had known him for twenty years and we could talk freely and in confidence. He was deeply concerned about the deterioration in the Sudan, and as we were flying on to Khartoum he requested us to give him our impressions and opinion.

The spiralling inflation was immediately obvious on our arrival at the Khartoum Hilton, where a bottle of mineral water cost £5.00, a pot of tea £6.50 and the bill for one and a half nights including only one meal was £375.00. We speedily moved to the Grand Hotel which was less expensive.

Sadig who had returned, briefed me on the latest developments; the most important being that Dr Abdel Hamid Saleh had flown to Cairo to see the then Prime Minister Fuad Mohieddin, and President Mubarak. Dr Saleh had told the Egyptians that they could not go on without a real understanding with Sadig, and that he had resigned from his post in the Sudan Government. This was reported back to Numieri who was furious, refusing to acknowledge receipt of the resignation and sending Azzadin el Sayed to

---

[4] G F Thomas. Mss notes.
[5] G F Thomas. Mss Diary, Vol. IV, p. 78.

talk with Dr Fuad Mohieddin and Dr Saleh. No minister had
had the temerity to resign from Numieri's Governments;
they had always been dismissed. Dr Abdel Hamid was
frightened to return to the Sudan, or to remain in Cairo, so
he had withdrawn to London.

Ahmed Abdel Rahman, Minister of the Interior and Sherif
Touhami, Minister of Energy, said that it was believed in
Government circles that I had prepared the way for Dr
Abdel Hamid Saleh on my visit to Egypt the previous
January which was totally untrue.

Ismay and I spent a lot of time gathering material for the
Pictorial Biography I was preparing of Sayed Abdel
Rahman, but the political situation impinged on this. Sayed
Ahmed Abdel Rahman, who had most of the photographs,
was not on the best of terms with his nephew Sadig, the
leader of the Sudan Opposition. Relations were very
strained, so much so that on the previous Friday, Ahmed
had been greatly rebuffed by the Ansar when he had gone
to the Gubba to lead the Friday prayers, and as he
attempted to do so a voice had said 'We came to hear THE
descendant of the Mahdi". This was a terrible insult to a
grandson of the Mahdi. Sadig, a great-grandson, when he
heard that Ahmed was at the Gubba wisely left and led the
prayers at the Wad Nubawi mosque. The faithful left the
Gubba in hundreds leaving Ahmed with only a handful of
some twenty souls. It was said that one man had been
injured by a pen-knife wound in his bottom.

A few days later Numieri sent twelve soldiers and police
at 1.30 am to occupy the Ansar offices at the Mahdi's house
adjacent to the Gubba, as an act of provocation to Sadig.
When Sadig was wakened to be told the news and asked
what the Ansar guardians should do, he said that they were
to give beds, blankets, and tea to the occupying forces. I
was pleased that Sadig had taken my advice to play it very
coolly and not to react to such acts of provocation. Our

round of social activity and political discussions continued into our fourth week. The day Sherif Touhami and Fatma his wife, (daughter of Sayed Abdel Rahman) entertained us, Numieri had sent all the Mahdi family letters announcing that their possessions were to be returned to them. Everything had been confiscated and now, after the reconciliation, restoration was forthcoming. The Dairat el Mahdi, built up during the lifetime of Sayed Abdel Rahman was now, because of inflation, worth many more millions which were to be split into the agreed proportions with Sadig el Mahdi receiving twenty per cent more as willed to him by Sayed Siddig through the will of his grandfather. The return of this wealth was long and complicated and led to much bitterness within the Mahdi family, giving Sadig's opponents the opportunity of suggesting that this was the real reason for his agreeing to the reconciliation.

A rather puzzling situation arose during a meeting I had with Vice-President Omer el Tayeb. As was usual it was frank and free ranging, and suddenly he posed the question "What would you do. I am torn between the President and Sadig. Which should I choose?" Frankly, I suspected a trap. I thought that the conversation could be being taped. So I prevaricated, trying to play for time, talking about Sayed Abdel Rahman at the time of abrogation. He interrupted me saying "I asked you a straight question", so I replied, "Well, Your Excellency, you have given your oath of allegiance to the President. You must honour that unless you think that other factors override that. Then it is a matter solely between you and God".[6] I was not then, and neither am I with hindsight, proud of that answer. It was much too much a politician's reply. On reflection I am sure that he was sincerely torn. He conveyed to me that the President was convinced that Sadig was plotting against him. Omer el

---

[6] G F Thomas. Mss Diary, Vol. IV, p. 86.

Tayeb said that Numieri was receiving information not through Omer but with the help of the Egyptians and the CIA; he had also established his own back-stairs security who informed him that Sadig was surrounded by armed men, that he travelled in convoy with cars full of armed men and that his house in Omdurman was an armed camp. I said that this was absolute malicious nonsense; that when Sadig came to see me at the hotel he had been accompanied by one bodyguard which was not unreasonable in view of the state of the country. I had also visited his house in Omdurman, and it was full of old retainers and young people. I was sure that Sadig was not deceiving me, and was certainly not plotting against the President. I protested most vigorously adding that Sadig was, in fact, avoiding all possibilities which might lead to a confrontation and I begged Omer to reassure the President on this adding that Sadig was in a "no win situation", as if he were out of the Sudan he was suspected of plotting, and if he was at home it was to organise a conspiracy, quoting the incidents with Ahmed Abdel Rahman at the mosque and the occupation of the Ansar offices. I had asked to see the President, but either it was not possible because of a busy schedule, or more likely, he wanted to slight Sadig by refusing to see me. Prior to my seeing the Vice-President, the Egyptian Ambassador to the Sudan, Ahmed Izzat Abdel Latif had asked to see me, and after the usual courtesies he suddenly asked "Where is your friend?" This was rather aggressively expressed, and at first I thought that he meant Sadig, but it transpired that he was referring to Dr Abdel Hamid Saleh's recent visit to Cairo which I was supposed to have arranged. I was annoyed and expressed this forcibly saying "I had nothing to do with the visit, nor did I know what Dr Saleh's aims were" adding "I bitterly resent that my confidential talks in Cairo last January had been relayed by Egyptian Intelligence to Khartoum". We then talked about Sadig, and the

Ambassador said "I would like to talk to him but the situation is too delicate". I pointed out that my sole objective was a real and effective reconciliation between Egypt and the Sudan, and that in this I had helped Egypt as much as the Sudan.

On our last evening in Khartoum I went to say farewell to Sadig who was sitting with a group of Southerners. We went apart for privacy and talked for well over an hour. There were things that I felt I had to say to him which might well hurt him but I felt it was imperative to do so. Foremost among these was the fact that a number of the Sudanese middle class and the educated elite considered him to be aloof and arrogant; and that even those close to him were deterred by his manner from discussing matters frankly with him. I impressed on him that he could not, as he was inclined to try, do everything himself, that he needed to delegate, and that he lacked his grandfather's gift for choosing men. Finally I warned him that he was relying too heavily on people whose loyalty was beyond doubt, but whose ability was limited. I know that he was hurt, but although it was painful to me I felt it right to give my advice. He accepted that I was speaking with my heart, and that thirty-five years of friendship lay behind it. I think that his public image is not the true Sadig who is warm, humorous, humane and kindly. He has indeed softened with time and now relaxes more easily. Sadig had intended to return to London, but I begged him not to leave too soon as some of the younger members of the Ansar felt that his policy was 'too passive' and they needed his leadership, and for him to reassure them that it was the right policy in the circumstances.

Our final dinner in the Sudan was at the house of Hassan el Turabi and his wife Wisaal (sister of Sadig). Hassan is the leader of the Muslim Brothers, and Attorney General in the Numieri Government. With us were Ahmed Abdel Rahman and other Muslim Brothers. The arguments were fast and furious, although certainly not complimentary to the President even by some of his ministers. One of them told the following story "Numieri was under the shower when the water went off. He called to his wife to telephone to the water engineer to re-connect it. She replied that she would do so except the telephones were not working. Then get me a pen so that I might send a note. Buthayna said that she would do so but the electricity was not functioning so she could not see so to do. The President then told her to summon the chauffeur and send him with the message to which her reply was that that too was impossible as the driver had been in the queue for petrol for the whole day. In exasperation Numieri said "Well we still have a cook don't we? Send him". His wife "I'm very sorry dear but he has been queuing for calor gas since this morning". With a shrug Numieri replied "What a country. If I were not its President I would be leading a coup".

It seemed a fitting story on which to end a record of our Sudan visit. On the following day we flew to Cairo and on to London. We were to hear Dr Abdel Hamid Saleh's version of the saga as soon as we arrived home, he had been waiting impatiently to relate the sequence of events. As he explained "I had reached the point that Numieri did not believe any more in the Reconciliation and I do not believe that he can go on longer without broadening the base of his Government, so I went to Egypt to see Dr Fuad Mohieddin". He then said that Mohieddin had taken him to see President Mubarak and they were joined by Kamal Hassan Ali. Dr Abdel Hamid explained that he had resigned from the Numieri Government and had given his reasons. There were several meetings, at some of which Shirbini, Head of the State Information Service (Intelligence), attended. When Azzadin el Sayed had arrived he had revealed that not only was Dr Saleh's resignation "not received" but that he had no right to go to Egypt, nor to talk about Foreign Affairs. Azzadin had apparently done his best to effect a compromise between Numieri and Abdel Hamid but the latter said "I withdrew to London to avoid further pressure". He also claimed that Sadig had sent Mubarek el Abdullahi to Cairo to persuade Dr Saleh to return to the Sudan, as Sadig needed him. I was frankly sceptical but Dr Abdel Hamid assured me that he had read his resignation to Sadig before sending it to the Palace. Shortly after this he returned to Cairo.

The Sudanese and Egyptian governments had agreed to 'integrate' and the ceremonies to celebrate the integration were to be held in Khartoum in late December, but they were postponed. Numieri explained this by saying that he had to go to the South, but I suspected from my Cairo talks that the Egyptian Government had cooled towards the project[7] as I was sure that Kamal Hassan Ali believed that Numieri should consult the Sudanese (ie Sadig) before proceeding. I had the feeling that nemisis for Numieri was just beginning.

Indeed, 1983 was to mark the beginning of the end for Numieri. News arrived from the Sudan very early in the New Year when Ahmed Abdel Rahman, the Minister of the Interior, flew in from a visit he had made to Morocco. He said that Sadig had made an excellent and constructive speech on the economy, and that all was the same in the Sudan, "only worse". Indeed this was confirmed by Sadig el Mahdi when he arrived in London during February. The South was once again involved in an armed uprising, some Dinka tribesmen had attacked a police post killing eleven people; an army unit had refused to be moved from their garrison and tribal fighting had broken out at Bantu near to the newly discovered oil deposits. Perhaps more serious was

---

[7] G F Thomas. Mss Diary, Vol. IV, pp. 92–93.

that the Riziegat and Messaria tribes were indulging in their traditional pursuit of fighting each other.[8] The Government had lost control and had been totally unable to restore order. During this period President Mubarak of Egypt had appealed to the USA to prevent Gaddafi invading the Sudan. The Americans had responded by sending a battleship into the Mediterranean off the Libyan coast and dispatched surveillance aircraft (AWAC's) to Egypt. Sadig had no knowledge at all of Libyan troops massing on the border, or of them trying to organise a coup in the Sudan. The reports had emanated from Washington, and a few days later Egypt denied the reports while Numieri declared that he had no knowledge of the affair. Whereupon George Shultz, the American Secretary of State, announced that a battleship, The Nimitz, had been sent to the Eastern Mediterranean on 'normal duties' not just to Libya; but he confirmed that the AWAC's were sent. The Times reported that Egypt was annoyed and that it had suggested that they be withdrawn. An Egyptian spokesman said "We are the third world, non-aligned".[9]

Sadig el Mahdi was still travelling and lecturing or attending Islamic Conferences. After attending a Muslim Conference in Pakistan he decided that he would return to the Sudan. We had news of him from Osman Mirghani who came back from Khartoum at the beginning of August. Things were looking blacker, and very depressing. Sadig was back in England by August and came on September the sixth, to see us before he once more returned home. He reviewed the situation in the Sudan in great detail. The prospects were bleak, he told me that the country was at a standstill; the public utilities had almost completely collapsed. Water was intermittent and blackish (called Sherbet

[8]G F Thomas. Mss Diary, Vol. IV, p. 112.
[9]The Times, 21.8.83.

Numieri); electricity almost non-existent. Schools had all been closed and the professional classes were in turmoil; even the judges were on strike. There was much activity on the opposition front with meetings being held by Sadig with the other opposition groups, and a national Charter had been drawn up. Vice-President Omer el Tayeb had sent several messages of support and he, Sadig, felt that even the Army was confused. It was a chaotic situation, with the Muslim Brothers being split. Sadig also said that he had spoken to leaders of the Egyptian opposition who considered President Mubarak inadequate, and who felt that if it were left to the Egyptian people and the Sudanese people they could cooperate on an equal basis.

The final point in this very thorough survey concerned the Ansar. They had offered the Imamate* to Sadig, but he had refused as he felt that the election for the spiritual leader of the Mahdists should be based on the qualities and abilities of the incumbent rather than dynastic and family connections. They had however taken an oath of allegiance to him.[10] There was no doubt the crisis was severe and Numieri was trapped by his own policies or lack of them. He was once more having to seek another tactic to survive, but his options were running out. He had laid the responsibility for the condition of the Sudan at first on the old corrupt parliamentary politicians, and on the Mahdists, then on the Communists. He had sought solutions by initiating grandiose projects, for example the Sudan was to be the bread basket for the Middle East. These adventures were utterly unrealistic and had proved to be financially disastrous, so that even the bonanza of the discovery of oil could not produce the billions of pounds which had been frittered on massive unfinished buildings, factories, roads,

---

*Statement issued 30.11.83.
[10]G F Thomas. Mss Diary, Vol. IV, p. 193.

and bridges. One of the most extravagant schemes was the grandiose Kenana Sugar project which was declared to be able to produce sufficient sugar for the world. Initially its costs had been estimated as likely to be two hundred million pounds, this was revised upwards again and again until it reached over one thousand million. The Sudanese Pharaoh rushed around the country laying the foundation stones for buildings destined never to rise above the first footings.

Corruption, incompetence, and maladministration had resulted in serious inflation. Numieri was becoming more isolated, no one dared to advise him, and the President was desperately seeking yet another way, mainly by consulting his 'Fekir' (religious adviser) who urged him to seek a solution by turning to Allah; and by introducing the Islamic 'Sharia' Laws. It has been suggested that Hassan el Turabi was one of those who originated the idea, but I myself doubt this, although he certainly did not dissuade Numieri.

Suddenly, overnight, in search of yet another possible solution to his problems the President declared the Sudan, with a population of whom one-third were non-Muslim, to be an Islamic State, and that 'Sharia Laws' should be enforced. This occurred on the twenty third of September 1983, and like every dictator in a tight corner he staged a dramatic spectacle. He himself emptied bottle after bottle of whisky into the Nile; and as is typical in such situations turned on the poor and the needy who had been forced into stealing simply to keep alive. The era of amputations had begun, not only at Kober Prison where a special viewing arena was built, but throughout the Sudan. Non-Muslims were beaten for contravening the so-called 'Sharia Laws', including a Catholic Priest found in possession of a bottle of communion wine. Arbitrary courts were established and punishments administered immediately. A tolerant, fair-minded Sudan, had turned into the plaything of a despotic tyrant only concerned to take attention away from the sorry state into which he had led the Sudanese people.

Some have suggested that Numieri had been enraged to hear that the Ansar had taken the 'Ba'ia' oath of allegiance, (contract of fealty) to Sadig el Mahdi which he had accepted whilst not consenting to the title of Imam. In any event, Numieri later demanded such an oath from his Ministers, and the country as a whole, and indeed, declared the regime to be a Khalifat. Immediately following the declaration of Islamic Laws, Numieri left for Dongola, and the Ansar asked permission to hold a meeting in Omdurman which was granted by Vice-President Omer el Tayeb. At the meeting on the twenty fourth of September 1983, which was attended by over fifty thousand people, Sadig el Mahdi made a powerful speech against the Proclamation. During his declaration of opposition to the newly instituted laws he said, "If the distribution of wealth is unjust and if the doors of 'Hallal' (Sustenance) are closed on the unemployed and the poor, while the opulent have acquired their wealth by unlawful means, then the application of punishments for theft in such a society will only lead to enhancing social injustice".

He made a clear denunciation of the corruption surrounding Numieri's regime. He went on to say that the Islamic 'Hudoud' (Punishments) cannot be separated from the political system which must be a system ensuring justice in all spheres of life "Cutting off the hand of a thief in an unjust society is like throwing a person into the sea, tied up with ropes, and then asking him not to get wet". It was a courageous challenge to the regime, which Numieri could not ignore. Sadig had emphatically declared that the introduction of 'partial' Sharia Laws was completely contrary to the true spirit of Islam.[11]

Sadig was immediately and arbitrarily arrested without

---

[11]Speech by Sayed Sadig el Mahdi Omdurman, 24.9.83.

charges or trial, together with Mubarek el Abdullahi, Omar Nur el Diem, Nasr Eldin El Hadi, a venerable Judge Abdel Rahman el Nur and scores of other Ansar leaders, but not before the Ansar had repeated the 'Ba'ia' at the conclusion of Sadig's speech. By strange coincidence this happened as we were celebrating Ismay's birthday, at which Sara (Sadig's wife) and Faisal (Sadig's brother) with Ibrahim el Nur, were among the guests.

As President Numieri was proclaiming his so-called 'Sharia Laws', Sir James Robertson (Civil Secretary in the Condominium Administration) died. We were deeply grieved at the death of this great man; the integrity and courage he had always demonstrated was universally appreciated by the Sudanese. I was glad that he had not lived to see the abyss into which the Sudan had sunk. At the Thanksgiving service for Sir James' life which was attended by many Sudanese the words

"Look backward with gratitude
Look forward with hope
Look upward with confidence"

were hardly appropriate to the Sudan in its darkest hour, but we could only hope that at last the downfall of the regime was imminent.

The next eighteen months were to be amongst the most hectic in our lives for Ismay and I threw ourselves wholeheartedly into a campaign for Sadig's release and the overthrow of Numieri's infamous regime. There was no longer any thought of reconciliation, no man of conscience could continue to support this dictator who had passed the point of no return.

We inserted, with the help of Margaret Morgan, an advertisement in the Guardian early in October.

PRISONERS
OF CONSCIENCE
PRISONERS
OF NUMIERI

Amnesty International and The Islamic Council have
protested to President Numieri of Sudan against the
arbitrary arrest and detention of Sadig El Mahdi, former
Prime Minister and leader of Muslim Ansars and 150
other distinguished religious Sudanese. Sadig's contribution to Islamic thought and practice is world known.
They have requested everyone interested in "Prisoners of
Conscience" to cable/airmail protest to President
Numieri, Khartoum, Sudan.

Sudanese and Friends of Sudan

October 1983

Both the Guardian and the Observer wrote items on the
situation, and Amnesty International were persuaded to
declare them Prisoners of Conscience. A strong appeal was
also made on their behalf by the Islamic Council, and we
personally wrote over seventy letters seeking the support of
churchmen and political leaders to condemn Numieri's
actions. The response was gratifying. The Rt Hon David
Owen took up the cause with the Secretary of State for
Foreign Affairs while the Rt Hon Roy Jenkins wrote to the
Minister of Overseas Development, and the Rt Hon Dame
Judith Hart wrote a very strong protest direct to Numieri.

At the end of October Sadig managed to smuggle a
letter out of Kober Prison, to his wife Sara, who was in
England. It only took fourteen days to reach her, and
contained the news that he was fit and that seventeen of his
followers were imprisoned with him, and three hundred
elsewhere. I learned from officials in the Foreign Office that
President Mubarak of Egypt had flown to Khartoum on the
eighteenth of October, and a statement had been issued

which was 'anodyne', obviously designed to cool things. Ismay visited the House of Commons to lobby all the parties by talking to many senior MP's. David Owen who had questioned the wisdom of the British action in sending 100 troops to the Sudan informed me that Sir Geoffrey Howe had defended the decision, as it was suitable terrain for training purposes and assured David Owen that the exercises were not jointly conducted by the Sudan and British forces as Numieri had been saying. Richard Luce confirmed to me the same information. I was advised by an old friend Amin Hassoun not to visit the Sudan that winter, as he put it cryptically "most of our friends will not be in Khartoum".

We continued to campaign vigorously and even went to see the Egyptian Ambassador who was very hostile to Sadig, arguing that he was getting huge sums from Saudi Arabia and from Libya, while the Egyptians were giving very little to Numieri. I repudiated the myths about Sadig's close ties with Gaddafi or receiving much support from Saudi Arabia. Eventually after much heated discussion, in which he displayed a virulently anti-Saudi and anti-American stance, he did admit that Numieri was "not necessarily the best but what could Egypt do?"

Oliver Miles of the Foreign Office confirmed to me that the Egyptians were frustrated, and that Saudi Arabia was determined that Egypt should not be welcomed back into the Leadership of the Arab World. He believed that President Mubarak was not fully in control.[12] His Excellency the Egyptian Ambassador kept closely in touch with us presumably on orders received from Cairo, and we were invited to a dinner party at the Embassy where we were the only British present. It was a strange mixture, the High Commissioners from Sri Lanka, Zambia, Singapore, and

---

[12]G F Thomas. Mss Diary, Vol. IV, p. 204.

Mauritius, together with the Ambassadors for Senegal and the Sudan. The later was Abdullahi el Hassan who had sentenced Sadig to death 'in absentia' but had been arbitrarily sacked as a Provincial Governor, before being recalled to serve as Ambassador. I was amused at the way in which he attacked the British media which was, he said, "of no importance". When I asked him why in that case he was so angry; he replied "It was all caused by a few people and a handful of dissidents".

He was very anxious to know whether I had seen Sadig before he had returned to the Sudan, and what was his mood. I assured the Ambassador that Sadig wanted to restore the Ansar movement and go along the constitutional road to reform. This was brushed aside by a heated retort that Sadig had returned in a militant mood and had been making hostile speeches. To cool the heat which was being engendered I asked if he knew why Numieri had introduced the 'Hudoud' (Punishments) and was it in order to get some Saudi gold. Abdullahi wearily replied, "I honestly have no idea why he did it".[13]

Protests continued to be organised by Ansars throughout the world, and internally too, individuals and groups courageously declared their disapproval of the newly instituted laws. A petition was submitted to the High Court by the President of the Omdurman Bench of Magistrates and that of the el Obeid Bench (Eitidal Muhammed Fadl and El Rayah Hassan Khalifa), requesting that the so-called 'Sharia' Laws should be declared unconstitutional. They were brave men, and they were not alone. The Southern Students organisation at the University of Khartoum wrote a long letter of protest to the President, but the most telling protest came in a fifteen page statement by the Sudanese Islamic Movement, declaring that the decrees were a

---

[13]Ibid, pp. 210–211.

'manipulation of Islam, an exploitation of it'. They appealed
to all Sudanese to "save God's religion from fabrication".
They sent an open letter to the British Government and
copies to all members of Parliament.

We had no further news of Sadig so I decided to go to
Cairo to put some pressure on Egyptian friends. General
Kamal Hassan Ali was very sympathetic. We had two hours
talking with him and he assured us that "We are doing all
we can. I went to the Sudan three days after the President's
announcement of the so-called 'Sharia' Laws and the
President (Mubarak) two days after that". He had been told
by Numieri "I had to do it. I know these people; they go to
the Mosque, then they drink until they are drunk and do no
work". Kamal Hassan Ali had been unimpressed, and
thought that he, Numieri, had hoped it would gain Saudi
financial assistance. It had also, in his view, been aimed at
outflanking the Muslim Brothers and the Ansar.

After long discussions Kamal Hassan Ali said that the
matter was difficult and delicate, and urged me to go to talk
with Numieri saying "We and you can tell him the truth
there is no one else". I told him that I would go if I had an
invitation from Numieri, but I had no wish to go on my
own initiative as the President might interpret my going as
being a supplicant for Sadig. Kamal said that he was
expecting Numieri within a few days and would put it to
him, but Numieri delayed his journey to Cairo and nothing
came of the suggestion.[14]

We spent a while touring in Egypt travelling from
Alexandria to Aswan, but on our return to Cairo we were
due to have discussions with the Prime Minister Fuad
Mohieddin. The train journey from Aswan was a nightmare,
our train was many hours delayed because of a derailment,
so that at the time of our appointment we were still many

---

[14]G F Thomas. Mss Diary, Vol. IV, pp. 214–215.

miles away in Upper Egypt with no means of informing the Prime Minister of our plight. However, as soon as we ultimately reached Cairo in the late afternoon, we were informed that the meeting had been rescheduled. Dr Fuad listened most patiently while I asked for his help. He was very polished, had a good 'bedside manner' (he had been a practising medical man) but I cannot say that I was impressed although he convinced me of his high intelligence. I felt that there was not much depth or strength, but he had survived for many years in the muddy waters of Egyptian politics. He drew my attention to the fact that "Sayed Muhammed Osman el-Mirghani and his brother Sayed Ahmed come frequently to Cairo and always come to see me. We never see Sayed Sadig el Mahdi or any of his people". I assured the Prime Minister that should he be invited, I was sure Sadig el Mahdi would visit him but as he was in prison it was not possible. I then asked him to use his good offices but did not press him to give any answers.[15]

We also met Mustafa Khalil a former Prime Minister, who was Vice-President of the Egyptian National Democratic Party, (President Mubarak is the President of the NDP), and Chairman of the Arab International Bank. He was quite forthright about Numieri, and highly critical of him. He was trenchant in his assessment of the political and economic situation, and his outspoken comments had a frankness which was very un-Egyptian. I felt little had been achieved and when I again returned to Egypt in February 1984 there was little difference in attitude. The comments were always variations on the theme of "What can we do?" The official circles in London too were unhelpful, both there and in Cairo I was told that Numieri could not be wholly bad as respectable men like Sherif el Touhami and Dr Abdel Hamid Saleh continued to support him. Returning once

---

[15]G F Thomas. Mss Diary, Vol. IV, pp. 227–228.

more to appeal to the British Foreign Office I was assured by Richard Luce (then Minister of State at the Foreign Office) that he was "despairing of doing anything with Numieri".[16] We talked at length and Richard told me that they had considered a number of possibilities, including the scaling down of aid, and even visiting the Sudan personally but it was very difficult to do much.

Yet another bizarre episode was to occur in the Sudan towards the end of March, when a single plane was reported as having dropped bombs on Omdurman Television Station and on the house of Sadig el Mahdi on the opposite side of the road. A bomb had landed on Sadig's study but had not exploded. No one was injured, but the rumours were incredible some suggested that Numieri himself had organised it but the Sudan News Agency said it was a Russian plane and that it came from Kufra in Libya.

Sara had a message to say that President Mubarak had flown to Aswan to meet President Numieri, and that Numieri had been told that he must come to an understanding with Sadig, and further that Sadig had been visited in Kober Prison and told that he would be released if he would come to an agreement with Numieri. Sadig had replied "I will fulfil the Port Sudan Agreement of reconciliation if Numieri fulfils his promises". He had further said that he would only leave prison if all prisoners were released, reminding Numieri that he had agreed to an amnesty at Port Sudan. Sadig was adamant that he would not leave prison alone when there were many older men who should be released first. It was alleged that Numieri, furious with Sadig's attitude and reply, had reacted by sending the bombers from Wadi Seidna airbase. There were several strange aspects to the whole affair. The Americans leaked news of the bombing in Washington; it was reported

---

[16]Ibid, p. 228.

that General Abu Ghazala the Egyptian Defence Minister was in Khartoum at the time, but official reports said that he was there one-and-a-half hours later and the Libyans denied all knowledge of it. Eye witnesses to whom I spoke later said that Numieri arrived at the scene in mufti with all the others, (including Abu Ghazala), in uniform and they could be seen quite clearly laughing. There were certain questions which remained unanswered. If it were a foreign plane why was no alert given, no general mobilisation, or emergency declared? Khartoum was ringed by anti-aircraft gunposts. Her Majesty's Government had serious doubts about the bombing, but they did confirm the Mubarak-Numieri meeting and Christopher Long added that a senior Foreign Office official had gone with a brief to Washington.[17]

The Times carried a good third leader written by Edward Mortimer and the following day printed an excellent account of the bombing, also by Edward Mortimer, and the media gave a highly critical account. Richard Hall was making an effective contribution in The Observer and Colin Legum was very helpful with his freelance writings. Dr Chris Terrill of the BBC Africa Network came to tape an interview with me on the Sudan and Numieri, which was broadcast on the first of April and caused a bitter row with the Sudanese Ambassador at the first anniversary party of At Tadamon. Mansour Khaled, who was also at the anniversary, was vituperative, declaring that he was writing a book in which he was exposing the regime. This he has since done, calling it "Numieri and the Revolution of Dis-May".

We arranged a series of meetings and luncheons for Sara to meet the media and Chris Terrell, Charles Meynell (Africa Confidential), Richard Hall, Edward Mortimer, and Malise Ruthven all were very co-operative.

---

[17]G F Thomas. Mss Diary, Vol. IV, pp. 247–251.

Ahmed Abdel Rahman, then Minister of the Interior, together with another Sudanese Member of the Muslim Brotherhood arrived and Ahmed was persuaded to give an interview to the BBC. He was unwise enough to include several points in this to which undoubtedly Numieri would take exception, and I warned him that he was likely to be sacked on his return to the Sudan once the President had heard the tapes. He told me that had the doctors not gone on strike Sadig would have been released, but he then added that the ground had been cut from under Sadig's feet, and that the introduction of Sharia law united the whole of the Muslim population behind Numieri. He was however deeply worried about the war in the South.[18]

A few days later Sherif Touhami came to see me, late one evening. He was looking tired and dispirited and had aged considerably. All his ebullience had gone. He claimed that he had spent two hours with Sadig in Kober Prison and was a negotiator between Numieri and Sadig. He told me that Sadig had agreed on two points; that there should be no fragmentation of the Sudan, and that there should be no foreign interference (from Ethiopia, Libya or Egypt). I offered to go to Khartoum as an objective mediator and suggested that a meeting be arranged between Sadig, Numieri, and President Mubarak, but he felt that the President "would not take kindly to that idea". He was personally very hostile to Egypt, and like Ahmed Rahman depressed about the South being very caustic about one of the Southern Leaders, John Uduho whom he had helped in various ways. I urged Sherif to leave Numieri, and withdraw from the Government, but he gave me the impression that he was a frightened man. I told him bluntly that he had blood on his hands, after the introduction of the 'Hudoud' punishments. I urged him to break away adding that he was

---

[18]G F Thomas. Mss Diary, Vol. V, pp. 1–2.

financially secure with monies enough to live on comfortably abroad which of course he denied, but he left me with the distinct impression that he realised a change was inevitable, but was unable to make the break perhaps it was fear.[19] Sherif returned to Sayeda Rahma, Sadig's mother and Sara, and asked Rahma to write a letter begging Numieri to release Sadig. He said that Wisal had telephoned to arrange this. Sara was furious, threatening to leave the house if the letter was written. She knew that Sadig himself would have been deeply angry, and it appeared as if Numieri or Sherif were seeking an excuse to release Sadig.

It was fairly widespread knowledge that Egypt was also concerned about the Sudan and that they could not see Numieri going on for much longer but they were "waiting for a suitable alternative to appear".[20] The West was taking no action, and the terrible siege and shoot-out at the Libyan Embassy, during which a young British policewoman was killed, did nothing to help the Arab Cause and hardened the attitudes of ordinary people towards the Arabs in general.

Sha'ma el Siddig (Sadig's sister) brought news from Khartoum that Sadig approved of the actions being taken by Sara and me. He said "the Egyptians had done what they could and that they wanted a dialogue with him to which he had agreed when the time was opportune". The opposition parties were coming to an understanding and Muhammed Ibrahim Khalil reported from Kuwait that the opposition was now "comprehensive and would include the southerners and communists". by the end of April, Numieri was becoming even more repressive. Martial Law was declared and arbitrary courts were set up with a Judge and a military man at the head. Ten courts were established in Khartoum, including one for passports, and one for food

---

[19]G F Thomas. Mss Diary, Vol. V, pp. 2–3.
[20]Ibid, p. 4.

offences. Rationing was introduced and Waheed, a well known grocer was found to have two bottles of wine and was summarily charged and sentenced to twenty five lashes and a fine of £1,000, administered immediately. Afterwards it was revealed that he was a Coptic Christian. All workers were ordered to leave their offices at prayer times and pray collectively for half-an-hour, and simultaneously the President dismissed Parliament and his Cabinet, assuming supreme powers, but as he was already de-facto a complete dictator, this was only a 'paper' declaration. As I forecast, Ahmed Abdel Rahman was dismissed together with Bahaa Eldin one of the President's closest cronies. Only Azzadin el Sayed, Hassan el Turabi and Sherif Touhami survived. It was reported from Khartoum that Numieri was "furious with Graham Thomas"[21] presumably because of the media campaign.

Charles Meynell told me that President Arap Moi of Kenya had been taken to talk with Numieri in Khartoum by Tiny Rowland in his private jet. Holmes of the Foreign Office confirmed that this was true, and also that the President had instructed his ministers to be "ready for prayers at anytime". There was now considerable concern that Numieri's physiological condition might be having a mental affect. His behaviour was becoming increasingly unpredictable. At an interview with Numieri, Fouad Matar (Editor-in-Chief of At Tadamon) had asked whether Sadig was to be released to keep Ramadan in his own home. The reply was abrupt: "No I am going to put him on trial in the Sharia Court for not supporting Islamic Law". This gave us renewed impetus for a vigorous lobby through the Foreign Office, the Egyptian Ambassador, and the media.

The fiscal and economic situation in the Sudan was increasingly alarming(Ibrahim Muhammed Khalil who was

---

[21]G F Thomas. Mss Diary, Vol. V, p. 5.

in a position to know because of his position in the Kuwait
Investment Bank, said that the Sudan's foreign debt stood at
an horrendous nine billion US dollars. Dr Tigani el Ibrahim
of the World Bank said that Numieri needed another 1.9
billion US dollars to survive for the next twelve months. He
also went on to say that the US was going to provide thirty
to forty million dollars, and Saudi Arabia two hundred to
three hundred million dollars, for immediate needs, Dr
Tigani also believed that the Americans were grooming
Omer el Tayeb to take over from Numieri and certainly
some of the new appointees in Government were General
Omer el Tayeb nominees. I found it difficult to accept this
as I feared Omer was not strong enough, although the
Americans, I believed, were capable of anything.
Christopher Long of the Foreign Office told me that Chester
Croker the US second deputy had informed Her Majesty's
Government that the Americans had found Numieri was
saying all the 'right things' to which he added "Arabs
would, would they not". The Americans had also passed on
to HMG that Numieri had complained strenuously to them
about the British Press and Radio, and of the unhelpful
attitude of the British Government and pressed for it to be
more supportive of Numieri. Christopher Long was in
despair with Washington.[22]

Meanwhile in Khartoum, Numieri had established a
commission to revise the constitution with Dr Abdel Hamid
Saleh as Chairman. The chameleon had changed his colours
yet again. Numieri was still changing Ministers at the drop
of a hat. The Palace announced the dismissal of Dafalla Haj
Yusef, Kamal Hassan Ahmed and El Banna (a high ranking
army officer) one of whom had only held office for ten days.
The Islamisation process was continuing with Numieri
declaring that he would be proclaimed "Khalifa el

---

[22]G F Thomas. Mss Diary, Vol. V, p. 16.

Muslimein" while reports from Medina in Saudi Arabia and from Abu Dhabi of an interview given by Hassan el Turabi gave the information that a separate University was to be opened for girls, and that sex segregation in offices was to be introduced. What was perhaps more significant was that he announced that two hundred political prisoners including Sadig el Mahdi were to be released shortly. The political temperature was naturally rising, especially among a new generation of highly educated Sudanese who were becoming increasingly active, in a network of contacts that spread throughout the world.

I spent Ramadan in Morocco where I discussed the Sudan with a number of high ranking Moroccans close to the King, who were introduced to me by Dr Kenneth Sinclair Louttit. On our return we again increased our lobbying as we were deeply concerned about Sadig's safety, having heard that he had been admitted to the military hospital for a long standing hernia operation. Sara was showing increasing signs of strain and fatigue as well she might. The Rt Hon Roy Jenkins at this time was extremely helpful in discussing the Sudan with the Foreign Secretary, and in writing a number of letters to the Foreign Office.

In late July Dr Abdel Hamid Saleh arrived, declaring that he had not taken the "Baia" to Numieri, that he had never attended the amputations, that he was not supporting the regime and was "completely with the opposition". He told Sara that he had seen Sadig at Kober, and convinced her that Sadig trusted him by introducing things into the conversation that only she and Sadig knew. If not as she said "They were undone". She explained to me the code she used to communicate with Sadig, but I warned her to take care as all codes could be broken.

Within the Mahdi family the strains were emerging into the open. Fatma Abdel Rahman, on a visit to England told Sayeda Rahma, (Sadig's mother) that Sara and her committee were plotting to assassinate Hassan el Turabi, and a furious family quarrel erupted. In order to legitimise any statements I issued on behalf of Sadig, and to give some authority to them, Sadig smuggled out of prison a statement which micraculously arrived safely through normal postal channels. It read "Mr Graham Thomas was a trusted and worthy friend of my late grandfather (Sayed Abdel Rahman) my late father (Sayed Siddig) and has been a friend to me for the past thirty six years. May he be blessed with long life and good health Sadig el Mahdi."[23]

Sara brought Dr Abdel Hamid Saleh to see us, and I told him, as I had told Sherif Touhami that he had blood on his hands. I verbally lashed him for his activities, and Ismay (although more quietly) effectively and cuttingly told him that his ambivalence was abhorrent. He tried unsuccessfully to justify his continued association with Numieri, and even had the effrontery to claim that he had kept Sadig alive, and that he, Abdel Hamid was wholly with Sadig.[24]

I was still contacting my Egyptian friends. Dr Abdel Kader Hatem who had been in London took a letter back to General Kamal Hassan Ali, and also brought news of the death of Neguib, the first Egyptian President, at the age of eighty two. He had been very kind to me in 1954 when he had received me at the Abdin Palace. It was interesting to note that he had outlived Farouk, Nasser, and Sadat.

Sadig was continuing to get messages out whenever possible, and this time it was a tape, which Sara translated. It was exciting to hear his voice and to have evidence of his continued courage and fortitude, his ability to come to terms with political imprisonment. Here it is transcribed in its entirety.

"Graham, I hope that you have completed the pictorial

[23] G F Thomas. Mss notes.
[24] G F Thomas. Mss Diary, Vol. V, p. 45.

biography (of Sayed Abdel Rahman) would you believe it I am outlining an autobiographical novel which will portray the eventful and colourful history of our family from the Libab days—up to date. An adventure into literature, another weapon in the arsenal of killing time. Anyway, events in the country today depict a huge amphitheatre in which a thrilling tragi-comedy is being enacted. There is not a boring moment. The tearful people of the Sudan are bleeding, suffering, laughing. It only makes sense as a chapter in the process of political maturity. We all hope that the lesson is not wasted on us like the silence of a wilderness flower. Full many a flower is born to blush unseen and waste its sweetness on the desert air."[25]

It was very moving, and Ismay and I were in tears hearing his voice and thinking of him having to watch the amputations. We increased our activities as the anniversary of his detention drew near, and persuaded Chris Terrill to do a profile of Sadig on the Africa Network of the BBC.

By September there was a rift between Numieri and the Muslim Brothers because he feared their infiltration into Government Departments and thought they were becoming too powerful. A reporter from the Armed Forces Newspaper had suggested in an interview with Hassan el Turabi that Numieri was moving away from 'Sharia Laws', and Hassan had replied "If that is so Numieri is an unbeliever and ought to be killed". He added that he was speaking off the record, but the reporter was so horrified he discussed it with his editor Babiker Abdel Rahim, who promptly reported the matter to Numieri. The President's reaction was to denounce Hassan el Turabi and the Muslim Brothers in 'rude' language saying that he would insult them so much that they would react publicly and then he would retaliate.[26]

---

[25]Tape recording by Sayed Sadig el Mahdi.
[26]G F Thomas. Mss Diary, Vol. V, p. 67.

There is a ring of truth about it in the context of Numieri's character and psychological make up.

Spiralling inflation was continuing. The failure of the rains resulted in a doubling of grain prices, while meat and fish, being in short supply were expensive. Universities, schools and hospitals were without adequate facilities, grossly lacking equipment, medicines or drugs. We continued to mount our campaign, joined at this time by Dr Abdel Karim el Goni who acted as a liaison officer.

In yet another unpredictable move, the President of the Sudan was reported in the World News on BBC to have declared that the 'Sharia Laws' had cleaned up the country, put down corruption and that he was revising the judiciary. Chris Terrill telephoned me to let me know of a telex message from Khartoum that Numieri had suspended Sharia Law and ended the State of Emergency. It seemed strange that in his coup of fifteen years earlier, he had justified his seizure of power as being the means to end corruption.

It was obvious that both America and Egypt were exerting such pressure on him that he had to make a gesture of putting his house in order or there would be no US dollars to help him meet the 'creditor's club' in Paris. The previous year America had given him two hundred million US dollars to meet the IMF loan. The Islamic Conference was being held in Khartoum, and this too influenced him as, no doubt, many Muslim leaders had told him that his so called 'Sharia Laws' were scarcely Islamic. Sadig sent me a long document which destroyed point by point Numieri's psuedo-Islamisation. Within days Numieri appointed Fouad el Amin, a Sufi, to be Chief Justice. ✗

We had escaped from the English winter to Morocco and it was there, in Asilah, that we had a telephone call from Sara, in the early hours of the morning of the twentieth of December telling us ecstatically that Sadig had been released. It was a joyful Christmas message, but things were still not at all satisfactory. On the eighteenth of January 1985 an event happened which I am convinced marked the real beginning of the end of the Regime. This was the hanging of Mahmoud Muhammed Taha, an old, somewhat eccentric Sudanese who was essentially a man of peace.

Mahmoud had been released at the same time as Sadig. He was the guru of the Republican Brothers, and was deeply read in Islamic studies. For years he had advocated women's rights, and firmly believed that the Southern Sudan should determine its own future. He had published a new interpretation of the Koran which had upset the fundamentalists, but he was widely respected and held in affection as a teacher, thinker, and writer. On his release Taha with four of his colleagues openly and peacefully distributed leaflets condemning Numieri's abuse of Islamic Law. They were immediately arrested, charged with sedition and later apostasy (a heinous crime in Islam) and sentenced by venal courts subservient to Numieri's regime to be hanged. Having initially given them one month in which to recant, Numieri imperiously shortened the period to three days. Most Sudanese were appalled, and the news quickly circulated throughout the world. All the Ambassadors in the Sudan, including those from Arab States appealed for clemency, even the US State Department sent a special message urging a stay of execution but all to no avail, and the execution took place in Kober Prison as a public spectacle.

Sudanese in London, such as Dr Khalil Osman and Dr Mansour Khaled urged us to organise a protest to which we immediately responded by arranging a Memorial and Protest meeting at the House of Commons in the Grand Committee Room. It was supported by all the Political Parties. Sponsors were the Rt Hon Dame Judith Hart (Labour) Cyril Townsend MP (Conservative and Chairman of CAABU) and David Alton (Liberal-Alliance) while speakers included Lord Caradon, Don Anderson MP, and Lord McNair, and the room holding two hundred was crowded. From the chair I read messages from the Rt Hon Roy Jenkins, the Rt Hon David Steel, and the Bishop of Salisbury; Cardinal Hume was represented by Bishop James O'Brien. A colleague of Mahmoud Taha, Malik Beshir Malik gave a highly charged speech on Taha, and Michael Smith of Amnesty International was followed by Dr Khalil Osman who spoke movingly and effectively about the influence on him that Taha had exerted when the two were imprisoned together for nine months. It was an emotional experience and made a deep impression on all who came many of them members of Parliament. A report by Malise Ruthven went out on the BBC Arabic Service and on the BBC Africa Network by Deborah Pugh. I understand that it was broadcast in Arabic, Hausa, and Swahili, and it was also carried in The Observer on the following Sunday. After the meeting Don Anderson hosted a dinner in the Harcourt Rooms of the Houses of Parliament attended by Dr Mansour Khaled, Dr Khalil Osman, Jeffrey Thomas QC, Ismay and myself. Later I wrote the following

> I grieve for Taha
> Who was this Taha?
> He was a man
> He hurt no man
> No man's enemy
> Full long he lived
> Seventy years and seven
> Loving, giving, teaching
> Passionate and peaceful
> "Human rights for all"
> A few leaflets given
> Was his heinous offence
> For this they hanged him
> Publicly in Kober Prison
> 18 January 1985

Mahmoud Muhammed Taha

Since Christmas, I had been receiving reports that Numieri was going to Washington and that he would not be allowed to return to the Sudan. Neither the Foreign Office, nor my friends in the media would believe this but the reports were persistent and came from a wide cross section of Sudanese.[27] Dr Khalil Osman who was commuting frequently to Khartoum was emphatic, as were several other reliable Sudanese friends.

In March, Numieri, irritated and fearful of the influence of the Muslim Brothers had rounded up two hundred of their leaders, and imprisoned most of them in El Fasher. There were reports that the Muslim Brotherhood had received arms from Iran, and Numieri accused them of creating para-military structures, battalions, companies and cells in strategic areas. The imprisonment of Hassan el Turabi and the other leaders was to be the last poisonous act of Numieri, for, when the new Transitional Military Council came into being, one of its earliest acts was to release all political detainees.

Numieri had probably hoped that by getting rid of the Muslim Brothers he could reach some sort of accommodation either with the Mirghanists and/or Sadig el Mahdi and the Ansar. He had become completely isolated and out of touch with reality. He was surrounded by corrupt syncophants. Numieri bitterly denounced his erstwhile allies saying "I seek refuge from the Devil" and that the brotherhood was a "satanic group". The extensive arrests certainly showed how successfully the infiltration of the Muslim Brotherhood had been in significant and powerful positions within the legal, academic, and business structures. Together with Hassan el Turabi they included the Leader of the National Assembly (Ali Muhammed Taha)

---

[27] G F Thomas. Mss Diary, Vol. V, p. 133.

Ahmed Abdel Rahman (ex Minister of the Interior), the President of the Criminal Court of Appeal (Ahmed Magid Haj Nur) two other judges, a number of senior lawyers and Abdel Rahim Hamdi (Director of the Bohkara Bank).

George Bush the Vice-President of the USA visited Khartoum during March, and, besides meeting the President, had meetings with the Vice-President Joseph Lagu who had written a trenchant memorandum criticising the Numieri regime. He also met a Southern Sudanese delegation, Abel Alier (a Southern Minister), Sadig el Mahdi, and a number of eminent Sudanese from the professional academic and business communities. George Bush was left in no doubt of the unpopularity of the regime, and the appalling state of the economy, and the country. Lagu publicly criticised the introduction of the September '83 Laws declaring that they had made Southerners "second class citizens", and that this was unacceptable to them. Sadig el Mahdi warned Bush that "the American support for the present regime had alienated the Sudanese people". Cairo was well aware of the situation, and as a warning to Numieri and to reassure the opposition, especially the Southerners, they withdrew three hundred Egyptian troops that they had sent in response to an appeal from Numieri who considered Gaddafi to be threatening him.

It was at this time that Dr Mansour Khalid published his condemnatory book 'Numieri and the Revolution of Dis-May' which merely served to confirm what was already known of the widespread corruption which had overtaken the country. Mansour declared at the end of the book that "The Sudan had reached its Nadir". What is remarkable is that men as distinguished as Mansour had continued for so long their support of Numieri.

At the beginning of April the Sudanese President went to Washington for talks and a medical check up. He saw President Reagan and others and it was announced that the fifty-four million (dollars) which had been blocked, were to be released.

The day after Numieri's departure for the States, rioting broke out in Khartoum. It was reported that the attitude of the Armed Forces was ambivalent, but a few people were killed in minor skirmishes. I was informed by messages from Khartoum that loudspeakers were broadcasting in Khartoum and Omdurman announcing that the police would be with the people. The Foreign Office were sceptical when I told them. The following day was quiet, relatively speaking, but Dr Khalil Osman telephoned me to say that the professional groups were organising and would take action, which they did, originally calling for a general strike on the Sunday, but later postponing it until Wednesday the fifth of April. The Foreign Office informed me that General Omer el Tayeb was not only in charge but was in control. Numieri announced in Washington that he was not worried as the forces were loyal. I then heard that Bahaa-Eldin Idris had arrived in London and the President of the SSU had flown to China the very day that the SSU had called for a demonstration of support for Numieri. The SSU demonstration was a complete flop—only 3000 people at the most, rallied on the fourth of April. It was clear that power was rapidly flowing away from the dictator. On the following day, despite all efforts and the closing of the Khartoum North and White Nile Bridges, over thirty thousand people converged on the Palace demanding Numieri's resignation. The forces kept a low profile, a few canisters of tear gas were thrown, but the crowds dispersed peacefully.

On Thursday the sixth of April Christopher Long told me that it had been reported that things were quiet in the Sudan and seemed to be under control in Khartoum[28] and

---

[28]G F Thomas. Mss Diary, Vol. V, pp. 134–135.

while this may have been true it was obvious that huge changes in the power structure were taking place. Numieri announced that he would leave Washington a day early to see President Mubarak and give a press conference in Cairo before flying home. Late on Thursday evening I heard that the army had cut off Khartoum and that rioting was spreading. El Obeid and Gadaref were involved and it appeared that at the latter the army was supporting the demonstrators. By Friday the seventh of April all tele-communications were cut off to the Sudan and all airports were closed.[29]

Numieri arrived at Cairo, where he met a group of Egyptian security officials after which he returned to the aircraft. Later reports said that he was 'bundled' into the plane. Certainly no press conference was held. Sara was told by an informant in Cairo who telephoned her, that the pilot refused to fly on to Khartoum, but I suspect that the Egyptians, either told the pilot not to go or refused him clearance. At any event, the security cars left and Numieri embarked in a helicopter to go to an Egyptian Palace, it was not clear which one.

General Sawar el Dahab, who had only been appointed Commander-in-Chief three weeks earlier by Numieri announced that Numieri was deposed, and that he had taken over.[30] The armed forces had established a military council of fifteen, and that they would shortly be arranging to hand "power back to the people" by the institution of a civilian government. There was of course great jubilation in Khartoum, and Ismay and I quietly celebrated too. I did still have some reservations for all fifteen of the military council were Numieri's men what else could they be after sixteen years of Numieri rule.

---

[29]Ibid, p. 135.
[30]G F Thomas. Mss Diary, Vol. V, p. 135.

In the South, John Garang, the SPLA leader announced that he would suspend hostilities for seven days in order to allow the army to hand over to a civilian administration, but this was obviously an impossible task so the war was renewed, while in the North in the euphoria of freedom twenty nine political parties and numerous trades unions emerged. All demanded representation in the Government; democracy was reborn, but confusion and dissension was rife. Sadig telephoned us to congratulate us on all our efforts, but could say little concrete in this first flush of freedom.

On his return to Khartoum, Bahaa Eldin Idris was beaten up, while General Omer el Tayeb and others were arrested and put into Kober Prison. Dr Abdel Hamid Saleh was as I had expected in Cairo. The Sudan Ambassador in London Abdullahi el Hassan was dismissed, but the luckiest person of all was Hassan el Turabi, who with other members of the Muslim Brotherhood had been imprisoned three weeks earlier and were now released as 'Prisoners of Numieri'.

CHAPTER VIII

TOWARDS DEMOCRACY

"A democracy, that is a government of all the people by all the people, for all the people"

THEODORE PARKER

Undoubtedly, the public execution of Mahmoud Muhammed Taha removed the last vestige of credibility from Numieri. Even his most faithful supporters realised that this was a crisis point. They hesitated to take action, which they thought might be counter productive, for they feared the alternative. They were convinced that the Armed Forces should be kept intact but passive and that it was essential to prevent the NCOs joining with the communists to seize power. There were negotiations, and conversations between the opposition groups and leading Army Officers. Eventually it was agreed that the Armed Forces should take over, depose Numieri and form a transitional Government. General Abdel Rahman Sawar el Dahab emerged as the agreed leader. He was a devout Muslim of the Khatmiyya tariqa and related by marriage to my old friend the late Mirghani Hamza. He was a respected, if not outstanding soldier, but he was an appointee of Numieri, and had only a month earlier, been promoted by the President to the post of Commander-in-Chief, when Numieri himself assumed the title of 'Supreme Commander'. On the tenth of April it was announced that a transitional Government would be composed of a Military Council of fifteen members. I was

224

frankly doubtful and had serious reservations, indeed I even distrusted the Transitional Military Council as all fifteen men had been appointed to their senior army posts by Numieri. Dahab and the Council made repeated statements to the effect that they would hand over to a civilian administration, but this was not universally believed. John Garang did not believe them, and to be truthful neither did I. But I was wrong and they honoured their promises. An almost continuous series of meetings was held between the Transitional Council and the civilian groups who had opposed Numieri. Omar Nur el Diem represented Sadig while the Umma Party spokesman was Salah Abdel Salaam. Haj Meddawi and Mubarek Shadad were delegated by the Unionists while the Sudan Communist Party, the Baathists and the Islamic Socialist Party all joined in the talks. When I attacked Omar Nur el Diem for agreeing to a Transitional Military Council he replied "If we had not agreed the Armed Forces would have split and it would have been Civil War".[1]

With the downfall of Numieri there had come a rash of political parties. Among them were the traditional groups such as the Umma Party (Mahdist) and the Democratic Unionist Party (Mirghanist) led by Mahmoud Hasanaya; the communists were now led by Muhammed Ibrahim Nugud, but there was little cohesion between the multiplicity of newly created party groupings. The Muslim Brothers had split into two Hassan el Turabi leading the one faction and Sadig Abdel Majid the other. The Islamic Socialist Party under Nasr el Sayed wanted an Islamic Government but with modern conditions. There were also the anti-Egyptians calling themselves the Nasserite Arab Socialist Organisation; while Ali Abu Sin headed the National Democratic Party which favoured the Sudan as part of an Afro-Arab

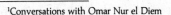

[1]Conversations with Omar Nur el Diem

Community. All these together with the Communists, the Arab socialist Ba'ath Party (closely allied originally with Iraq) and the so-called Bureau of the General Secretariat of Professionals and Trades Unionists emerged. To add to this there was the SPLM of Garang but this refused to participate until full democratic Government was established.

Meanwhile, many young intellectual Sudanese had no real wish to return to the pre-Numieri sectarian regimes, and some like Mansour Khalid had been caught up with that dictatorship. He was typical of many. After the downfall of Numieri, Mansour, alas found that he had no popular grass-roots following and had alienated his natural allies (The Umma) by his close association with Numieri. His high intellect and his general air of superiority made him personally unacceptable in the transitional period which was a tragedy for him and for his country for he could have contributed much. He asked my advice after the downfall of Numieri and knowing the feeling of many Sudanese I advised him to remain abroad and let things heal quietly and naturally. Mansour, still a comparatively young man, was impatient and rushed into discussions with John Garang of the SPLM. A few injudicious remarks, exaggerated and embroidered by his opponents made him unacceptable to most Northern Sudanese.

By the end of April a civilian government, under Dr Ghizali Da'Fallah (Professional and TU Group) was formed and had to face twenty-nine political parties and seventy-seven trades unions. The Army had had to negotiate with fourteen civilian groups. As the year progressed the Transitional Military Council and the civilian government tried to reach some understanding with Garang and Ethiopia but failed, so the hard-liners in the Army increased the military presence in the South. In the meantime the Northern political groups and factions struggled ineffectually to make coherent policies and efficient organisations.

The question of whether the Army would hand over to a civilian government was the primary one in everyone's mind; or would the intransigence of Garang and the war in the South be used to prolong their own control. It was inevitable that the new military leaders, the newly liberated politicians and the people should experience a period of confusion. After all the country had had for sixteen years an arbitrary and ruthless dictator who had made all the decisions.

However despite the continuing decline in the economy and the almost complete collapse of the infra structure which they had inherited, the Transitional Military Council repeatedly expressed their determination to have free elections by April 1986. It was evident that the army leaders wanted to ensure that their continued rule should be with the consent of the main parties.

The problems facing the credibility of the administration to achieve aid from the world organisations, and the necessity to end the fighting in the three Southern Provinces were in the forefront.

A number of Ansar leaders were now free to come to London, and it was very obvious that there was disunity even among the Mahdists. The leadership of the Ansar by Sadig was challenged by his uncle Ahmed Abdel Rahman who was conspiring with Wali Eldin el Hadi to take over the Ansar, although Dr Ahmed A A Yacoub assured me that only about five per cent supported their splinter group. There were also rumblings among the younger Sudanese of the influence on Sadig el Mahdi of Omar Nur el Diem and Mubarek el Abdullahi. I still felt uneasy about the Military regime but Omar again reiterated that the promises made by the Transitional Military Council would be honoured although he accepted that a young army colonel or even a sergeant like Rawlinson in West Africa might attempt a coup. He insisted that he and Sadig had been in full negotiations with "all sections of the army and that the armed forces had acted at their request".[2] Omar told me that Sadig el Mahdi would take office "if the people wanted it" which was what Sadig had continuously reiterated, and he was convinced that Sadig was the only "strong character" available.

I opposed the idea of Sadig accepting office, and his brother Salah el Siddig[3] agreed with me. My argument was that whoever took over had an appalling mess to face economically and in every other way and that one man could not do it. I feared that Sadig would get bogged down with the minutiae of Government and after eighteen months would be toppled and blamed for not having cleared away the corruption of sixteen years of dictatorship. My suggestion was to put someone else into power, and for Sadig to concentrate on thinking on a much larger scale than of "the sewers of Wad Medani" as I put it.

It was, in some ways, a time for celebration, and Sara gave a luncheon party in Fokkereldin's Restaurant in Piccadilly to thank the journalists who had helped to publicise the atrocities of the Numieri regime, and campaign for a return to human rights. Charles Meynell, Edward Mortimer, Richard Hall, John Ryle, Malise Ruthven, Deborah Pugh, Nick Cater, and Colin Legum had all played a valiant part in informing the world of the true situation in the media and press.[4] Martin Hill of Amnesty International who had done so much in declaring the Sudanese Prisoners of Conscience, also attended.

After the Memorial Service to Lord George Brown at St Margaret's Westminster David Owen greeted me with the words "Well you have toppled him (Numieri) at last". He

---

[2] G F Thomas. Mss Diary, Vol. V, p. 114.
[3] Conversations with the late Salah el Siddig.
[4] G F Thomas. Mss Diary, Vol. V, p. 145.

then added that he had recently seen President Mubarak in Cairo and had asked him—"Why don't you pull the rug from under Numieri's feet?".[5] Sadig phoned from Geneva where he had been trying to get the help of UNRAA in the resettlement of the Sudanese refugees in Libya and Ethiopia back in the Sudan. He arrived in England shortly afterwards and we began a week of intense activities. On the fifteenth of July 1985 he was interviewed on Newsnight, and I gave luncheons on successive days so that Sadig could meet the Rt Hon Roy Jenkins who had some penetrating questions, Dr Chris Terrill, Edward Mortimer, Richard Hall, and Ali Bahaijoub (Head of the Moroccan Press Agency).

He saw Denis Healey in the House of Commons, but it was disappointing as it seemed that he was already resigned to the Labour Party losing the next General election. We then went to the Central Lobby where we were graciously greeted by David Owen and David Steel who were waiting for us and they took us to tea in the members tea-room. David Steel had to leave fairly soon as he had another meeting, but David Owen who was very well briefed, and very shrewd in his probing, told Sadig that "Graham kept him well informed" and again repeated that he had told President Mubarak "to get rid of Numieri".

A meeting with Ted Heath at his Walton St home was next on the programme. He was very sympathetic about Third World Problems, and his questions were incisive, going right to the heart of the problems. Their discussion was at some depth, including the problems of financial aid not only in the Sudan, but as a world wide problem. There was no social chit-chat; just pertinent stacatto questions which indicated that Edward Heath was "much more personally interested in the Sudan that I had expected".[6] As

[5] G F Thomas. Mss Diary, Vol. V, pp. 148–153.
[6] Ibid, p. 156.

we rose to leave I found difficulty in getting up from his very low settee, and it was a cause of amusement that it was the first time I had been 'raised' by two ex-Prime Ministers. He was much warmer personally than his public image conveys.

A significant encounter took place on Friday the nineteenth of July when I took Sadig to call on His Eminence Cardinal Basil Hume at Archbishop's House Westminster, which is a Palace on a grand scale with a sweeping marble staircase. Portraits of past Clerics and Cardinals in purples and reds with lace in profusion 'upon their cottars' looked down on us from every wall. We were ushered into a large sitting room and there joined by the Cardinal Archbishop, who wore no purple vestments, nor was his ring in evidence. A real aura of saintliness and humility emanated from the slightly stooping slim figure, who immediately indicated his sympathetic understanding. The rapport between the two men soon became evident, both clearly sensed the deep spirituality of the other. Cardinal Hume was most appreciative that Sadig, a Muslim, had gone to see him, and was most impressive, and warm, with a very keen intelligence but with no hint of superiority or arrogance. His immediate concern was to enquire "What can I do to help? I am willing to come to the Sudan personally if you think I can be of any assistance". He asked to be kept informed of developments, and revealed that he had for several years had a member of his staff liaising with the Muslims in the Archdiocese, and that these quiet unpublicised developments had been most fruitful.[7] As he escorted us back down the stairs I teased him about the grandeur of the house built by his Victorian predecessors. He laughed saying "Oh, it was to keep up with the Jones's over the river" meaning the

---

[7] G F Thomas, Mss Diary, Vol. V, pp. 156–159.

Archbishops of Canterbury at Lambeth Palace. His humanity shone through.[8]

As Sadig and I shared a breakfast at Holyport the next day we talked over the programmes we had just completed, and of hopes for the future. Sadig expressed his willingness to go along with the new Military Junta, but once again I expressed my reservations and fears that the war in the South was a perfect excuse for not proceeding to free elections. I added that although I was reluctant to say so I felt that if this was so, he might have to think about a pre-emptive coup and I think he had given this some thought. However for the present he intended to go along with the Agreement. He was very concerned about the southern problem and told me that he was trying to make contact with Southern Sudanese, and asked me to do the same in London. I tried but there was no response although those based in London had supported the Taha memorial meeting at the House of Commons.

Within days, on the eleventh of August, Sadig telephoned to say that he and Sara were flying to Nairobi to see President Arap Moi and John Garang about the South. He was undecided whether they would return to England or go from Kenya to the Sudan. I detected the hand of Tiny Rowland of Lonrho in this and possibly Chester Croker of the USA in this move for I was certain they wanted their commitments in the Sudan to continue. The oil exploration of Chevron and the work on the Junglei Canal were at a standstill and millions of pounds of investment were at risk. Sadig travelled directly to the Sudan after his Kenya visit and had obviously decided that the time of exile was at an end. He asked me to sell his house at Holyport, and his family all left for the Sudan to prepare for the elections in the New Year.

[8]Ibid, p. 165.

The war in the South dragged on and the Transitional Military Council with the Civilian cabinet seemed to be simply overwhelmed with the enormity of their problems, and there was no evidence of any policy being pursued with the exception of their determination in April 1986 (the first anniversary of Numieri's overthrow) to hold the elections. The Council attempted to persuade the Ethiopians to stop supporting John Garang, and sent General Tagidin Abdulla, second in the hierarchy, to Moscow to request that pressure be put on Mengistu in Addis Ababa but to no avail.

With the advent of 1986 there was once again a flurry of activity by the political parties. In addition to the traditional Umma, DUP, Communists, and the Muslim Brothers, a group of Southerners who had been connected with Numieri in his 'pre-Sharia' days formed the new Sudan Liberation Front and had a very high profile. There were dozens of fringe and splinter groups including the pro-Libyan Sudanese Revolutionary Movement and the Workers and Farmers Party which was Marxist but not attached to the Sudan Communists. A number of parties had conflicting Southern Interests. The Sudanese Africa Congress Party (mainly Southerners resident in Khartoum); The Nuba Mountains Union (with close links with Garang) and the Sudanese National Party of Father Philip Abbas Ghabbush (non-Muslim Nubians) to name but a few. The most militant group, who violently opposed both democracy and the SPLM, called themselves the Islamic Jehad Organisation.

Eighteen parties, trades unions and professional groups signed a Charter for the protection of democracy and were known as 'The National Alliance for the Salvation of the Country'. The Muslim Brothers refused to sign. In accord with the Government's avowed intentions, elections were called for April and when held they were surprisingly free from violence. A number of constituencies in the war-torn

South were unable to hold elections but the remainder of the country polled effectively and fairly. The Umma Party emerged as the single largest party with one hundred seats and in May Sadig el Mahdi was elected as Prime Minister of a coalition Government of the Umma Party with the Mirghanist DUP. So the first freely and democratically elected Government of the Sudan since the nineteen sixties took office, to face the consequences of a regime which had utterly ruined the whole economic structure and had corrupted, divided, and demoralised a whole nation.

POSTSCRIPT

With the advent of a newly elected democratic government the aspirations of the people soared beyond all hopes of realization. Seventeen years of corrupt, arbitrary, and brutal dictatorship had virtually destroyed the whole fabric of society. The economic situation was so desperate that to say the country was bankrupt was to 'understate the gravity of the situation'.[1] The infra-structure had collapsed; there were few all-weather roads, the railway (both track and rolling stock) and air transport were underfunded and chaotic. The country continued to face an appalling rebellion in the South, but perhaps the most serious problem facing the new government was the virtual impossibility of finding trained and efficient personnel. Thousands of educated and competent Sudanese had many years earlier judged the Numieri regime, by leaving the country to work elsewhere in the Middle East or the western world. These are now in senior positions in government, education, commerce or trade elsewhere and have grown roots outside the Sudan. Patriotism brought back a few, but not sufficient to rebuild the administration, so senior officials with talent and experience are lacking.

Inevitably too, after any long period of dictatorship and in a revolutionary situation every individual believed that he had the answer to all the ills of society. A multitude of political parties, pressure groups and factors came into being; all contesting for power.

Alas, history was to repeat itself, for, as in 1953 in the

---

[1]Colin Legum—3rd World Report, 21.5.86.

old Legislative Assembly, no one group had a clear decisive majority. The Transitional Military Council had led the way to the elections which were fought in April 1986 with surprising fairness and little violence (except in the southern constituencies over-run by the war). The results were: 100 seats to the Umma Party, 63 to the DUP, 51 for the National Islamic Front, 10 for the Progressive Peoples Party. The southern Sudanese Political Association gained 8 seats, the Sudanese Nationalist Party 8, the Sudan African Peoples Congress 13; while 13 seats were won by a miscellany of candidates.

As a result a Coalition Government was formed between the Umma and DUP, in which Sadig el Mahdi (Umma) became Prime Minister, and Ahmed el Mirghani (DUP) became Head of State. As had happened under earlier periods of party rule in the Sudan, ministries were allocated between the two main parties, 9 going to the Umma Party and 6 to the DUP. Other, mainly minor portfolios, went to the smaller groupings such as the southern alliance. The National Islamic Front remained outside the government as were the SPLM led by John Garang and the small, but highly organised, Sudan Communist Party which has enormous influence totally out of proportion to its members of Parliament, or even actual party membership. It was particularly influential in the Trades' Unions.

Apart from the Prime Minister and a few of his colleagues, the Umma Party lacked strong, efficient, and experienced men, while the DUP had serious divisions within its ranks. There was no clear government policy or even direction of purpose, and sadly, it must be said that partisan prejudices and personal considerations were placed above national need. Quite open animosities and divisions arose between Ministers leading to a constant game of musical chairs in re-shuffled administrations. The situation was exacerbated by the continuation of the bloody insur-

Muhammed Ibrahim Nugud, Communist Leader

rection in the south led by John Garang and the SLPM which had refused to participate in the elections, preferring the bullet to the ballot box. It should be remembered that the Southern Revolt took place in 1983 months before President Numieri introduced the so-called Sharia laws; it did not have its origins in religion.

In November 1985, on an initiative, inspired by the Transitional Military Council, Dr T Mohd Ali and Professor Muhammed Omer Beshir saw Garang but met with no response other than the totally unreasonable ultimatum that the TMC should hand over power 'within seven days'. In view of the position in the country after the downfall of Numieri this was utterly impracticable, and even the SPLM knew this. Within a few months Garang ordered a boycott of the first genuinely democratic elections in seventeen years.

Even before the elections, Sadig el Mahdi had flown to Kenya to see President Arap Moi in an attempt to negotiate a settlement, and after the elections various missions were dispatched to Ethiopia to see John Garang and Mengistu. Sadig el Mahdi went on the 10th of August 1986 but in spite of offering to take "two steps for every one taken by Ethiopia"[2] it was of no avail.

Garang was demanding the abolition of the September Laws which was impossible for the Coalition Government to do immediately. The Sudan Government had already frozen the 'Hudoud' punishments pending a revision of the laws, which it was felt should be done constitutionally, rather than in an arbitrary way.

Unfortunately for both the Sudan and Ethiopia, natural forces added catastrophically to the already almost insuperable problems as famine swept through Ethiopia and Sudan. The world was aghast and huge sums were raised to aid the sufferers. In the UK, Band Aid and Sports Aid contributed millions of pounds but as the agencies poured in supplies and personnel so further problems arose because of the multiplicity of agencies some of which were activated by political rather than humanitarian motives.

Foreign affairs proved to be a major difficulty for the new democracy; these problems were partly historical with personal overtones, and involved relationships with Egypt, Libya, and the United States of America.

I have always believed that Egypt had a legitimate interest in the Sudan because of the Nile Waters, and have consistently advocated an understanding. The Egyptians, however, by their superior attitude to the Sudanese, almost regarding them as 'Abd' (slaves and black) aggravated the tensions, and the Sudanese resented this. There was a reflection of this in the relationship between the United States and the Sudan. It was alleged that in the last days of the Numieri regime, President Reagan had remarked to a

---

[2] G F Thomas. Mss Diary, Vol. VI, p. 131.

Sayed Sadig el Mahdi

senior British politician "we know that he (Numieri) is a bastard, but he is one of our bastards".

Despite much pressure, Sadig el Mahdi remained adamant, refusing to visit Cairo, while undertaking many foreign trips to Iran, the Middle East, and Europe. He also visited Moscow in 1986 before coming to London where he was warmly welcomed by Mrs Thatcher during his official visit. At a luncheon at Number 10 Downing Street she said "your return to office . . . marks Sudan's return to democracy. That is an achievement of which the Sudanese people can justly be proud. It is an example to Africa and more widely that even in adversity, democracy can win through. I know that all of us . . . are confident of your courage and your determination to overcome the problems which Sudan faces. I pledge to you the support and good will of the British Government and people as you confront this challenge"[3] and as I left she commented to me "he is indeed a remarkable and impressive man".[4]

The Sudan Government, however, found it difficult to understand the contrast between her warm reception and the subsequent 'cold and unhelpful'[5] attitude of Her Majesty's Government. The Sudanese Prime Minister believed that Britain had no distinctive policy from the Americans, although as he put it "The Dutch, French, Germans and Italians had written President Reagan off concerning the Middle East"[6] Relations between Britain and the Sudan have improved under the ambassadorship of John Beaven, who was described to me on one of my recent visits to Khartoum as "very forthright and friendly—a good choice".[7]

---

[3] G F Thomas. Mss Diary, Vol. VII, p. 4.
[4] G F Thomas. Mss Diary, Vol. VII, p. 53.
[5] G F Thomas. Mss Diary, Vol. VII, p. 56.
[6] G F Thomas. Mss Diary, Vol. VII, p. 56.
[7] G F Thomas. Mss Diary, Vol. VII, p. 27.

As a result of repeated urging concerning Egypt, Sadig el Mahdi promised to consider the matter further and initially Mubarek el Abdullahi was sent as an emissary to Cairo; He and Nasr Eldin Imam el Hadi had always agreed with me on this subject.

In February 1987 the Sudanese Prime Minister again visited London for talks with Sir Geoffrey Howe at the Foreign Office and to address the Oxford Union where his warm reception befitted an Oxford graduate. During our long conversations he told me that he had planned to go to Cairo on 16th February stressing that he proposed to speak "people to people rather than Government to Government".[8] He was proposing to give talks and lectures. I told him privately that he should be more conciliatory as by visiting almost everywhere else before going to the Sudan's nearest neighbour he had humiliated the Egyptians and this would be resented bitterly. My advice was to "give a little but charm a lot". Before leaving England the next day Sadig telephoned me to say that he accepted what I had advised. The same day the Egyptian Embassy telephoned to ask me to see Anwar Galal the Press Director and an old friend. He asked for my advice on Sadig el Mahdi's visit and this I gave him saying "let him speak people to people". This they did and within days I heard that the visit had been a great success. Unfortunately, relations soon became strained once more and indeed deteriorated seriously.

During my visit in February 1988 I had a long talk with the Prime Minister at Numieri's old house in the Military Headquarters. He agreed that he should meet President Mubarak again but he was insistent that Egypt must treat the Sudan as a sovereign and independent state. The Sudan Government was resentful of Egypt's "neutrality" over Ethiopia's relations with the Sudan suggesting that as water

---

[8] G F Thomas. Mss Diary, 12.2.87, Vol. VII, p. 53.

consumers the Sudan and Egypt should work together, and proposing a joint working party might be set up.

After careful thought, I went to see the Egyptian Ambassador in Khartoum, His Excellency Sherbini, to discuss matters. Events moved swiftly much to my surprise. At a tea party given by Prime Minister Sadig el Mahdi to celebrate our 39th wedding anniversary on the Government launch which was attended by His Excellency John Beavan, Jim Lester MP, the Chairman of a visiting Parliamentary Committee, His Excellency the Jordanian Ambassador and many of our old Sudanese friends, the Prime Minister received a message. Turning to me he said "I have just heard that Mubarak is coming tomorrow, very un-expectedly—it is what you wanted". Regretfully, the meeting which lasted for less than an hour and a half was reported to me as being 'not helpful' and Sudan-Egypt relationships showed no sign of improvement.

It must be said that to these tremendous problems of foreign affairs was added an additional burden to the poor and distressed Sudan. Following the famine came the floods which although causing few deaths did tremendous physical damage to houses, buildings and roads as well as disrupting agriculture. These problems put heavy pressure on the administration and led to even more internal problems.

The immediate future must see the resolution of two major problems which are inter-related and almost insuper-able. These are the settlement of the war in the south and an economic reconstruction for the whole country—north and south. The solution for these problems depend for success on the stability of the Government and this in turn implies an efficient, incorrupt, and just administration. It is this, the third factor, which seems most elusive.

Intrigues and disputations have prevented cohesive government. The difficulties of coalition have been con-stantly highlighted. Shortly after our Khartoum visit, a new

Sayed Ahmed el Mirghami

coalition was formed comprising of the Umma Party, the DUP, the Southern parties, and for the first time the National Islamic Front. It was doomed from the beginning; the contrary views of the participants on policy matters ensuring this. There can be no doubt that the Egyptians were gravely disturbed by the new administration which included Muslim Fundamentalists, but this government was not to last long.

By December 1988 Sayed Mohd Osman el Mirghani, at the suggestion of the Prime Minister instigated discussions with John Garang in Addis Ababa, and there is no doubt that Egypt saw its opportunity to interfere and encouraged the DUP, which had reached an accord with John Garang, to withdraw from the coalition. Certainly Egypt had played a part in the negotiations and wanted to secure the removal of Sadig el Mahdi from the office of Prime Minister. So once more the country was faced with a divided government and Sadig el Mahdi sought for time to search for a consensus with all parties.

In January 1989 General Abdel Magid Hamid Khalil resigned as Defence Minister, accusing the Prime Minister of failing to endorse the DUP and SPLM agreement. The rift between the Prime Minister and the army became public. Now they presented an ultimatum to the Prime Minister to expedite the peace; to change his foreign policy, and to take the DUP back into government within seven days. This was to be the fourth time the armed forces had intervened in politics since independence.

Once more, behind the scenes negotiations took place; the army was reluctant to act; the Prime Minister defended his foreign policy and demanded that the army withdraw its ultimatum. After a month of discussion, argument and negotiations yet another compromise was reached. The DUP returned to government, the NIF left, and Sadig el Mahdi remained as Prime Minister. Once more the ministries were allocated on a proportional basis between the parties. Stability remains elusive and will remain so until an administration can be formed on the basis of the appointment of Ministers because of their ability and suitability for the post, not on their loyalty and allegiance to a party or religious sect. If this stability is not achieved the two main aims of peace and economic reconstruction will not be resolved. There are serious dangers of the fragmentation of the Sudan.

Insha'allah, the Sudanese will find a unity of purpose and policy for their future.

Footnote

Since the above was written the Sudanese armed forces have once again, on the thirtieth of June 1989, overthrown a democratically elected Government in a Military Coup. Leaders of all the political parties and trades unions have been detained. Among them are, the Prime Minister, Sadig el Mahdi (Umma Party), Muhammed Osman el Mirghani (D.U.P.), Hassan el Turabi (National Islamic Front), and Ibrahim Nugud (Communist). Most are imprisoned in the notorious Kober prison, being detained without charges or trial.

BIBLIOGRAPHY

I Manuscript Sources

MSS   Journal of Ismay Thomas 1950–55

MSS   Diaries of Graham F Thomas 1964–87

MSS   Letters from Graham Thomas and Ismay Thomas
      1950–1955

MSS   Letters from
      Sayed Abdel Rahman El Mahdi, Imam
      Rt Hon Clement Attlee, MP (Earl Attlee)
      Tom Driberg, MP (Lord Driberg)
      Sir Arthur Gaitskell
      Rt Hon James Griffiths, MP, CH
      Rt Hon Roy Jenkins (Lord Jenkins)
      Rt Hon H A Marquand, MP
      Rt Hon Dr David Owen, MP
      Sir James Robertson, KT, GCVO, GCMG, KBE
      Sadig El Mahdi

MSS   Notes of Graham Thomas

II Newspapers and Periodicals

The Financial Times	London
The Guardian	London
The Observer	London
The Sunday Times	London
The Times	London
The Economist	London

Africa Confidential	London
Africa Analysis	London
Third World Reports	London
Voice of the Arab World	London
At Tadamon	London
Al Ahram	Cairo/London
Al Sahafa	Khartoum
Sudan News Agency Reports	Khartoum
The Sudan Times	Khartoum

III   Biographies, Memoirs, Published Works

Adel Amin Beshai
  Export performance and economic development in
  Sudan 1900–1967
                                                Ithaca Press
              For St Anthony's College, Oxford 1976

Beshir Mohammed Said
  The Sudan—Crossroads of Africa
                                            Bodley Head 1965

Bedri, Dr Yusif and George Scott (Editors)
  The memoirs of Babiker Bedri Volumes I and II
                          Oxford University Press 1969
                                                        1980

Bell, Sir Gawain
  Shadows on the Sand
                                            C Hurst & Co 1983

Collins, Robert O and Francis Deng (Editors)
  The British in the Sudan 1898–1956
                                              MacMillan 1984

Driberg, Tom
  The Best of Both Worlds (A personal diary)
                                      Phoenix House (Dent) 1953

Duncan, J S R, MBE
    The Sudan's Path to Independence
                    William Blackwood 1957

Grafftey-Smith Sir Laurence
    Hands to Play
                    Routledge and Kegan Paul 1975

Henderson, K D D, CMG
    The Making of the Modern Sudan
                    Faber & Faber 1952

Hill, Richard
    A Biographical Dictionary of the Sudan
                    Frank Cass & Co Ltd, 2nd Edition 1967

Holt, P M
    The Mahdist State in the Sudan 1881–1898
                    Oxford University Press, 2nd Edition 1970

Lloyd, Selwyn
    Suez 1956
                    Jonathan Cape 1978

Mansour Khaled
    Numieri and The Revolution of Dis-May
                    KPI 1985

Ministry of Information and Culture—Sudan Government
    Sudan Today
                    University Press of Africa 1971

Mohammed Ahmed Mahjoub
    Democracy on Trial
                    André Deutsch 1974

Mohamed Heikal
    Autumn of Fury
                    André Deutsch 1983

Mohamed Omer Beshir
The Southern Sudan—From Conflict to Peace
C Hurst & Co 1975

Mohamed Omer Beshir
Educational Development in the Sudan 1898–1956
Oxford—At The Clarendon Press 1969

Mekki Shibeika
British Policy in the Sudan 1882–1902
Oxford University Press 1952

Muddathir Abdel Rahim
Imperialism and Nationalism in the Sudan
Oxford University Press 1969

Nelson, D Harold *et al* Editors
Area Handbook for the Democratic Republic of
Sudan
The American University 1973

Nelson, Harold D (Editor)
Sudan A Country Study 1983
Foreign Area Studies The American University

Robertson, Sir James
Transition in Africa—From Direct Rule to
Independence
C Hurst 1974

Sudan Government PRO
Sudan Almanac
1951

IV   *Secondary Sources*

Sudan Notes and Records   1950–1955

INDEX

Ab Bakr al Senussi 143

Abboud Ibrahim, General, President of Sudan 85–88, 91

Abdel Fatah Hassan, Colonel 54, 71

Abdel Fattah Mograbi, Member of Supreme Council 30, 79

Abdel Gadir Yusef 161

Abdel Halim Ahmed 33

Abdel Halim, Dr 89

Abdel Hamid Saleh, Dr 146, 148, 150, 152, 154, 155, 166–168, 170, 171, 178, 181, 182, 189, 190, 192, 194, 195, 205, 211, 212 213, 223

Abdel Kader Hatem, Dr 115, 116, 134, 140, 161, 162, 164, 213

Abdel Karim el Goni, Dr 215

Abdel Khalig Mahjoub 90, 100, 110

Abdel Magid Hamid Khalil, General 180, 183, 188, 243

Abdel Moneim, family of 173

Abdel Rahim Hamdi 220

Abdel Rahim Shannan, Brigadier 88

Abdel Rahman, Judge 162, 200

Abdel Rahman Abdoun 19, 22, 30, 161

Abdel Rahman Ali Taha 19, 23, 85

Abdel Rahman el Mahdi, Imam 13, 17–19, 22, 23, 30, 34–40, 42, 43, 46, 47, 50, 52, 55–59, 65, 66, 69, 75, 81, 82, 83, 85, 86, 89, 95, 108, 117, 120, 167, 171, 190, 191

Abdel Rahman el Siddig 170, 171

Abdel Rahman Sawar el Dahab, General, Head of Civil Government. See Sawar el Dahab 00

Abdel Rasoul el Nur 175

Abdel Salaam Aboul Ela 122

Abdul Daiem 143

Abdullah Khalil, Prime Minister of Sudan 19, 23, 30, 37, 43, 45, 49, 50, 65, 66, 81–83, 85

Abdullahi el Fadl 55, 95, 97

Abdullahi el Hassan 115, 203, 223

Abdullahi el Ta'aishi, Khalifat el Mahdi 7, 9, 22

Abel Alier 184, 220

Abu Dhabi 212

Abul Gassim Muhammed Ibrahim, Vice President 144, 167, 170, 171, 173, 174, 181, 182

Abu Ghazala, Field Marshal 207

Ahfad College 127

Ahlia School 33, 118

Ahmed Abdalla Hamid, Lt. General 88

Ahmed Abdel Aziz Yacoub, Dr 165, 227

Ahmed Abdel Halim 167

Ahmed Abdel Rahman 190, 193, 195, 208, 210, 220

Ahmed Abdel Rahman Sayed 106, 135, 157, 172, 181, 192

Ahmed Abdel Wahab, General 86

Ahmed Adam 29

Ahmed Anis, Dr 126, 127

Ahmed el Fekki 107

Ahmed el Mirghani, Sayed. Head of State. See Mirghani (el) 00

Ahmed Izzat Abdel Latif 192

Ahmed Magid Haj Nur 220

Ahmed Muhammed Saleh, Member of Supreme Council 79

Ahmed Muhammed Yassin, Member of Supreme Council 79

Ahmed Sulieman Muhammed Ahmed 90, 113, 133

Ahmed Zein el Abdin 143

Al Ahram, Egyptian Newspaper 32

Al Sadig Ball 143

Al Sahafa, Sudan Newspaper 143

Al Shafiee Ahmed el Sheik 34, 112

Ali Abu Sin 225

Ali Bahaijoub 229

Ali Maher Pasha, Egyptian Prime Minister 40, 41

Ali Muhammed Taher 219

Ali el Mirghani, Sayed 19, 22, 30, 38, 41, 46, 50, 52, 57–59, 81, 86, 89

Ali Neguib 45

Ali el Siddig 106

Alton, David, M.P. 216

Aly Khan, Prince 29

249

Amin Ali Hassoun 202
Amin el Sayed 63
Amir el Sawi 117, 149, 165, 176, 178, 180
Amnesty International 201
Anderson, Donald, M.P. 217
Anglo-Egyptian Agreement 30
Anglo-Egyptian Co-Domini 2, 9, 10, 32
Anglo-Egyptian Convention 9
Anglo-Egyptian Treaty 17, 36
Ansar 38, 61, 66, 67, 81, 89, 109, 113, 118, 125, 164, 165, 171–173, 178, 185, 219, 227
Anwar Sadat, President of Egypt (See Sadat) 00
Anya Nya 90, 93, 94, 100, 155
Arap Moi Daniel, President of Kenya 210, 231, 236
Aru Samuel 184
Ashigga Party 13, 61
Atabani, family 129
At Tadamon 207
Attlee, Rt Hon Clement, M.P., Prime Minister U.K. 16, 39, 65, 74, 75, 76
Awad Jahia 148
Azhari, Ismael, Prime Minister and President of Sudan 13, 30, 38, 52, 61, 63, 66, 73, 79, 85, 94, 95, 100, 102, 105–107
Azzadin el Sayed 158, 170, 189, 194, 195, 210

Ba'athists 225, 226
Baballa 69
Babiker Abdel Rahim 214
Babiker Awadalla, Prime Minister of Sudan 91, 104, 107, 108, 115, 121, 125, 160
Babiker el Nour, Colonel 111, 112
Babiker Karrar 143
Bache, Iranian Politician 180
Bahaa Eldin Muhammed Idris 170, 210, 221, 223
Baker, Sir Samuel 5
Baker, Stanley, Judge 42
Baring Sir Evelyn 9
Beaton, A C 33
Bedri, Ali, Dr 19, 161
Bedri, Ghassim, Dr 138
Bedri, Ibrahim 58
Bedri, Yusif, Dr 89, 138, 161, 166
Begin,Menachem, Prime Minister of Israel 177, 178, 188

Bell, Sir Gawain 53
Beshir Muhammed Said 158, 182
Beswick, Frank, M.P. 76
Bevin, Rt Hon Ernest, M.P. 18, 35
Bona Malwal 158, 170, 176
Bowker Sir (Reginald) James 74
Bridges, Lord 131
Brocklebank-Fowler, Christopher, M.P. 150
Brown, Rt Hon George, M.P. 228
Bukhari Ahmed Salem 131
Bush, George, President U.S.A. 220
Bushra el Sadig 179
Buthayna Khalil 131, 187
Buxton James 165, 182

Caffery Jefferson 47
Cailaghan, Rt Hon James, M.P., Prime Minister of the U.K. 147, 175
Camp David 171
Caradon, Lord 217
Carden, Derek Charles 158, 169, 172
Carter James, President of U.S.A. 177, 179
Cater, Nicholas 228
Chapman-Andrews, Sir Edwin 89
Chappell, Frank 131
Chevron Oil Co 184, 231
Churchill, Rt Hon Sir Winston, M.P., Prime Minister of U.K. 16, 40, 46
Clark, William 39
Contomichalos 160
Craig, James 116, 130
Cripps, Lady Isabel 76
Croker, Chester 211, 231
Crouch, David, M.P. 150

Dafalla el Haj Yusif 211
Dairat el Mahdi 191
Dardiri Muhammed Osman 30, 41, 49, 50, 63, 73, 79
Davies, Rt Hon John 150
Democratic Unionist Party 99, 100, 225, 233, 235, 243
Deng, Dorothy 160
Deng, Francis, Dr 133, 160, 176
Deng, William 93, 100
Dongala 4, 199
Driberg, Tom, M.P. 39, 76
DuCann Edward, M.P. 131

Eden, Rt Hon Anthony, M.P., Prime Minister of U.K. 40, 46, 49, 74

Eitidal Muhammed Fadl 203
El Banna, General 72
El Fatih Muhammed Beshir, General 133
El Hadi Abdel Rahman, Imam 23, 35,
36, 47, 95, 97, 100–102, 106, 108,
109, 146, 153, 167
El Rayah Hassan Khalifa 203
Etherington-Smith, Gordon 121, 123,
126, 131–132
Ethiopia 226, 229, 232, 237

Fadalah Ali el Tom 61
Fadl el Abdallahi 161
Fadl el Imam el Hadi 109
Faisal el Siddig 200
Farida, Queen of Egypt 30
Farouk, King of Egypt 17, 29, 33, 37,
38, 40, 43, 45, 46, 72, 73
Farouk Hamad' Allah, Major 111, 112
Fatatery 158
Fatah el Rahman el Beshir 148, 158,
166–170, 173, 178
Fatma Abdel Rahman 86, 155, 212
Foot, Sir Dingle 131
Foreign Office 116, 123, 127, 135, 144,
147, 157, 174, 201, 210, 219, 221
Fouad el Amin 215
Fuad, Mohieddin, Dr., Prime Minister
Egypt 189, 190, 194, 204, 205

Gaddafi, Muamar, Libyan Leader 111,
112, 140, 141, 145, 155, 167, 168,
172, 173, 176, 177, 187, 195, 202, 220
Gaitskell, Sir Arthur 27, 130, 131
Gamal Abdel Nasser, President of Egypt
(See Nasser) 00
Garang, John 223, 225, 226, 227, 231,
232, 235–237, 243
Garang, Joseph 112
Gezira Aba 34, 35, 108, 109, 146, 172
Ghabush, Father Philip Abbas 232
Ghizali Da'Fallah, Head of Civil
Government (Transitional Military
Council) 226
Gibbon, John, Lt. General 133
Gillan, Sir Angus, Civil Secretary,
Sudan 130
Gordon, Charles G., General.
Governor-General of the Sudan 5, 7,
51, 109
Graduates Congress 11
Greenhill, Sir Denis 131
Griffiths, Rt Hon James, M.P. 35, 45,
73, 75, 76

Hafia Mamoun Sherif 179
Haggar, family of 160
Haj Meddawi 225
Hall, Richard 207, 228, 229
Hamed Tewfiq 63
Hart, Rt Hon Dame Judith, M.P. 201,
216
Hashim Al Ata 111, 112
Hassam Muhammed 143
Hassan II, King of Morocco 101
Hassan, Prince of Jordan 179
Hassan el Turabi 164, 167, 175, 179,
193, 198, 210, 212–214, 219, 223 225,
244
Hawkesworth, Desmond 27, 57
Hayhoe, Barney, M.P. 150
Hayward, Ronald 150
Hayworth, Rita 29
Healey, Rt Hon Denis, M.P. 113, 229
Heath, Rt Hon Edward, M.P. Prime
Minister of the U.K. 131, 229
Helm, Sir Knox, Governor-General of the
Sudan 79
Hill, Martin 228
Hillali Pasha, Prime Minister of Egypt
42
Hillard, R J 27, 28
Holding, Michael 130
Holmes, Timothy 210
Home, Rt Hon Sir Alec Douglas, M.P.,
Prime Minister of the U.K. 131
Hosni Mubarak, President of Egypt. (See
Mubarak) 00
Howe, Rt Hon Sir Geoffrey, M.P. 131,
202, 240
Howe, Sir Robert, Governor-General of
the Sudan 18, 73, 76, 79
Howe, Lady 18, 76
Huddleston, Sir Hubert,
Governor-General of the Sudan 18
Hudoud, Sharia Punishments 199, 203,
208, 237
Hume, Cardinal Basil 217, 230
Hussein, King of Jordan 179
Hussein Zulfikar Sabri 73

Ibrahim Abboud, President of the Sudan
(See Abboud) 00
Ibrahim Ahmed 19, 30, 75, 125
Ibrahim el Nur 153
Ibrahim Faraj Pasha, Prime Minister of
Egypt 33
Ibrahim Mufti 61, 63
Ibrahim Muhammed Khalil 210

Idi Amin, President of Uganda 144
Ishag Khalifa Sherif 30
Islamic Jehad Organisation 232
Islamic Socialist Party 225
Ismael, Khedive of Egypt 5
Ismael el Azhari, President of the Sudan
  (See Azhari) 00
Ismay Thomas 19, 21, 26, 30, 31, 49,
  55, 56, 61, 68, 101, 106, 108, 126,
  127, 129, 153, 159, 162, 186, 187,
  190, 202, 214, 217, 222

Jaffar Muhammed Numieri, President of
  the Sudan (See Numieri) 00
Jamal Muhammed Ahmed 31, 106
Jenkins, Rt Hon Roy, M.P. 127, 201,
  212, 217, 229
John 145
Johnson, James, M.P. 174
Jordanian Ambassador 241
Judd, Frank, M.P. 174

Kamal el Jack 31, 113
Kamal Hagras, Dr 106
Kamal Hassan Ahmed 211
Kamal Hassan Ali, General, and Prime
  Minister of Egypt 189, 194, 195,
  204, 213
Kamil George 126
Kamil Shawki 30, 70, 113
Kenana, Sugar Enterprise 198
Khalid, King of Saudi Arabia 179
Khalid Farah, Dr 155, 173, 181
Khalid Mohieddin 65
Khalil Osman, Dr 112, 147, 148, 173,
  216, 217, 219, 221
Khatmiyya Tariqa 5, 35, 49, 59, 61, 86,
  109, 172, 224
Khidr Omer 30
Khomeini, Ayatollah 176, 179, 181, 188
Kissinger, Henry 134
Kitchener of Khartoum, Field Marshal
  9–11, 22, 25, 51
Kober Prison 198, 201, 206, 208, 212,
  216, 223, 244
Kronfli, Joseph 159, 160
Kyle, Keith 174

Lagu, Joseph, General 93, 155, 172,
  174, 175, 184, 187, 220
Lawes, Glenville 144, 145
Legislative Assembly, Sudan 25
Legum, Colin 207, 228
Lester, James, M.P. 241

Libya 229
Lloyd, Rt Hon Selwyn, M.P. 51, 74
Long, Christopher 207, 211, 221
Luard, Evan, M.P. 144
Luce, Richard, M.P. 150, 202, 206
Luce, Sir William 39, 53, 69, 73

McGuigan, Hugh 67, 68
McNair, Lord 217
MacNally, Tom 147
Maghboul el Amin 88
Mahdi Mustafa 68
Mahmoud el Feki 63
Mahmoud Fahim 129
Mahmoud Hasanaya 225
Mahmoud Muhammed Taha 216, 224
Mahmoud Salih 146
Maitland, Patrick, M.P. 75, 76
Malik Beshir Malik 217
Mamoun Bihairi 175
Mansour, Khalid, Dr 31, 113, 115, 122,
  128, 130, 133, 138, 139, 146, 147,
  149, 167, 175, 207, 216, 217, 220, 226
Marquand, Rt Hon Hilary, M.P. 35, 45,
  47, 76
Matar, Fouad 210
Mayhew, Rt Hon Christopher 131
Mauritius, High Commissioner 203
Mengistu, Mariam, President of
  Ethiopia 232, 237
Meynell, Charles 207, 210, 228
Mian Ziauddin 73
Miles, Oliver 202
Mirghani (el) Ahmed, Head of State
  205, 235
Mirghani, the family 5, 109, 219
Mirghani Hamza 30, 41, 49, 61, 63
Miriam el Sadig 137
Mohieddin Ahmed Abdullaha 88
Moore, George 129, 130
Morgan, Gwyn 123, 127, 150
Morgan, Margaret 200
Morhigs 160
Morocco 212
Morrison, Rt Hon Herbert, M.P. 35, 45
Mortimer Edward 207, 228, 229
Mossadeck, Prime Minister of Iran 35
Mubarak Hosni, President of Egypt
  109, 189, 194, 197, 201, 202, 204,
  206, 222, 229, 240
Mubarek el Abdullahi 166–168, 195,
  200, 227, 240
Mubarek Shadad 225

Mubarek Zarroug 30, 61, 65, 70, 79, 91, 113
Muhammed Abdel Rahman Nugdallah 90, 98, 155, 180
Muhammed Ahmed Abu Sin 61
Muhammed Ahmed el Mahdi, The Mahdi 1, 5, 7, 46
Muhammed Ahmed el Sadig 23, 139
Muhammed Ahmed Mahjoub, Prime Minister 25, 30, 41, 59, 70,79, 81, 86, 87, 90, 91, 94, 95, 98, 99–102, 105, 106, 108, 133, 149
Muhammed Ahmed Omer 75
Muhammed Ali Pasha, Khedive of Egypt 4
Muhammed Ali Shawki 19, 36, 37, 52, 55, 66
Muhammed el Baghir, General 112, 123, 126, 128, 129, 139, 142
Muhammed Hamad el Nil 70
Muhammed Ibrahim Khalil 209
Muhammed Ibrahim Nugud 225, 244
Muhammed Khalifa Sherif 55
Muhammed Neguib (See Neguib), General, President of Egypt 00
Muhammed Nur-el-Din 38, 56, 57, 63
Muhammed Osman el Mirghani, Sayed 205, 243, 244
Muhammed Omer Beshir 236
Muhammed Said Telba 21
Muhammed Saleh Shingetti 18, 36, 43, 49, 69
Muhammed Tewkik Ahmed 30, 57, 70, 72, 113, 128, 161
Murphy, Robert 43
Mustafa Gabaley 129
Mustafa Khalil, Prime Minister of Egypt 205

Nadeem Adawi 117
Nahas Pasha, Egyptian Prime Minister 17, 23, 26, 33, 37, 40
Narriman, Queen of Egypt 30
Nasr Eldin Imam el Hadi 165, 166, 167, 200, 240
Nasr el Sayed 225
Nasser Gamal Abdel, President of Egypt 46, 63, 71, 82, 83, 106, 107, 110, 116
National Islamic Front 235, 243,
National Unionist Party 54, 57, 59, 71, 94, 99
Nefissa el Amin 127, 128

Neguib Muhammed, General, President of Egypt 47, 49, 50, 52, 59, 63, 65, 66, 68, 71, 72, 82, 213
Newbold, Sir Douglas, Civil Secretary of the Sudan 15
Newman, David 25
Nicholas, Sir Harry 123
Nimitz, U.S. Battleship 196
Noel, Cleo 129, 130
Nokrashi Pasha, Egyptian Prime Minister 18
Noon el Abdel Rahman 170
Numieri, Jaffar Muhammed, President of the Sudan 102, 104–106, 108, 109, 111–113, 115–118, 122, 125, 126, 128, 130–132, 135, 138–145, 147–159, 162–195, 197– 207, 210, 211, 214, 219, 222, 224, 225, 228, 229, 234, 236, 239
Nuba Mountains Union 232

O'Bang, Philip 123, 125, 127, 133, 137
O'Brien, Bishop James 217
Omar el Hag Musa 126
Omar el Sheikh 174, 183
Omar Nur el Diem 143, 168, 183, 200, 225, 227
Omer el Tayeb, General Vice-President 183, 186, 191, 192, 197, 199, 211, 221, 223, 227
Omer Dindish 143
Osman, Colonel 148
Osman Mirghani 196
Owen, Rt Hon David, M.P. 201, 202, 228, 229

Palmer, Richard 158, 165, 169
Parsons, Sir Anthony 116
Peoples' Democratic Party 81, 82, 93, 94, 99
Priddie, Sir Eric 130
Princess Ann H.R.H. 127
Progressive Peoples' Party 235
Pugh, Deborah 217, 228

Raschid el Taher, Prime Minister of the Sudan 167, 175
Rahma Abd'Allah Ja'Allah 117, 137, 157, 164, 209, 212
Rajwadi, Rao Rajah 66, 71
Rawlinson 227
Reagan Ronald, President U.S.A. 220, 237, 239
Reddaway, Norman 116, 123
Roberts, Michael, MP 150

Robertson, Sir James W, Civil Secretary of the Sudan   15, 18–29, 31, 33, 34, 35, 37, 39–47, 49–52, 57–59, 74, 79, 97, 130, 137, 149, 153, 200
Robertson, Lady   20, 31, 51, 74
Rowland, Tiny   210, 231
Ryle, John   228
Ruthven Malise   207, 217, 228

Saad el Shazli, General   134
Sadat, Anwar, President of Egypt   109, 111, 112, 116, 122, 125, 126, 134, 145, 162, 171, 173, 177–179
Sadig Abdullah Abdel Magid   225
Sadig el Khomeini (Iran)   180
Sadig el Mahdi, Prime Minister of the Sudan   23, 34, 49, 59, 86, 95, 97–102, 105, 106, 108, 110, 118, 122, 125, 128, 135, 137, 139–148, 151, 152, 154, 156, 157, 159, 161, 164–182, 184, 185, 187–193, 195–197, 199, 201, 203–206, 208, 212, 215, 220, 223, 227–231, 233, 236, 237, 239, 240, 241, 244
Saleh Abdel Salaam   225
Salah Salim, Major   50, 52, 63, 65
Salisbury, Bishop of   217
Samir Sabri   123
Sara el Fadl Mahmoud   139, 146, 155–157, 164, 167, 168, 182, 200, 201, 206, 207, 209, 212, 215, 222, 231
Saudi Arabia   204, 211, 212
Sawar el Dahab Abdel Rahman, General   222, 224, 225
Seif-el-Din Abdullah   148
Senegal, High Commissioner   203
Shah-in-Shah   175–176
Sharia Laws   198, 199, 204, 208, 210, 214–216, 236
Sha'ma el Siddig   183, 209
Sherbini   241
Sherif Hussein el Hindi   140, 143, 154, 156, 164, 166, 172, 173, 176–178, 186
Shefiq Shawki   30
Sherif Touhami   146, 154, 182, 183, 190, 191, 205, 208–210, 213
Shultz George   195
Siddig el Abdel Rahman, Imam   23, 30, 37, 55, 56, 66, 70, 73, 75, 85, 89, 90, 95, 97, 108, 117, 120, 191
Siddky-Bevin Protocol   15, 17, 18, 42
Sinclair-Louttit, Kenneth, Dr   212
Singapore, High Commissioner   202

Sir-el-Khatim el Khalifa, Prime Minister of the Sudan   91, 100, 106
Sirhan Sirhan   129
Siricio Iro, Member of the Supreme Council   73, 79
Slatin Rudolf, Pasha   9
Smith, Michael   217
Socialist Republican Party   57, 58
Souad, Dr   130
Souad Ibrahim Ahmed   125
Southern Front   93, 100
Southern Sudanese Political Association   235
Sri Lanka, High Commissioner   202
Stack, Sir Lee, Governor-General of the Sudan   11
Steel, Rt Hon David, M.P.   217, 229
Stevenson, Sir Ralph   47
Stewart, Rt Hon Michael, M.P.   45, 101, 102, 106
Stonehouse, John, M.P.   131
Sudan African National Union   93, 99, 100
Sudan African Congress   232, 235
Sudan Communist Party   90, 93–95, 99, 100, 105, 109, 110, 111, 125, 126, 143, 169, 171, 172, 178, 197, 225, 226, 235
Sudan Liberation Front   232
Sudan Peoples' Liberation Army   231
Sudan Peoples' Liberationa Movement   226, 235, 236, 243
Sudanese Socialist Union   128, 153, 164, 165, 173, 174, 177, 181, 182
Sudanese Revolutionary Movement   234
Sudanese National Party   232, 235
Sukamar Sen   53–67

Tag el Din, Abdullah, General   232
Taylor, Bernard, M.P.   76
Terrill, Christopher, Dr   207, 214, 215, 229
Tewfik Salih Osman Salih   143
Thatcher, Ron Hon Margaret M.P., Prime Minister of UK   150, 179, 239
Thomas, Jeffrey, QC   217
Thomas, Radwan   116, 130
Thomas Rhiannon   158, 183
Thorpe Jeremy, M.P.   150
Tigani, Ibrahim, Dr   211
T. Muhammed Ali, Dr   236
Tombra, Joseph   174
Tomkys, W R   174, 178
Torry, Peter   169, 174

Townsend, Cyril, M.P. 216
Transitional Military Council 219, 225–227, 232, 235, 236

Uduho, John 208
Umma Party 13, 17, 19, 23–25, 35, 37, 38, 46, 47, 55–57, 59, 66, 70, 71, 79, 82, 85, 94, 95, 99, 102, 103, 225, 233, 235, 243
Urwick Alan Bedford 144, 145

Vanian 160
Vance, Cyrus 181

WAFD Party of Egypt 17, 37
Wahaab, Lt General 88
Waheed 210
Wali Eldin Imam el Hadi 125, 126, 135, 165, 166, 167, 227
Waller, Mrs 19, 20

Walters, Denis, M.P. 131
Waterhouse, Captain Charles, M.P. 75
Watkins, David, M.P. 150
Wingate, Sir Reginald, General, Governor-General of Sudan 9, 10
Wisal el Siddig 193
Wogan Patrick 135
Wolwol, L 174
Workers and Farmers Party 232
Wright, Pearce 174
Wilson, Rt Hon Harold, M.P., Prime Minister of the UK 116

Yahia el Fadl 63
Yasser Arafat 176
Younger, Sir Kenneth 131

Zambia, High Commissioner of 202
Zein el Abden, S.A.R.'s Servant 36
Zubeir Hamad el Melik 30

The translation of Arabic names and place names is extremely difficult as there are a number of differing systems. The author has attempted to be consistent.